IN SHEEP'S CLOTHING

The Arcane, Profane and Subversive in Shakespeare

written by
Sidney Wade Stout
© 2008

In Sheep's Clothing
The Arcane, Profane and Subversive in Shakespeare

Sidney Wade Stout
Copyright © 2008
ISBN-13: 978-0-9784483-1-8

Library and Archives Canada Cataloguing-in-Publication

Stout, S. W. (Sidney Wade), 1955-
In sheep's clothing: the arcane, profane and subversive in Shakespeare / Sidney Wade Stout.
Includes bibliographical references.
ISBN 978-0-9784483-1-8
1. Shakespeare, William, 1564-1616--Criticism and Interpretation. 2. Philosophy, Renaissance--Influence.
I. Title.
PR2976.S76 2009   822.3'3   C2009-903329-1

To

Janice Mackett

"she doth teach the torches to burn bright"

(Romeo and Juliet, 1.5.45)

"There is layer upon layer in the words of the sages. In your reading of them, penetrate deeply. If you simply read what appears on the surface, you will misunderstand. Steep yourself in the words; only then will you grasp their meaning."

Chu His (twelfth century CE)

Learning to be a Sage. Selections from the Conversations of Master Chu, Arranged Topically, translated by Daniel K. Gardner, Berkeley, 1990.

TABLE OF CONTENTS

IN SHEEP'S CLOTHING
The Arcane, Profane and Subversive in Shakespeare

Introduction   10

    About Hermetism   12

    The Essays   15

    A Help to All Involved   16

    Footnotes   18

Abstract for *Hamlet*   20

    Hamlet's Hermetic Soul   21

        Which Planet Are You From?   21

        7 Planets for 7 Actors   25

        Hamlet's Ascent of the Soul   31

        The Copernican Connection   36

        Reprise: About Hermetism   39

        Conclusion   41

        Footnotes   43

        Bibliography   46

Abstract for *Macbeth*   48

    Macbeth's Imaginings and the Logic of Evil   49

        Introduction   49

        A Civil War of Biblical Proportion   49

        Ramism   51

        A Closer Look at the Mind   54

        The Heart of the Disagreement   55

The Hermetic Mind 58

Hermetic Macbeth 61

Holinshed Versified 62

Macbeth as a Capricorn 63

Lady Macbeth as a Scorpio 64

Why We Love Macbeth 66

Logic: The Real Villain 68

Conclusion 70

Footnotes 71

Bibliography 73

Abstract for *The Merchant of Venice* 76

The Character of Cabala 77

Introduction 77

The Character of Cabala 78

Adam Smith as the Merchant of Venice 87

Usury and the Deuteronomic Double Standard 90

Levels of Meaning 91

Conclusion 93

Footnotes 95

Bibliography 97

Abstract for *The Winter's Tale* 98

White Magic in *The Winter's Tale* 99

Introduction 99

Pico's Concepts Create Characters 100

The Sun God Apollo 106

The Magic of Redemption and the Rites of Spring 107

Pico's Breakthrough 111

How to Bring a Statue to Life 113

Conclusion   117

Footnotes   119

Bibliography   123

Abstract for *A Midsummer Night's Dream*   126

Hekate Weaves *A Midsummer Night's Dream*   127

Introduction   127

The Moon, Shakespeare and Hekate   127

The Goddess Hekate   129

Hekate and the Soul   131

Ficino's Theory of Love and Magic   131

Hekate, Eros and Magic   140

Imagination in the Elizabethan Age   150

Bottom is at the Bottom of it All   154

Harmony for Bottom's Ballad   159

Conclusion   162

Footnotes   164

Bibliography   168

Abstract for *King Lear*   170

King Lear and the Blinding of Cupid   171

That Dark Place   171

King Lear is no Dream   172

Marriage in *King Lear*   173

Lear's Character   176

The Daughters' Characters   177

Character Arcs   181

Idle Weeds   186

Reconciliation of Opposites   188

Chaos and the birth of love   190

A Civil Society   192

A Moral Society   195

Conclusion   199

Footnotes   200

Bibliography   202

Abstract for *Love's Labour's Lost*   204

Bruno's Labour's Not Lost   205

Introduction   205

What's the Matter in Shakespeare   206

Love's Labour's Lost as an "Arsy-Versy" Genesis   209

A Matter of Ideas   212

A Matter of Fact   214

Hunting for Fame   218

Nothing Desires What it Already Possesses   220

Fame and Death   221

Universal Becoming   223

Intelligible and Sensible Worlds   223

Conclusion   227

Bibliography   229

Abstract for *Othello*   230

Bridling Othello   231

Introduction   231

The Objects to be Bound   234

The Honest Broker   235

The Power the Binds   237

The Hunter of Souls   241

We Cannot All Be Masters   242

Potions and Charms   247

The Handkerchief's Poisonous Magic   248

Phantasy and the Power of the Imagination   250

Gates of the Senses   253

Opportunity Knocks   254

Why he hath thus ensnared my soul and body   255

Obedient to the End   256

Seeds of Bonds   258

Conclusion   259

Bibliography   262

Conclusion to *In Sheep's Clothing*   263

In Sheep's Clothing

The Arcane, Profane and Subversive in Shakespeare

Introduction

This collection of essays was created to summarize my research into several of Shakespeare's plays. Each essay reveals an underlying philosophy that winds its way through the play examined. This philosophical backbone comes from the Hermetic tradition. Each essay focuses on one play and reveals the incorporation of material from this tradition. By reading all the essays one gradually comes to realize that Shakespeare had extensive knowledge of this tradition and applied many of its concepts throughout his works. The frequency of references to Hermetic sources and the sophistication with which Shakespeare integrates these ideas into his plays indicates he was proficient in these concepts and was not just introducing ideas from the general zeitgeist of his times. It also indicates he was making a special effort to contribute ideas from this philosophy to play after play. His use of such controversial material indicates that Shakespeare believed in the importance of this material and that by integrating these ideas into his works he was hoping for both their dissemination and their survival.

Shakespeare was aware of the censors and the problems that could arise from living in a too restrictive intellectual environment. He understood the role that art could play in circumventing these restrictions. That ideas could be hidden in images and symbols. That his plays could act as a forum for the debate of ideas 'frowned on' if discussed openly. That his art could act as a pressure relief valve for society allowing a safe place for people to rehearse possible futures, to see possibilities and be offered a chance to empathize with 'the other'. Art could be used to lubricate the wheels of change. People could discuss 'the play' rather than their personal beliefs. The anonymity of 'the play' as a topic could provide safety for debate. Change becomes possible because people see change acted out.

The tradition and source materials that exerted an influence on his plays came from the major writers associated with the Hermetic or Neoplatonic movement: Marsilio Ficino, Pico della Mirandola, Giordano Bruno, and others.

Francis Yates, John Mebane, and many others have presented arguments that link Shakespeare to the Hermetic movement in a 'general' way. What the following essays will show is 'specific' points of contact between Hermetic sources and Shakespeare's work and they will reveal just how deeply these ideas penetrate into the structure of his plays.

The essays are annotated with quotations from or references to works that Shakespeare could have been exposed to. All these works are presented in their English translations and not the Latin or French versions he probably had access to. I do not believe this to be a problem since it is the general ideas that influenced Shakespeare and the translations are 'true enough' to this essence. Let me be clear, we are talking about an Elizabethan poet reading some type of translation of an Hermetic work, daydreaming on it, and taking elements of what he thought was important and incorporating those ideas into his work. We are looking for influence not plagiarism.

The essays present novel ways of viewing the plays and I hope people can use the ideas to help reinterpret some of Shakespeare's work. I also hope that this brief exposure to works not normally encountered on the Elizabethan reading list might encourage a wider awareness and knowledge of these works.

All the quotations from each play are from The Arden Shakespeare version of that play. Each essay introduces ideas and concepts from the Hermetic movement that will assist in understanding the next play and give a fuller picture of the belief system. Because of this the plays are not presented in chronological order [1] but rather in an order determined by the concepts presented and how they might assist the reader in understanding subsequent essays.

About Hermetism

The *Hermetica* and the *Asclepius* were understood (in Shakespeare's day) to be profoundly ancient documents describing Egyptian beliefs and containing the wisdom of Hermes Trismegistus. The documents were believed to have predated and contributed to the philosophies of Moses, Pythagoras, Plato and Christ. During the Renaissance the rediscovery of the ancient philosophers rekindled a hope for a better world. Unlike today where we look towards the future for improvements through technology, they looked to the past, to the ideals of the Greeks and to the Golden Age for hope.

Life hadn't changed a lot from the ancient ways. Transportation was still by boat, horse or foot. The speed at which news could travel was limited by these modes of transportation or at best the speed of a pigeon. Wars were still fought by hand to hand combat. Everything was still handmade. Humans were contained within Nature. Technology hadn't yet exerted its muscle through mass production or economies of scale. Cities existed but England was largely an agrarian society. How that society was structured had changed but not necessarily for the better. A return to Eden offered much hope. New ideas and maybe better ideas could be found in the past.

The madness of the Renaissance was religion. Religion controlled everything. In order to introduce new ideas it was necessary to make them seem acceptable to the religious establishment. Virgil was 'seen' to prophesy the coming of Christ so his work was acceptable to the Church since he could be regarded as a 'pagan prophet'. The same was true of the *Hermetica*. It was argued that it supported the New Testament and prophesied the coming of the Son of God. So by dressing the classical philosophies in Christian clothes (an act of imagination) it was possible to introduce those ideas into a Christian culture and in effect broaden the discussion.

The *Corpus Hermeticum* was translated into Latin by Marsilio Ficino in 1463 and published in 1471. The Greek manuscript had come to Florence and the Medici court from Byzantium at the fall of Constantinople (1453). Hermes (a.k.a. Thoth or Mercury), the god whose writings are contained in the *Corpus Hermeticum* or *Hermetica*, was actually two gods. The first was a type of Prometheus character who brought the secret of writing in hieroglyphics to the Egyptians. The second was known better as Hermes Trismegistus and he was more like a prophet akin to Moses. He came after the flood and showed the Egyptians how to make books and transfer the hieroglyphs to paper. Hermes Trismegistus was teacher to Orpheus, who taught Aglaphemus, who taught Pythagoras, who taught Philolaus, who taught Plato. It was a line of gentile theology that ran concurrent with that of Moses. Moses and Hermes were seen as contemporaries in some traditions. Because of its pedigree the Hermetic philosophy easily broadened to include all the works of Orpheus (like the Orphic Hymns), the teachings of Pythagoras, the Chaldean Oracles (a series of Greek oracles), the works of Plato and the Neoplatonic philosophers that came later.

Clement of Alexandria (200 C.E.) knew of 42 books of Hermes, some texts were philosophical, some astrological, some about alchemy, still others about occult technology. Each of Shakespeare's plays focuses on a different aspect of Hermetic philosophy, for instance, *Hamlet* explores and improvises on the astronomy/astrology aspect of the *Hermetica*. The *Hermetica* that Shakespeare probably encountered was the Basel Edition of Ficino's works. It was printed in 1576 and included *The Corpus Hermeticum* up to book XIV and the *Asclepius*. I don't mean to imply that Shakespeare was tied to just one book of Hermetic wisdom, but rather, he explored the work of philosophers (like Pythagoras, Plato, Julian the theurgist, Ficino and Bruno) whose ideas were reflected in this rather eclectic starting point.

The translated *Hermetica* only began to run into trouble with the Church after the publication of Copernicus's heliocentric view of the solar system (1543). Copernicus had used the text to support his views. It was after this that others began to use the contents of the *Hermetica* to not only support the Heliocentric system but also to promote the resurrection of the long dead Egyptian religion.

The Hermetic philosophy had much to offer the 16th century. It was a gnostic religion, meaning salvation was obtained through knowledge; it was also a self actualized religion that did not require the intercession of a priestly class. Since the Protestant Reformation of 1517 this idea of personal responsibility for one's salvation was becoming commonplace. The Hermetic philosophy also did not support the idea that any Scripture was infallible and it held that all religious texts should be seen only as books offering wisdom. Hermeticism had no dogma, no holy book, and no one set of rules; it was a search for God through all philosophies and through the study of nature (the creation). Because of this, tolerance formed the bedrock of its belief system. Disagreements were to be resolved by knowledge and study. Because of this, Hermeticism is more a philosophy than a religion, it is amorphous in character, contains contradictions and debates, its holy book is really the library of all human knowledge and it constantly expands its vision and absorbs other religions and philosophies. What it did share with religion was a quest to understand our place in creation, to understand the nature of the soul, and to understand who, what, or if God was.

For those of the Elizabethan age that had witnessed the violent and rapid swings in fortune of first being under a Protestant government (under Edward VI, 1547-1553) then a Catholic government (under Mary, 1553-1558) and then back to a Protestant government (under Elizabeth, 1558-1603) the Hermetic philosophy must have seemed exceptionally civil and possibly offered a way out from under the intransigence of other systems.

The Essays

Recognizing the texts an author improvises on or references in their work adds to the understanding of that work. Sometimes one can recognize what the author's intensions were in updating a particular story. What changes are made to update the story, what bits are left out, all these choices reveal decisions made by the author. Not only is it possible to see the work but one gets a glimpse of the mind behind it.

In the case of understanding Shakespeare these changes can give a clear idea as to his goal in writing various works. Shakespeare wrote in layers. These layers not only involved Concept, Character, and Plot but also ideas involving history, science, religion, and mythology.

In regards to Plot, Shakespeare, in general, did not so much create a plot as he did borrow one to improvise on. These plots, taken from 'other sources', have been extensively examined elsewhere. In my essays I only briefly touch on them in order to demonstrate how his particular choice of plot could be used to support and contribute to what I feel is the more general idea or concept behind the work.

In the essays that follow you will see that Concept and Character for Shakespeare are deeply connected. Character often being directly drawn from the Concept he wishes to investigate; often to the point of personifying the Concept.

It is the integration of Concept, Character, and Plot that produces such a unity and synergy in his work. In the essays I limit my scope to a discussion of the Hermetic sources that I believe have contributed to concepts central to each play and my reasons for believing so. I never deal with the genius required to distill prose into poetry, or how clever a turn of phrase is, or comment on the rhythm, timing, and pacing of the plays. In short, I never deal with any of the aspects that make Shakespeare a great poet.

A Help to All Involved

Just as one's actions can reveal one's intensions, so can what an author writes reveal certain concepts he wishes to explore in a piece of work. Recognizing what these concepts could be is a great benefit to actors and directors. It presents these interested parties with a way into the piece and a way to understand the characters. It alerts them to precedents for the work and to details that may not have made it into the present version of the tale. It gives them both backstory and access to related stories.

By understanding concepts central to a play a director is empowered for when a question of interpretation comes up not only do they have the context of the play around the disputed piece of dialogue but they have the context for the play itself. They know the overall intent of the work so they, in fact, have a context for the context. They are privy to the 'Big Picture' and can now shape each scene or edit the play while staying true to its intent.

For an actor, by knowing where a character comes from, by knowing the character from a previous work, they may find themselves better equipped to understand that character's motivations. They have a context outside of the play itself to understand the character's past and hence their present incarnation. This may include their mythological symbolism or the role they play in the overall concept of the piece. It equips their characters with baggage so that the script can be delivered as a conversation coming from an embodied individual and not just as a piece of written dialogue.

Shakespeare almost always dealt with familiar plots but the concepts he brought to them made them fantastically new. For an audience this is where the fun lies, in surprise. Surprise is why we enjoy variations on a theme, the same story told in slightly different ways. The variations delight us because they surprise us. How clever the actors, directors and writers can be with familiar material is the source of our delight.

In the essays to follow I hope you will enjoy seeing how clever Shakespeare could be in his introduction of unique concepts to pre-existing plots.

Footnotes

[1]   The chronological order for these plays based on the dates found in the Arden Introductions of each play. They are roughly:

(1594-1595)   *Love's Labour's Lost*

(1595-1596)   *A Midsummer Night's Dream*

(1596-1598)   *The Merchant of Venice*

(1599-1601)   *Hamlet*

(1602-1603)   *Othello*

(1603-1606)   *Macbeth*

(1605-1606)   *King Lear*

(1610-1611)   *The Winter's Tale*

Hermetic ideas will be found in many of Shakespeare's plays throughout his career. He did not tentatively introduce these ideas with increasing boldness over time. *Love's Labour's Lost* (one of his earliest plays) is as bold as *The Winter's Tale* (one of his later works) in integrating complex Hermetic ideas into its structure. This carries implications as to his education as well as his continual adherence to a marginalized belief system. It gives one the impression that this is a man with a plan.

Abstract for *Hamlet*

Hamlet's Hermetic Soul

Many of Shakespeare's works have been associated, in a general way, with the Neo-Platonic/Hermetic views of his age. What this essay argues is that with *Hamlet* Shakespeare drew directly from an Hermetic work, *The Corpus Hermeticum*, to both define the play's characters and to structure Hamlet's soliloquies.

Hamlet's Hermetic Soul

Which Planet Are You From?

Many of Shakespeare's works have been associated, in a general way, with the Neoplatonic/Hermetic views of his age [1]. This essay demonstrates that, in *Hamlet,* Shakespeare draws conceptually from the *Hermetica* to both define the play's characters and to structure Hamlet's soliloquies. The use of the *Hermetica* in both an overt and covert way suggests that Shakespeare was probably not just influenced by Hermeticism (like a bystander indirectly affected by its philosophy) but was very well versed in its major texts. To reveal Shakespeare's dependence on this text let me first quote from *The Corpus Hermeticum* (Libellus I 25,26a) as translated by Walter Scott [2]. The passage is in response to the question of what happens to the soul once the body is dead.

(And thereupon the soul) "*mounts upward through the structure of the heavens. And to the first zone of heaven (the sphere of the Moon) he gives up the force which works increase and that which works decrease; to the second zone (that of the planet Mercury), the machinations of evil cunning; to the third zone (that of the planet Venus), the lust whereby men are deceived; to the fourth zone (that of the Sun), domineering arrogance; to the fifth zone (that of the planet Mars), unholy daring and rash audacity; to the sixth zone (that of the planet Jupiter) evil strivings after wealth; and to the seventh zone (that of the planet Saturn), the falsehood which lies in wait to work harm. And thereupon, having been stripped of all that was wrought upon him by the structure of the heavens, he ascends to the substance of the eighth sphere (the sphere of the fixed stars; heaven), being now possessed of his own proper power; and he sings, together with those who dwell there, hymning the Father.*" [3]

To appreciate this passage it helps to understand that the reverse was also believed to be true, that when the soul was incarnated at birth it descended through these same planetary spheres. Only this time instead of removing vices from the soul each sphere (or planetary god) would impart gifts [4]. The gifts were unique to each sphere and were given to the developing soul (for instance, pride and wisdom could come from Jupiter, aggression and courage from Mars, etc.). Different gifts were given to the soul as it descended through each planetary sphere, beginning with the outer planetary sphere of Saturn and ending with the sphere of the Moon. When the soul arrived at the Moon it was ready for birth in a physical form. The Moon being farthest from God (the outer celestial sphere) was seen as the crudest planet, it being subject to change and imperfection (through its phases). It was also seen as the Mother, spiritual womb, to all humanity. Her imperfection was an asset that helped the Moon relate to and have empathy for the human condition. Once the soul passed through the lunar sphere it had reached its final destination (hence the birthing analogy). The Earth rested at the center of the universe surrounded by these celestial spheres. Home to this newly incarnated life.

The personality traits each planet could contribute (positive and negative) were well defined and can be found in Ptolemy's *Tetrabiblos* (III, Chapter 13,14) or in William Lilly's *Christian Astrology (1647)* (Chapters 8-15,108,115) or in any number of ancient or modern resources [5]. The following paragraphs summarize the characteristics of each planetary sphere as you would find them defined in these books. I should point out that these seven planetary spheres represent seven distinct character types that have little overlap with each other [6]. Each planet represents or 'has dominion over' several personality traits as well as trades and objects associated with these trades. They are listed in the order a soul would encounter them on their ascension to heaven i.e. in the order they appear in the passage quoted from the *Hermetica*.

The Moon rules over women, fertility, motherhood, family and cyclic activities like marriages and funerals. It also rules over the processes of growth and decay; this can apply to plants or any number of other things. It also rules over anything to do with water or moisture. It represents traits like versatility, a capacity for change, sensitivity and caring (the emotions), but also dark qualities like grossness, crudeness, instability, forgetfulness, confusion, and self-absorbance. The Moon is also associated with the night and with hiding things.

Mercury is associated with thought, memory, imagination and is also linked to communication both written and spoken. The planet is associated with diplomacy and commerce. Character traits include a quick wit, a logical and inventive mind, eloquence, wisdom and all aspects of memory. Its dark aspects include nervousness, lying, cunning, and craftiness.

Venus rules over traits such as beauty, manners, harmony, and affection but also over darker qualities such as egotism, hedonism and jealousy. She is associated with trades involving fashion, cosmetics, beauty, poetry, dance, music, theatre and eroticism.

The Sun represents the life-force. Its traits are self-reliance, success, dignity, generosity, and leadership but it can also manifest dark qualities like egotism, overconfidence, and tyranny. It's instrumental in bringing hidden things to light.

Mars represents qualities like nobility, aggression, courage, pride, strength, but also anger, pitilessness, rashness, selfishness, and being a spendthrift. Mars rules over people and objects connected with warfare and bloodshed such as swords and knives, noxious agents like poisons as well as things related to Hell.

Jupiter along with the Sun and Venus is seen as a benefic planet and its traits reflect this by manifesting themselves as optimism, wisdom, jovial nature, spirituality and justice. Jupiter is associated with lawyers, philosophers, and religious leaders as well as all who seek knowledge and truth. Jupiter can also manifest darker qualities like a sense of entitlement, recklessness, and vanity.

Saturn is the Roman name for Kronos, Father of time, Father of the gods, and so not surprisingly represents parental authority, conventional views, narrow mindedness, stubbornness, rigidity, repression and control, a love of earthly life and property. The planet also represents the 'awful virtues' of discipline, hard work, patience and contemplation. Saturn can manifest dark qualities like malice, blasphemy, greed and covetousness.

From this list of characteristics it may come as no surprise when I point out that Shakespeare peopled his cast with souls derived from these pure types; Gertrude (Hamlet's Mother) is modeled on the inconstant, forgetful Moon, Polonius after the scheming, language loving Mercury, Ophelia after the beautiful, loving Venus, the King (Hamlet's Father) after the Sun. Laertes is modeled after the vengeful Mars, while Hamlet himself is an immature form of the knowledge seeking, justice seeking Jupiter and Claudius (Hamlet's Uncle) is modeled after the covetous Saturn.

The match becomes very obvious especially when one starts reflecting on their behavior, characteristics, and dialogue as offered up in Shakespeare's text. The reason for it is easily understood. Shakespeare did this as a form of type casting. His audience would have easily recognized the planetary types (astrological almanacs were the top selling books of his day) [7] so it provided a kind of shorthand for the actors, the audience and the writer; everyone knew the backstory of the characters so they were fully developed personalities the moment they stepped on the stage.

7 Planets for 7 Actors

The seven planetary types carry with them a complete classical history of stories and traditions. It is a deep well that Shakespeare tapped and it afforded him a generous body of knowledge to exploit in his poetry. Not only can one associate the astrological qualities with each character but all the classical myths related to each of the planetary gods can also be evoked. It is a body of knowledge I can only hint at in the following text.

King Hamlet (Hamlet's father) is certainly the most one dimensional character in the play. He is referred to as Hyperion, the Sun god, twice (1.2.140) (3.4.56) just in case we didn't pick up on his solar attributes. Tradition certainly held that monarchs and the Sun were related, the royal crown being a solar symbol (gold with its rays ascending to heaven). Hamlet's father is presented as the embodiment of virtue (1.2.140-145) but then what dead father isn't. The Sun was also regarded as that which brought hidden things to light and that is the role of the ghost in this play. He reveals his murder to young Hamlet and demands justice.

Hamlet's mother, Gertrude, is a wonderfully tainted character. She has the best qualities of the goddess Salene, but also some of the worst qualities of the Moon including stupidity, inconstancy, and corruption all of which are revealed in Hamlet's tirade against her in (3.4.39-88). This scene also reveals the Moon's attribute of hiding things as she stashes Polonius behind the arras (3.4.6)

Withdraw, I hear him coming.
[Polonius hides behind the arras].

The Moon was the most human of the gods and was associated with ritual practices such as weddings and funerals (because of her association with concepts of growth and decay). In this play we are given both in rapid succession (1.2.12). Gertrude, like the Moon, is also the doting mother recognizable to us all (1.2.118-119).

Claudius possesses qualities of Kronos. Kronos was regarded as the Prime Mover of the cosmos and it's Claudius's murder of the King (his brother) that sets the play in motion. Kronos went through a name change to Saturn, the agricultural deity, when adopted by the Romans. He was celebrated during the festival of Saturnalia which occurred around the Winter Solstice. It was a time when social roles were reversed. The King would step down and let a boy or fool take his place as 'King for a day'. At the end of the day the old King, representing the new born Sun, would again take up his position to serve for another year. This festival is of no incidental interest to the play. The days around the winter solstice are cold and short. This helps create the claustrophobic atmosphere of the play. Denmark is a prison this time of year. It is also the time of year that spirits can cross over (*Hamlet's Mill*; *"Macrobius…has it that souls ascend by way of Capricorn"*, p. 242) and this affords Hamlet's father the opportunity of communication before he crosses over.

Claudius is our Saturn, the contemplative, controlled god, the symbol of parental authority. He is tied to the earth and to his possessions as evidenced in his confession (3.3.51-56)

> *- but O, what form of prayer*
> *Can serve my turn? 'Forgive me my foul murder?'*
> *That cannot be, since I am still possess'd*
> *Of those effects for which I did the murder.*
> *My crown, mine own ambition, and my queen.*
> *May one be pardon'd and retain th'offence?*

The ghost and its effect on Hamlet would prove to be a challenge to any step-parent but they pose a particular danger to this Kronos's manhood.

The one nice thing that can be said of Claudius is that as an agricultural deity he shares much in common with Gertrude, who as Moon goddess, has an affinity for both the soil and gardening. They do truly love each other, an observation made by Stephen Greenblatt (*Will in the World*, p. 137) who views their marriage as genuinely intimate and as powerful as that of the Macbeths.

Polonius and his family make up the bulk of the rest of the characters in the play. Polonius can be directly related to Hermes/Mercury messenger and scribe to the gods. He is intelligent, deceitful, and ambitious, a man of twists and turns (like Odysseus who was a descendent of Mercury). In productions of the play Polonius is often used for comic relief; I believe this to be a mistake, he is a trickster character not a comedian.

His eloquence and love for the arts of language and hermeneutics are part of this god's skill set. Skills he uses to facilitate commerce through the drafting of agreements and contracts. Because of this Mercury was also seen as the god of commerce. Love of language and business acumen are both presented in his speech to his son (1.3.55-81). That Polonius is also capable of devious plotting is also demonstrated in that he has his son followed (2.1.1-74) and it is he who hatches plans to figure out whether Hamlet is truly mad (2.2.156-168).

It's Polonius's son Laertes that provides the foil to Hamlet and his dithering. Laertes has the characteristics of Mars, the god Ares; he is arrogant and can be cruel; thinking is not his strong suit. Where Hamlet's character considers all aspects of revenge, Laertes can barely contain his blood lust when he finds out about his father's untimely death. He leads a near revolution (4.5.99-152) in pursuit of his goals. Laertes is the hound of hell, the only morality he understands is revenge.

Ophelia, Laertes's sister, in many ways is as complex a character as Hamlet. Representing Venus, the goddess of Love, Ophelia is inclined to both the virtues of caring for others as well as the vices of caring too much for herself (hedonism, egotism). She is a creature of light, caring for frivolities like fashion, theatre and dance. She loves life. She has little ability to deal with its dark side. In the play her effervescent social nature is at first isolated then exposed to great loss. Her brother, Laertes, has left for France, Hamlet has rejected her, and her father is murdered. These accumulating losses press on her psyche. Where Hamlet feigns madness at his loss Ophelia truly suffers in her isolation and despair.

Hamlet is a shell of a man. He is, in short, a liar. In his arrogance he boasts of his compassionate nature (1.2.76)

Seems, madam? Nay, it is. I know not 'seems'.

Hamlet implies that he feels the world deeply but from the action in the play we know he does not. He feigns madness from grief whereas Ophelia truly is grief-stricken. He feigns to make a vow of vengeance to the ghost, his father, but never quite gets around to it whereas Laertes is ready to kill anyone in sight at the news of his father's murder. 'Seems' is just what Hamlet does.

Hamlet is the last major character and in the pantheon of the gods, he represents Jupiter/Zeus. As such he is symbolically involved in the greatest generational conflict of all time. Every twenty years the planet Jupiter overtakes Saturn in the huge celestial clock of the cosmos and so too every twenty years the son should overtake his father on earth. In the tale of *Hamlet*, this natural process of one generation taking over from the previous is interrupted. Hamlet's father is unnaturally killed and Hamlet is too young to assume his role.

This explains how such a beneficent planet ends up being represented in the play by such a boob as Hamlet. Hamlet is inexperienced and young. The 'sphere of Jupiter' as well as the planet were seen as representing philosophers, religious leaders, and law makers. It was the planet one consulted over questions of law and justice. It is, in fact, Hamlet that the ghost (his father) appeals to for justice, but Hamlet cannot deliver.

He possesses the qualities and interests of a Jupiter but as of yet he is still an unripened version of Jupiter. He has the potential of becoming what Jupiter is but he is still too young and inexperienced; he does not know how to judge where the line is between a virtue and a vice or how to differentiate between justice and vengeance. Though thoughtful, Hamlet makes nothing but mistakes throughout the play. All his decisions are wrong! He does not appease his father's shade, he orphans and estranges the girl he loves, he orders the death of two innocent friends, he fails to act when he has a chance to kill Claudius only to mistakenly kill Polonius moments later. He has the potential to be a philosopher but has not yet the judgment. Hamlet is a fool thinking himself wise. He is reckless, entitled and out of sync with his true nature.

Hamlet is very much the headstrong teenager, thinking and feeling like an adult but without the experience to avoid mistakes. I believe Hamlet's youth is routinely underestimated both contextually and from an historical perspective. Shakespeare (1564-1616) was a contemporary of the Danish astronomer Tycho Brahe (1546-1601); Tycho was a part of Danish nobility and his schooling was reflective of that segment of society. He went to the University of Copenhagen at age 12, this was typical; Roger Bacon attended Oxford at age 13 (see B. Clegg, *The First Scientist*, p. 23-25) and John Dee went to Cambridge at age 15 (see W. Sherman, *John Dee*, p. 4). Primary school was mainly to learn Latin. Once one had sufficient schooling in Latin they went on to University to study the Quadrivium (arithmetic, geometry, music, and astrology) in addition to grammar and rhetoric (see K. Ferguson, *The Nobleman and his Housedog*, p.11-13). Astrology was taught in the first year before religion or philosophy because it was felt that astrology turned the mind towards the abstract and the heavens. Astrology/Astronomy, they made no distinction, were also felt to be essential in order to calculate when certain religious holidays occurred on the Church calendar. Hamlet is clearly in his first few years of University so he could easily be around 16. His actions support this level of immaturity. So does the Q1 edition of the play which states Yorick's skull has been in the ground only a dozen years (5.1.167-168), again making Hamlet about 16.

I am inclined to believe the argument referred to by Jenkins (*Hamlet,* Arden Shakespeare, in Longer Notes, v.i. 139-57, p. 552) that the script was adapted so that Richard Burbage (a leading actor at the time) could play the part while in his thirties.

When one looks at the source material for *Hamlet* there is more strong evidence that Hamlet should be in his mid-teens. The plot of *Hamlet* comes from *Amleth,* by Saxo Grammaticus, books 3/4 of his *Historiae Danicae* (a debt Shakespeare acknowledged in the title of his work) but an earlier Finnish story of Kullervo also echoes the play. Giorgio de Santillana and Hertha von Deschend in their book *Hamlet's Mill* also point to similar tales of Amolodi, Amlaghe, and Lucius Brutus. All these tales have several elements in common; a hero father who is murdered by his usurping brother; an orphaned son (whose name stands for simpleton or dumb animal) and who is too young to avenge his father but who feigns madness in order to buy himself the time needed to physically mature and exact justice.

It is Hamlet's youthfulness that allows him to believably make such large mistakes and that accounts for his being so self-absorbed. He is an immature Jupiter, not yet capable of delivering Justice. He has not grown up. The apron strings are still tight; that's why he is shocked by his mother's behaviour. He is still a little naive. His behaviours and responses are not those of a man approaching thirty.

Hamlet's lack of insight, his groping to try to understand things, in short his character arc is the focus of the play. His doubts and his emotional state are reflected in his soliloquies. But these are not normal soliloquies, these are special, they reflect his enlightenment.

Hamlet's Ascent of the Soul

The planets not only define the major characters in the play but they also define the path Hamlet's soul takes toward transcendence. This path is the Hermetic path of ascension quoted earlier, *The Corpus Hermeticum* (Libellus I 25,26a). In *Hamlet* there are seven soliloquies and these are structured around the seven celestial spheres that a soul must pass through on its way back to heaven. The soliloquies provide a unique glimpse into the state of Hamlet's soul. Although Hamlet does not understand himself it is in these soliloquies that he comes closest to revealing his true nature as he is not interacting with any other characters. Hamlet's first soliloquy (1.2.129-157) begins

O that this too too sullied flesh would melt,

Thaw and resolve itself into a dew.

The references to *"sullied"* or corrupted flesh, the references to water (melt, thaw, dew) are all references to characteristics attributed to the Moon. The topic of the soliloquy is itself directed at his Mother, Gertrude, who embodies the Moon and her all too hasty marriage to Claudius. Throughout the soliloquy are continued references to characteristics associated with the Moon, such as, *"unweeded gardens"*,

31

"things that are gross in nature", *"frailty, thy name is woman"*, and *"month"*, a word derived from Moon, is mentioned four times.

This kind of subjective word association could easily be ignored if the pattern did not then occur with the second soliloquy. This time we would expect words associated with Hermes or Mercury as Hamlet's soul rises still further along its path of Hermetic purification.

The second soliloquy (1.5.92-112) has to do with memory; memory of his father and the task appointed him. It is well known that Hermes (Mercury) is associated with memory, wit, and activities of the brain. In this soliloquy the word *"remember"* is repeated three times, the word *"memory"* twice and reference to the *"brain"* (distracted globe) twice. Other words in the soliloquy that can be associated with Mercury are: *"records"*, *"book"*, *"books"*, *"forms"*, *"word"*, *"commandments"*, *"volumes"* and *"tables"*, these are all things to do with written communication. Hermes brought the written language to the Egyptians and in this soliloquy we see Hamlet physically write down what he is thinking (stage direction (1.5.109) [Writes.]). All these associations to Mercury can be found in this brief soliloquy.

This idea of linking the planets to the soliloquies constitutes an important link to Hermeticism that has previously not been investigated. Although this is fundamentally a subjective act I feel the specific qualities associated with the planets adds a degree of objectivity which ensures that the interpretation is not arbitrary.

The third soliloquy (2.2.543-601) finds Hamlet condemning himself for lack of courage and scheming to touch the soul of Claudius through a trap. The content can be associated with Venus (the third sphere of ascension) as can the vocabulary chosen. Much of the soliloquy has to do with the theatre which is the venue of Venus (enjoyment, leisure, gaiety, beauty, harmony, dance and fashion). Much reference is also made about the soul, referred to as *"she"* (2.2.548). Venus was one of the trinity of good forces; she together with the Sun and Jupiter constituted Light, Life, and Love where she made up the female portion of this tripartite soul. In much of this soliloquy Hamlet berates himself as being like a female ((2.2.568) *Plucks off my beard and blows it in my face*) but the effeminate characteristics he says he possesses are actually those of Venus. Where he refers to himself as pigeon-liver'd and lacking in gall (2.2.573) this describes Venus whose bird is the dove which lacks bitterness. Other references that could be seen as alluding to Venus are "*muddy-mettled*" (2.2.562) which could actually refer to copper, the metal associated with Venus. The grief expressed would generally be regarded as the outward display typical of a woman (2.2.581-582)

Must like a whore unpack my heart with words
And fall a-cursing like a very drab.

The reference to a whore is also a reference to Venus for she was the goddess responsible for the arts of prostitution and all things erotic. The image of talking through one's grief very much describes how Ophelia tries to deal with her problems.

Following this, is a description of how an actor might portray a person that had a father murdered, how their sincere grief would enact itself (2.2.555-559)

Had he the motive and cue for passion
That I have? He would drown the stage with tears,
And cleave the general ear with horrid speech,
Make mad the guilty and appal the free,
Confound the ignorant, and amaze indeed
The very faculties of eyes and ears.

This, in fact, describes how Ophelia (Venus embodied) behaves when she finds her father murdered. Not only does the soliloquy foreshadow the event of Polonius' death but also Ophelia's grief.

This brings us to the fourth soliloquy (3.1.56-89) and in the Ptolemaic system this is represented by the Sun. The line from the *Corpus Hermeticum,* as quoted previously, is the requirement to give up *"domineering arrogance"* (attitudes of superiority, authority and domination). These are the negative attributes associated with the Sun. It is the most famous of the soliloquies and is easily recalled by its first line *"To be or not to be..."* The soliloquy is about the question of life or death, whether it's better to continue to exist in a world whose troubles you know or to chose to enter an unknown world. Since the passage of the soul through this fourth celestial sphere involves giving up domineering arrogance, a belief that you know-it-all, I believe nothing could be more suitable. Hamlet concludes he does not, in fact, know-it-all and chooses to continue to live.

The fifth soliloquy, again, is a perfect match to what one would expect from an ascent through the fifth celestial sphere, that defined by Mars. It is a short soliloquy and to the point (3.3.379-390). It contains phrases that originate from the attributes of Mars and becomes almost a declaration of war against Hamlet's Mother. Let me list just a few of the key phrases (3.3.379-381)

...the very witching time of night

When churchyards yawn and Hell itself breathes out

Contagion to this world. Now could I drink hot blood

Let me be cruel... (3.3.386)

I will speak daggers... (3.3.387).

The connection of this soliloquy with Mars could be no more obvious especially when realizing that Mars is associated with all things related to Hell.

The sixth soliloquy (3.3.73-96) brings us to the sphere of Jupiter, that occupied by ideas of philosophers, religious leaders, and law makers. It generally represents justice and that is exactly what is called for as

Hamlet contemplates killing Claudius who is busily praying. The soliloquy is full of questions that only philosophers, priests, or lawyers could solve (3.3.76-78)

> *A villain kills my father, and for that*
> *I, his sole son, do this same villain send*
> *To heaven.*

They involve questions of what is a just punishment for Claudius. Is revenge an inherited obligation? Does a repentant villain go to heaven? The concepts are so Jovian that I need not labor this discussion.

The seventh soliloquy (4.4.32-66) marks the ascension through the seventh celestial sphere, that of Saturn. It is the outermost sphere before the soul comes into contact with the lower regions of heaven. In the play this is, in fact, Hamlet's jumping off point as well. He is being shipped off to England and to his 'planned for' death. He will return to the play a changed man. In this soliloquy Hamlet is musing on the army he sees marching off to their imminent deaths in Poland to fight a war that they as individuals have little interest in. Hamlet muses that 'honor' provides the only motivation for these troops and that this 'lie' is not enough to justify their deaths (4.4.51-56)

> *Exposing what is mortal and unsure*
> *To all that fortune, death, and danger dare,*
> *Even for an eggshell. Rightly to be great*
> *Is not to stir without great argument,*
> *But greatly to find quarrel in a straw*
> *When honour's at the stake.*

When passing through this Hermetic sphere one was to give up "*the falsehood which lies in wait to work harm*" (*Hermetica* as quoted earlier). The falsehood is honor, the ultimate lie, that makes humans give up all their skills and god-like reason to perform the most beastly of tasks. Saturn is 'Father Time' and Hamlet, as he ascends through

Saturn's sphere, realizes he is out of time or at least sees the end of his time and he surrenders himself to the process. When he returns to play out the final scenes there is, as Harold Bloom believes (*Hamlet Poem Unlimited*, p. 100), a transcendent quality to him, he is playing out the story, not fighting, plotting, or brooding, he is at this point indifferent to all worldly ambitions and may be seen to be on the verge of enlightenment. Bloom's sentiment is also shared by Stephen Greenblatt (*Will in the World*, p. 363) and although both recognized Hamlet's change of attitude they did not understand the mythic reason for it. Saturn was the last gateway for the soul to pass through before it reached the stars and the enlightenment that they represented; it was also the last and greatest spiritual test. To pass through the sphere of Saturn required the renunciation of all physical possessions.

In *Hamlet* the 'planetary' character assignments were not arbitrary but contributed to the same undersong that the soliloquies did. Both helped to link the play to Neoplatonic ideas contained in the *Hermetica*. But now the question is: Why? Why did Shakespeare choose to use an overt connection of the planets to the characters that was plainly visible and understandable to a wide audience and also choose to use a covert connection by linking the planets to his soliloquies that very few would notice?

The Copernican Connection

Why would Shakespeare make reference to *The Corpus Hermeticum*? Part of the reason may have been to associate his play with ideas set forth in *The Corpus Hermeticum*. Copernicus had made reference to this work in his publication *De revoutionibus orbium caelestium* where he put forth his controversial argument that the Earth and all the planets orbited the Sun (the heliocentric model). The *Hermeticum* had at its roots the Egyptian sun centered religion and this may have piqued Copernicus's interest in alternative theories for the structure of the Cosmos or perhaps it just offered him some spiritual support for his work. Nevertheless *The Corpus Hermeticum* did become associated with this new heliocentric view of the Cosmos and not without good reason.

Corpus Hermeticum, Libellus XVI-7

"But it is not by conjecture that we contemplate the Sun; we see him with our very eyes. He shines most brightly on all the universe, illuminating both the world above and the world below; for he is stationed in the midst, and wears the Kosmos as a wreath around him."

Corpus Hermeticum, Libellus XVI-17

"And round about the Sun, and dependent on the Sun, are the eight spheres, namely, the sphere of the fixed stars, and the six planet-spheres, and the sphere which surrounds the earth".

Shakespeare (1564-1616) was born only a generation after Copernicus published his work on the true nature of planetary orbits (1543). He was also a contemporary with some of the leading astronomers in the world; Tycho Brahe (1546-1601), Kepler (1571-1630), Galileo (1564-1642) and Thomas Digges (1546-1595). This meant questions about the structure of the Universe would have been furiously debated during his lifetime. In fact Giordano Bruno spoke at Oxford in 1584, causing a near riot, as he tried to convince scholars of the importance of the Copernican idea of a heliocentric solar system. Shakespeare would have been 20 at the time and perhaps staying in the home of one of the people who invited Bruno to speak (*The Art of Memory,* Yates, p. 308-309).

The Church, both Catholic and Protestant, was taking a literal approach to scripture and allied itself with the very traditional views of Aristotle and Ptolemy holding that the Earth rested motionless at the center of the Universe. For them our sublunar home was made up of the four elements (Earth, Water, Air, and Fire) and was not like the other perfect planets and stars which were made up of a light airy stuff called the fifth element (quintessence). Aristotle's and the Church's view of the Universe did not allow for life to exist on other worlds since it did not believe matter existed outside of our imperfect world. They saw the heavens as a series of immutable crystalline spheres that expanded out from the central Earth.

When Kepler, Galileo, and Digges went on to confirm Copernicus's understanding of the Universe it meant that the Earth was just like the other planets and that they all orbited a sun that was no different from any other star in the heavens. Other stars; other suns; maybe other planets around these suns; the Universe was no longer finite and contained but was now infinite and unknowable. In 1580 Giordano Bruno wrote *De l'infinito universo e mondi* (On the Infinite Universe and Worlds); it was published in England in 1584. The cat was out of the bag. These ideas marked the beginning of a growing divide between the new emerging science and religion; a generational split between the old and the new; between stasis and change.

The Church dealt with the new information through book banning and inquisitions. In 1600 Giordano Bruno was burned at the stake in Rome. In 1615 Galileo was forced to recant his beliefs in the Copernican System. The Church appeared to be covering up the truth using violence and intimidation. Shakespeare would have been in the very heart of the debate in 1600 when he wrote *Hamlet*.

By using *The Corpus Hermeticum* to lend some structure to his play Shakespeare appears to be aligning himself with the 'new philosophy' of his day, a philosophy still not accepted by the Church. The play itself was a reflection of this controversy: the King (symbol of the Sun) was at the center of a conflict between Hamlet (the younger generation) and Claudius (the older generation); the play embodied the idea of change versus stasis with a very Copernican subtext.

Reprise: About Hermetism

The Hermetic philosophical system was a repository for various related religions and because of this its doctrines and writings often appear at odds with one another. The *Hermetica* itself can be divided into optimistic and pessimistic philosophies. Some critics believe this is the consequence of the different traditions' contributions to the writings; others believe this to be a result of having initiation texts from the different levels of enlightenment being mixed together in one document (*Hermetica*, Brian Copenhaver, Introduction, p. xxxix).

The optimistic views of a good universe touched by and embodying God, reflect beliefs that would be embraced by an initiate in the early stages. At this stage the initiate would still have strong physical needs because they are still tied to the joys of sensual life. For them the world was a miracle and God was in everything. By discovering God in nature, by discovering how to perfect creation they discovered how to perfect themselves. Understanding God in nature let them see and perfect the god in themselves.

The more pessimistic views of seeing the world as evil or like a jail would be more helpful to someone who is further along the path of enlightenment; the ones trying to disconnect from the physical, sensual world and just beginning to live the intellectual life of the mind. Those that have chosen celibacy and have given up their worldly possessions. They no longer see the world as their home for they have freed themselves of the body. They are ready for enlightenment. To live in the mind and join with the Mind of God.

The further the initiate was along the more they saw the world as a foul tomb and jail from which their higher soul (that part that belonged to God) had to escape. In the process their lower soul (that part belonging to the planets) also had to be shed. This is the process that was described in the *Hermetica*. Those attributes given to the newly incarnated soul as it descended from heaven are returned to each planet as it ascends back to the Divine. That which is God's returns to God; that which belongs to the planets are returned to the planets; and that which was the earth's, the dust of our physical bodies, was returned to the earth.

This is the setup for Hamlet. Not only do the soliloquies of Hamlet describe the ascension of the soul but the world Hamlet lives in is seen by him as a tomb and a jail (2.2.239-241)

> *What have you,*
> *my good friends, deserved at the hand of Fortune*
> *that she sends you to prison hither?*

also (1.2.133-134)

> *How weary, stale, flat, and unprofitable*
> *Seem to me all the uses of this world!*

also (2.2.309)

> *Man delights not me – nor woman neither.*

Hamlet has disengaged with the world. He becomes a celibate. He breaks off his friendships. He becomes an example of the Hermetic processes outlined in his soliloquies; he gives back to the planets what he received from the planets, and finally gives back to earth, upon his death, what he received from the earth. It is said of anyone planning revenge that the first thing to do is to dig two graves, one for the intended victim and one for yourself, this is certainly true in the case of *Hamlet*.

Conclusion

The philosophies of the *Hermetica* are embedded in *Hamlet*. They provided the well of ideas from which the poetic images were drawn. Shakespeare's plays were meant to be enjoyed as performances, they would wash over you. By reading Shakespeare we can take our time, we can dissect, we can follow up on allusions and see what lies beneath. *Hamlet* reveals its Hermetic bones in such a process and its strong connections to a new Copernican reality.

This essay has established that Shakespeare wanted to link this play with ideas related to the cosmos. Shakespeare's use of characters based on the planets, Hamlet's soliloquies, and Shakespeare's language all point to this conclusion. Stephen Greenblatt (*Will in the World*, p. 307-308) describes a rush of new words that Shakespeare introduced into the play *Hamlet*. They were words that Shakespeare had never used before in his plays or poems, and some of them were even new to the written record. Peter Usher's article (*Hamlet's Transformation*, Elizabethan Review Vol.7, No.1 p.48-64, 1999) indicates that many of these words were terms from astronomy and mathematics [8]. Clearly Shakespeare wanted his audience to consider the debate that was occurring over the structure of the cosmos as a backdrop to this play. His use of the *Hermetica* was two-fold, he wanted to direct people's attention to the heliocentric system and he wanted to make a personal statement about this newly rediscovered belief system.

Because the soliloquies mimic the Hermetic idea of the purification of the soul by ascension through the celestial spheres and because of its covert inclusion there appears to be something personal in Shakespeare's use of the concept. Since his audience would not have recognized its inclusion, it appears to be something he did for himself. It was an unnecessary constraint on the soliloquies and a challenge to his poetry. His willingness to take on this unnecessary complication demonstrates a sympathy with the Hermetic philosophy.

At the end of *Hamlet* all the planetary characters are dead. This marked the end of the Ptolemaic system and announced a new age of enlightenment. Aristotle's ideas were those of the previous generation and new ideas were yet to be discovered.

Footnotes

[1]   To find a detailed discussion of the Elizabethan world view when it comes to areas concerning Neoplatonic thought a few books that address this issue are: Tillyard, *The Elizabethan World Picture*; F. Yates, *The Occult Philosophy in the Elizabethan Age*; J. Mebane, *Renaissance Magic and the Return of the Golden Age* and Keith Thomas's *Religion and the Decline of Magic*.

[2]   Although I quote from Walter Scott's translation I should point out that Shakespeare may have read either the widely available Basel edition of Ficino's works printed in 1576 (a Latin version) or he may just have been exposed to these ideas second hand. One need not have the most accurate or up to date translation of the *Corpus Hermeticum* to assess the impact of the ideas on Shakespeare, in fact, these would probably not reflect the understanding or more precisely the 'misunderstanding' Shakespeare and his contemporaries would have been exposed to.

[3]   The Universe was seen as a regenerative force, one in a constant state of dynamic equilibrium (*Corpus Hermeticum*, Libellus XII (ii) 16). During incarnation gifts or virtues were given to the soul by each celestial sphere (planet); upon the body's death the soul would ascend back to heaven and each celestial sphere would remove specific vices (earthly corruptions) purifying the soul as it ascended back to God. In this way the Universe breathed "in with the good – out with the bad" constantly regenerating itself (see Yates F.A. *Giordano Bruno and the Hermetic Tradition*, Egyptian Regeneration, p.28-31).

[4]   *Psychanodia I, A Survey of the Evidence Concerning the*

Ascension of the Soul and its Relevance, Ioan Petru Culianu, E.J. Brill, Leiden, The Netherlands, 1983. See Chapter 7, *The Passage of the Soul Through the Spheres*, p. 48-54.

[5]   Keith Thomas points out that William Lily's work was not so much 'his' as a translation of much older Arabic works, more specifically the work of a medieval astrologer, Albohazen Haly filius Abenragel. When reading either Ptolemy or Lily or even modern books on astrology it becomes quite evident how conservative the field is in that the attributes of the planets do not vary greatly from one another regardless of the source or the time in which it was written.

[6]   The planets were very useful mnemonic tools because of their striking differences. In Francis Yate's book *The Art of Memory* (Chapter 6) she outlines in detail one of the most impressive memory systems of the 16th century developed by Giulio Camillo which was based on the planets.

[7]   Keith Thomas (Chapter 10, *Religion and the Decline of Magic*) points out that in 1600 over 600 astronomical almanacs were published in England and that these were exempt from copy limits imposed on other books. Conservative estimates show that sales of astrological almanacs far exceeded that of even the Bible during this period.

[8]   Usher also points to the origin of some of the characters' names; Claudius, he believed, alluded to Claudius Ptolemy and the traditional Ptolemaic view of the universe. Rosencrantz and Guildenstern he considered to be stand-ins for Tycho Brahe and his short lived compromise model of the universe; Rosencrantz and Guildenstern being two of Tycho's ancestors.

Tycho's model was a combination of Ptolemy and Copernican ideas that was quickly dismissed by Kepler's use of Tycho's data.

Bibliography

1) *Hamlet,* W. Shakespeare, Edited by Harold Jenkins, The Arden Shakespeare, Thomas Learning, Third Series, 2003.

2) *Hermetica: The Ancient Greek and Latin Writings Which Contain Religious Or Philosophic Teachings Ascribed To Hermes Trismegistus,* Hermes Trismegistus, Edited and translated by Walter Scott, Vol. 1. Boston, Shambhala Publications Inc., 1993.

3) *Hermetica,* Brian P. Copenhaver, Cambridge University Press, 1992.

4) *Tetrabiblos,* Claudius Ptolemy, Edited and translated by F.E. Robbins. Harvard University Press, 1980.

5) *Christian Astrology,* William Lilly, London, 1647. Reprinted by Astrology Classics, 2004.

6) *Religion and the Decline of Magic: Studies in Popular Beliefs in Sixteenth and Seventeenth Century England,* Keith Thomas, Penguin Books, 1991.

7) *The Elizabethan World Picture,* E.M.W. Tillyard, Vintage, London, 1959.

8) *De revolutionibus orbium caelestium,* Copernicus, Edited and translated by Edward Rosen, John Hopkins University Press.

9) *Psychanodia I, A Survey of the Evidence Concerning the Ascension of the Soul and its Relevance,* Ioan Petru Culianu, E.J. Brill, Leiden, The Netherlands, 1983.

10) *Giordano Bruno and the Hermetic Tradition,* Frances A. Yates, The University of Chicago Press Ltd., 1991.

11) *The Art of Memory,* Frances A. Yates, Great Britain, Pimlico, 1999.

12)   *The Occult Philosophy in the Elizabethan Age,* Frances A. Yates, Great Britain, Routledge, 2002.

13)   *The Rosicrucian Enlightenment,* Frances A. Yates, New York, Routledge, 2002.

14)   *Hamlet's Mill; An Essay Investigating the Origins of Human Knowledge and its Transmission Through Myth,* Giorgio de Santillana, and Hertha Von Deshend, A Nonpareil Book, David R. Godine, Publisher Inc., 1998.

15)   *The Nobleman and his Housedog; Tycho Brahe and Johannes Kepler: The Strange Partnership that Revolutionized Science.* K. Ferguson, Published by Review, 2002.

16)   *Will in the World; How Shakespeare became Shakespeare,* Stephen Greenblatt, W.W. Norton and Co., 2004.

17)   *The First Scientist; A Life of Roger Bacon, B.* Clegg, Constable publishing, 2003.

18)   *John Dee, The Politics of Reading and Writing in The English Renaissance,* William H. Sherman, University of Massachusetts Press, 1995.

19)   *Hamlet: Poem Unlimited,* Harold Bloom, Riverhead Books, Penguin Putnum Inc., N.Y., 2003.

20)   *The New Astrology: The Art and Science of the Stars,* N. Campion and S. Eddy, Trafalgar Square Publishing, 1999.

21)   *Renaissance Magic and the Return of the Golden Age; The Occult Tradition and Marlowe, Jonson, and Shakespeare,* John S. Mebane, University of Nebraska Press, 1989.

22)   *Hamet's Transformation,* Peter Usher, Elizabethan Review, Vol. 7, No. 1, 1999, p.48-64.

Abstract for *Macbeth*

Macbeth's Horrible Imaginings and the Logic of Evil

What I will argue in this essay is that *Macbeth* grew out of the debates (Dicson/Perkins debates) over Memory training. Conservative Protestants and Ramists were proposing an imageless memory system that would absorb Memory training into Logic.

The Classical system of Memory training was based on mnemonic imagery (outrageous phantastical images that could be used to store information by association). Because this imagery was often violent, shocking, and sometimes erotic the more conservative elements of the society sought to ban such imagery from people's minds.

Macbeth was constructed using the principles of mnemonic imagery in order to mount a defense for the Classical practice (by showing its potential for good) and at the same time reveal the potential for doing evil that was hidden within a system founded on Logic.

Macbeth's Horrible Imaginings and the Logic of Evil

Introduction

The play *Macbeth* describes a civil war fought on a very personal level. At first glance it is a family dispute fought between two legitimate heirs for the throne of Scotland [1]. It was a story Shakespeare's audience could relate to. A Scottish conflict brought close to their English home. But his intent was to get more personal. *Macbeth* is an allegorical tale. It takes a story from the macrocosm, that of a family struggle for the control of Scotland and parallels it with a story about the microcosm, the internal struggle Macbeth is experiencing between his faculties of Reason and Imagination for control over his Will. While Macbeth struggles in the macrocosm for control of Scotland his internal struggle is for his very soul.

To find the heart of *Macbeth* we must journey to the center of his mind and surprisingly to the center of religion.

A Civil War of Biblical Proportion

Macbeth was written in the same period as *Hamlet* and *King Lear* and yet *Macbeth* is virtually devoid of any reference to classical literature compared to either of these other plays. Instead most of the imagery in *Macbeth* comes from the Christian tradition. The Biblical allusions are too numerous to mention so only a few of the most significant will be examined; for further reading along this line see the paper by Jane H. Jacks entitled *Macbeth, King James, and the Bible*.

Throughout the play there are constant references to stories of both the Old and New Testaments but in particular to stories of the Old Testament Kings as sited in *Jeremiah, Kings(3,4), Samuel(1,2), and Chronicles*. *Macbeth* is Biblical in nature; the extremity of the character arcs, the depths of the tragedies are all in keeping with that tradition.

49

The stories of King Saul and King David are full of allusions to details that are found in *Macbeth*. For example, consider the advice given in Jeremiah to avoid the council of false prophets (soothsayers, or witches). It is a warning ignored by both Macbeth and King Saul and that ultimately leads to their downfalls.

"Thus saith the Lord of Hosts, Hearken not unto the words of the prophets that prophesy unto you: they make you vain: they speak a vision of their own heart, and not out of the mouth of the Lord.

They say still unto them that despise me, The Lord hath said, Ye shall have peace; and they say unto every one that walketh after the imagination of his own heart, No evil shall come upon you" (Jeremiah 23.16-17).

The story of King Saul and the Witch of Endor as told in 1 Samuel 28.3-20 is certainly the precedent for Macbeth and his increasing dependence on the witches. Saul's subsequent demise, where his head is impaled on a pole, can be found in 1 Samuel 31.9. This is an end which Macbeth comes to share with Saul (5.9.20). On a more general note the stories told in Samuel and Kings describe how both King Saul and King David are corrupted by power. This shared theme of ambition is certainly found throughout *Macbeth* and is dealt with by many other critics including Bradley.

The New Testament allusions are even more direct. Christ's temptation by Satan in the desert (Matt. 4.1-11) can be compared with Macbeth's temptation by the witches on the heath (1.2.47-78); the description of Macbeth's battle (1.2.41) as a scene from another Golgotha (Matt. 27.33); the fact that Macbeth denies his conscience three times just as Peter denies Christ three times (Matt. 26.75); the unnatural darkness that occurs at Duncan's murder (2.1.4-5)(2.3.53-59) and that which occurred at Christ's execution (Matt. 27.45); Lady Macbeth washing her hands of the crime (2.2.66) and Pilate washing his hands of the execution of Christ (Matt. 27.24); nor could anyone fail to notice King Macbeth's similarity to King Herod (Matt. 2.16) as he reenacts his own 'slaughter of the innocents' with the murder of Macduff's wife and son (4.2.79-86).

There is no doubt we are looking at a play founded in 'that old time religion' and the apocalyptic atmosphere it exudes is very similar to that found in the book of Revelation. The same darkness, death, and blood can be found there in equal abundance.

"And the second angel poured out his vial upon the sea; and it became as the blood of a dead man" (Revelation 16.3).

"And the fourth angel sounded, and the third part of the sun was smitten, and the third part of the moon, and the third part of the stars; so as the third part of them was darkened, and the day shone not for a third part of it, and the night likewise" (Revelation 8.12).

Because of these allusions and many more it is safe to say Shakespeare was creating a backdrop that was focused both on religion and it could be argued, on the dark side of these religious stories. Stories of doom, stories of massacres, stories of temptation, and stories of failure to do what's right.

These concerns can be linked to a particular debate that was going on at the time concerning religious education. I believe these changing attitudes were central to Shakespeare's play and may account for its doomsday, apocalyptic atmosphere.

Ramism

A major educational reform came about around the time *Macbeth* was written over differing views of memory training. It has been referred to as the Dicson/Perkins controversy of 1584 but it can be understood in more general terms relating it to a type of iconoclasm (*The*

Art of Memory, Frances Yates, Chpt.12, p. 260-278). What should have been a debate about education soon broadened into a religious debate (this was the 16th century after all).

In one corner were the Iconoclasts (Calvinists, Erasmians, Puritans, Ramists) and in the other corner the classicists (Catholic Church, Aristotelians, and surprisingly Bruno). At the heart of the debate was Aristotle's model for thought or more specifically memory.

One of the major educational reformers of the 16th century (by his own words) was Pierre de la Rame'e or more generally known as Peter Ramus. He was born in 1515 and died in 1572 at the massacre of St. Bartholomew [2]. This added to his prestige among Protestants. The 'Ramist' movement promoted a memory system where every subject could be arranged in dialectical order branching out from the general through a series of dichotomized classifications to the more specific. Memory was absorbed into Logic. Every subject could be summarized as a 'memory tree' devoid of any images and consisting only of a series of logical steps (chains of associations). There can be no doubt that a memory system based on imageless dialectical order went well with Calvanist (bare bones) theology. This method stood in contrast to and opposition with the Catholic tradition of memory training.

The Catholic tradition relied on the classical methods as passed down and modified by Simonides (556-468 BCE) to Aristotle to Augustine etc. It was a system founded on images known as mnemonic devices. The process involved the creation of highly emotionally charged striking images where every element within the image could hint to a piece of information you wished stored within this 'mnemonic device'. In theory later, when you recalled the image, each part of it would remind you of that stored information. The images chosen were easily remembered. They tended to be full of action, violence, strong emotion, unusual subjects, and often had erotic content; they tended to pound their way into the memory and were difficult to forget. <u>Memory was an imaginative process.</u> Advertisers today still employ these time tested techniques to slam their way into our brains with branded commercial content. At the time the Catholic Church used these mnemonic images and techniques to help train priests in techniques necessary for remembering sermons and other oratorical subjects. It has been suggested that the stained glass windows and sculptures in many Churches have been ladened with symbolic content so that they could function in this mnemonic fashion. I should emphasize that this technique was a classical technique employed by the Catholic Church but not exclusive to it. G. Bruno was a master of these techniques and no favorite of the Catholic Church.

Ramism was an extraordinary success in England (being a Protestant country) due to the fact that it provided a kind of inner iconoclasm of the mind. The Protestants felt that violent, sexually charged images had no place in the minds of the clergy or anyone else wishing to serve God.

It is against this historic backdrop that Shakespeare wrote *Macbeth*. I will argue that *Macbeth* was his response to a religious mania that was determined to create a type of censorship that was capable of reaching into the very thoughts of a person in order to drive out any devilish images. *Macbeth* was a defense of mnemonic theory and protest against the intrusive practice of trying to control how one stores memories.

Shakespeare employed the same techniques of violence, sex, unusual characters and emotionally charged scenes to create a play that pounded its way into history as one of the most popular plays he ever wrote. Shakespeare's play embodies the elements of mnemonic theory and makes them a part of its structure. The same principles that make advertisements memorable make *Macbeth* accessible to a modern audience.

A Closer Look at the Mind

Shakespeare, having received a classical education, would have been well aware of Aristotle's views of the mind as expounded in *De Anima*. In it Aristotle argued that information is received by the five senses and that the imagination acts on this information to create phantasma, images that the intellect can then work on. For Aristotle, to think was to speculate with images; cognition was an imaginative process. Without generating these images thinking would not be possible. Phantasms and Mnemonic Devices are both fanciful creations that mimicked one another. A mnemonic device was believed to copy how Nature worked; this was why it was seen to be so effective. This is one of the fundamental ideas in *Macbeth* for as Macbeth looses the ability to generate or be haunted by images (like the dagger before his eyes) he becomes increasingly tyrannical and instinctual in his behavior, he no longer thinks but rather just acts.

To appreciate *Macbeth* it may be helpful to understand the Elizabethan view on how the mind works (*The Elizabethan World Picture*, Tillyard, Chpt.5, p.71-79). The brain was divided into a triple hierarchy. The Lowest contained the Five External Senses (touch, taste, smell, hearing, seeing). The Middle contained what was called the Three Internal Senses, namely; Common Sense, Imagination, and Memory. The Common Sense received and summarized the reports from the five senses. The Imagination or Phantasy contained images/phantasms that were created by the imagination from information supplied by the Common Sense (its job being to create images that might account for all this sensory information). The Memory stored the Phantasms. Memory and Phantasm are closely related in that images created by the Phantasm were stored in the Memory and made available for the higher aspects of the mind to speculate on. This lower and middle region of the brain operated at a level of pre-cognition.

The highest form of brain function was Reason made up of Understanding and Will. Both required information retrieved from the Memory (in the form of phantasms) in order to function. The Elizabethans felt that humans were born ignorant and that through education they were able to develop and train their Understanding which in turn would bring them closer to God. Education was seen as a religious necessity; the angels "*knew themselves*", the beasts did not. It was the job of all humans to "*know themselves*" for only through knowledge could they know their weaknesses and thereby avoid sin as well as know their strengths so that they could employ these in the service of God. The Understanding had to speculate and sift through the evidence stored in the Memory (evidence contained in the form of the exuberant images constructed by the Phantasy from sensual information supplied by the Common Sense) to make reasoned presentations to the Will. The Will was concerned with possibilities; its job was to make 'just' decisions based on reasoned evidence presented to it by the Understanding. The Will was free to do as it chose. This is why choices of morality were considered acts of the Will rather than acts of Understanding. The correct use of Will was to do God's Will but the role of the Will was as controller, it determined which actions would be taken.

The Heart of the Disagreement

The Ramist attack on Memory was not just a minor disagreement over technique but it was perceived as a threat both to one's Understanding and one's ability to do the Will of God. Ramists did not trust the Imagination. It was considered a creative faculty, which means

55

it could generate false content, it could in effect lie to the Understanding by providing it with false information. Information that was perjured by the senses. Since the Imagination received its raw content from the Common Sense Ramists and Puritans believed the images it generated were weighted in favor of the sensual world and so would slowly draw people away from God. Rational control had to be exercised over the imagination, it could not be left to imagine just anything willy-nilly.

Aristotelians were worried, too, about the threat to their Understanding. They felt that Memory was a link to Divine Ideals. To censor memory or restrict its natural operation was seen as dangerous. Aristotle was a student of Plato's and one of Plato's views (nicely expressed in his *Meno* complete with an example of how a stable boy, who never studied math, could solve a complex problem involving square roots) was of how our pre-existent souls were exposed to all the secrets of creation.

"As the soul is immortal, has been born often and has seen all things here and in the underworld, there is nothing which it has not learned" Meno (81 d).

This knowledge the soul possessed was taken away just prior to incarnation but Plato felt that if we exercised our memories we could recapture some of this lost information. This understanding is implicit in Aristotle for he used philosophical speculation rather than observation to construct his 'science'. He too believed you could remember your way to the principals behind nature; remember your way to enlightenment; rather than experiment your way there

"...for searching and learning are, as a whole, recollection."
"...what we call learning is recollection" Meno (81 d).

This also helps explain one of the reasons for the Hermetic obsession with Memory training [3], it was a way to enlightenment. This is why so many of its practitioners like Giordano Bruno, Raymond Lull, and Giulio Camillo wrote extensively on the topic. Francis Yates' book *The Art of Memory* goes into great detail on the content of their work. For them it was a way of obtaining and storing knowledge (gnosis) and also of creating the conditions necessary for their salvation.

Since the fall of Adam it was felt that one's sensual appetite (senses) was at constant war with one's reason for control of the Understanding in order to have sway over the Will. This was a personal civil war waged within each of us. Humans were pictured in the position between beasts (given over to emotions and desires) and the Angels (serving God through the noblest of reason). Reason was seen as man's heavenly part, the Senses as his beastly part. Since Understanding was threatened when the Memory was undermined it meant we could be weakened in this fight for our very souls. Reason drew humans toward their spiritual home whereas the Senses drew humans to the earth and its pleasures. The Senses made us Earthlings and were seen as a corrupting influence on our spiritual potential.

Hermetica, Libellus X, 8b

"...the vice of the soul is lack of knowledge...such a soul is tossed about among the passions which the body breeds; it carries the body as a burden, and is ruled by it, instead of ruling it. That is the vice of the soul."

Hermetica, Libellus X, 9

"...the virtue of the soul is knowledge...Knowledge differs greatly from sense-perception. Sense-perception takes place when that which is material has the mastery; and it uses the body as its organ, for it cannot exist apart from the body. But knowledge is incorporeal; the organ which it uses is the mind itself."

At this point we can see how the Ramists and Aristotelians were polarized over the possible consequences posed by new methods of memory training. Aristotelians felt that without images thinking would be impeded (after all to think was to speculate with images) and people would become more instinctual in their behavior, more like animals. By removing images from our memories our Understanding would be compromised and our advantage in the battle between the appetite and reason could be lost, for our Reason would be diminished by our hampered Understanding. We could all become unthinking servants to our senses, and tyrants with each other (1.7.65-68)

> *Will I with wine and wassail so convince,*
>
> *That memory, the warder of the brain,*
>
> *Shall be a fume, and the receipt of reason*
>
> *A limbeck only.*

The Ramists feared the same thing only they believed that the Imagination was at fault for compromising the Understanding. They were fearful of its potential to supply misleading content and sensually biased content to the Understanding so felt it should be tightly controlled.

The Hermetic Mind

The Aristotelian point of view was seen as conservative compared to memory theories coming from the Hermetic camp (*Renaissance Magic and the Return of the Golden Age*, Mebane, Chpt. 7, The Renaissance Magus as Mock-Hero, p. 148-149).

The Hermetists agreed with most of Aristotle except on the how the Mens operated. This brings us to the last part of the brain, higher than all the rest, it was called the Mens, often thought of as our intuitive faculty. The Mens was considered the upper part of the soul, it was created divine, but upon falling into the body was considered to be trapped in the material world.

Aeneid Book VI (ll 724-732)

> *"First, you must know that the heavens, the earth, the watery*
>
> *plains*

Of the sea, the moon's bright globe, the sun and the stars are all
Sustained by a spirit within; for immanent <u>Mind</u>, flowing
Through all its parts and leavening its mass, makes the universe
work.
This union produced mankind, the beasts, the birds of the air,
And the strange creatures that live under the sea's smooth face.
The life-force of those seeds is fire, their source celestial,
But they are deadened and dimmed by the sinful bodies they live
in-
The flesh that is laden with death, the anatomy of clay."

The Hermetic view considered the mind to be linked to God's
Mind in much the same way as was voiced above by Virgil.

Hermetica, Libellus XII (i) 1

"Mind, my son Tat, is of the very substance of God...Mind then is not
severed from the substantiality of God, but is, so to speak, spread abroad
from that source, as the light of the sun is spread abroad."

The idea expressed in the *Hermetica* that knowledge is
incorporeal was important because God too is incorporeal so that it was
felt that the best way to get in touch with God was through the mind.
Some believed that through the Mens celestial influences could still flow,
that God or the Angels could still exert their influences or communicate
through the Mens. The Hermetic philosophers took these ideas much
further than Aristotelians and believed that it was also through the Mens
that the human intellect could climb, like Jacob's Ladder, (Gen.28.12)
through the planetary spheres to the Celestial Consciousness and regain
their divinity. They felt because the Mens was linked to the Divine that
it was also linked to the world of pure forms (this is a Platonic idea and it
refers to the pure ideas upon which the Demiurge based the creation).
They felt that these archetypal Ideas formed the basis of a
communication between the Divine and the human mind through its

imaginative faculties (i.e. the Phantasm). They felt the Mens was linked in some way with the Imagination. Dreams and Visions were a result of this Divine communication. The Hermetic Magus took the Aristotelian principal 'that to think was to speculate with images' as a way, through contemplation on dream images, to achieve Divine insight. These insights allowed the Hermetic magus to apprehend the meaning of the forms of created things [4], and to use this knowledge to bring the physical objects into greater conformity with the Ideas that governed them. To understand this concept think of it as an act of purification (like distillation) where, for example, a plant gives up its medicinal ingredients in a pure form; instead of chewing on raw birch bark you can isolate the salicylic acid from it. Alchemy was a Hermetic practice performed on the physical world as well as on the soul, it was an act of purification, it was an act of revealing the truth God put into every object of creation. In terms of Aristotelian thought it was akin to finding that object's purpose for being.

The traditional view held that the Mens was only linked to the higher rational mind, it dismissed the idea that dreams were a form of divine communication. On the contrary, it held that the Phantasy (imaginative power) was linked with the Common Sense (that part of the mind receiving sensory information) and that the imagination was therefore a slave to physical desires and that dreams were fundamentally earthly and potentially corrupting. Because of this danger Rational restraint had to be exercised over the imagination lest it inflame one's desires (passions) and lead them to sin (*The Three Books of Occult Philosophy*, Agrippa, Book 1 LXII).

"Passions which trouble the phantasy, though they dwell between the confines of sense and reason, yet they rather follow sense than reason, because they are drowned in corporeal organs of sense".

You can see here how Aristotelians and Ramists agreed on the point that the Imagination had to be controlled, what they disagreed over was on how to exercise that control. The Ramists pushing for a complete ban while the conservative Aristotelians would argue for disciplined control of imagination by examining its intended purpose. Hermetists disagreed with the idea that any control should be placed on the imagination at all.

The conservative Aristotelians supported the use of the imagination but still held the view that it was the Rational mind that was the only way to the Divine and that the Mens only represented pure Ideals (intuitive ideas of what was good) that could guide rational thought and help it find God's Will. The conservative view did not see the Mens as actively connected with God or as a channel for communication as the Hermetists did.

Hermetic Macbeth

In *Macbeth* we are presented with a character who sees visions, like the dagger (2.1.33-49). These visions do not feed his passions but rather cool them; they are warnings against his intended actions. Because of this they take on a moral quality and can be seen as coming from the Divine (Bradley states that Macbeth's visions are the form his morality takes shape in, that his imagination is the best part of him, something higher than his conscious thoughts, *Shakespearean Tragedy*, Bradley A.C., Lect. IX, p. 352). This is a Hermetic view of the Mind where the imagination (the phantasm) is linked to the Mens (the higher ideals that come from the Divine). This seems to be confirmed by the fact that Macbeth sinks deeper and deeper into moral depravity each time he ignores a vision. Had he but obeyed the first he would have been safe but having ignored them all he becomes nothing but a tyrant and a beast.

After the last vision Macbeth effectively turns off his mind. He has disconnected from God. He will think no more (4.1.146-148)

> *From this moment,*
> *The very firstlings of my heart shall be*
> *The firstlings of my hand.*

It is this moral role that is played by the imagination that suggests Shakespeare may have been exposed to Hermetic ideas. Although Hermeticism differed only slightly from the more conservative Aristotelian philosophy both still regarded images and phantasms as essential to a healthy rational mind and at odds with the imageless rationality and hampered thinking proposed by the Ramists.

Macbeth embodies the kind of tyrannical character that could result from the kind of unthinking imageless world that Shakespeare fears could be the consequence of a Ramist revolution. Without images we could become a little less human. For Shakespeare Images contain the power to convince, the power to shock, the power to shame, the very power to think. To abandon this to a form of dialectical rationalism would have been a denial of our humanity [5].

Holinshed Versified

The plot for *Macbeth* comes mainly from *Holinshed's Chronicle* (1587). It is surprising how closely Shakespeare sticks to the outline provided and the detail of information it contains; scenes one would think Shakespeare invented are actually present in this very fictive form of history. Holinshed does provide a nice background to the story that readers of *Macbeth* today may be unaware of. The fact that Shakespeare chose these 'bones' to improvise upon should not be surprising nor should it be surprising that he went to the Books of Kings and 1,2 Samuel in the Old Testament to find supporting material. This process of adding a new layer of meaning onto a pre-existing structure was a common practice in the past. In the Guild system a Master would have many apprentices under their direction; they would all help and work on the 'Master's piece'. When Shakespeare used Holinshed's outline it freed him to concentrate on improvising his poetry. He didn't have to imagine or construct a plot, he could channel his energy in developing characters and ideas that could exist within its structure. The work is similar to a collaboration between a lyricist and a composer.

   Macbeth was the last of the four great tragedies to have been written: *Hamlet, Othello, King Lear,* then *Macbeth*. In it we find characters that are again modeled after Zodiacal personalities. Shakespeare is once more taking advantage of pre-existing structures to help him tell his tale. In *Macbeth* we find that Macbeth and his wife are modeled after the zodiacal personalities of a Capricorn and Scorpio respectively. The use of astrology was not seen as a contradiction to religious belief nor was it seen as symptomatic of allegiance to any other belief system. Astrology operated much like a weather forecast; it could indicate forces that might influence you but it could not affect your Free Will.

Macbeth as a Capricorn

   The Sun's entry into Capricorn (Dec.21-Jan.20) marks the winter solstice. Capricorn is an earthly sign ruled by Saturn (because of this Macbeth has many similarities to Claudius, the Saturnine character in *Hamlet*). The hardship of winter was felt to foster, in those born in this season, a strong desire for security. This desire manifested itself in skills such as common sense planning and the ability to suffer in the short term if a long term gain was possible. The desire for security could also lead to vices like covetousness (for money or power) as well as to a general avarice.

Capricorns are symbolized as the Goat-Fish (a symbol derived from a Greek legend of Pan half transforming himself into a fish in order to save Zeus). Being an earthly sign it was felt that the senses dominated at least the Goat half of the personality while the imagination dominated the Fish half. The symbol indicated their dual nature allowing them to link the spiritual and physical worlds. Christ was a Capricorn. Capricorn is regarded as the sign of Patriarchs (Kings) and is generally consulted over any questions to do with governance. Finally, Capricorns were seen as those required to do those things that cannot be done and for searching after that which cannot be known (*Three Books of Occult Philosophy*, Agrippa, Book II,Chpt. XXXVI, XXXVII also *Christian Astrology*, Lilly, Chpt.7, The tenth House).

Although all these characteristics are easily seen in Macbeth's personality it is the need for security that is his major driving force. It is this unquenchable desire for reassurance that allows his wife such influence over him, it's this same need that drives him back to the witches (3.5.32-33)

> *And you all know security*
> *Is mortals' chiefest enemy.*

The murder of Duncan is also motivated by this same need; to finally rest securely at the summit of one's political career.

Although motivated by security Macbeth is also a creature of the imagination, it bullies and advises him, and he ignores it at his peril.

Lady Macbeth as a Scorpio

Scorpio (Oct.23-Nov.22) is a sign that is ruled by Mars. Ptolemy remarked that "*the sign of Scorpio as a whole is marked by thunder and fire*" (*Tetrabiblos* II.11). The Anglo-Saxons saw the month of Scorpio as a time when much blood would be shed as this was the time to slaughter animals and salt their meat for winter. Samhain was celebrated on

October 31 to mark the end of the year and the beginning of the descent towards darkness. Bonfires (literally bone fires, made from the bones of the slaughtered animals) were lit in celebration. The Greeks believed anyone born in Scorpio would only achieve greatness through violence. Scorpio was the sign that would be consulted regarding questions of absence and death.

The autumnal descent into darkness was linked to the experience of being abandoned or descending into the underworld. This was regarded as a time for self-reflection and a chance to improve oneself, a time for spiritual transformation. When Heracles kills the Hydra (regarded as a Scorpionic myth) he does so by dragging the creature from the darkness into the light.

Scorpio is a water sign and as such is associated with phantasy and the imagination. Scorpio was said to rule over the genitals and so was associated with lust. Comeliness and beauty are attributes of this sign along with impudence, deceit, and treacheries (*Three Books of Occult Philosophy*, Agrippa, Book II, Chpt. XXXVI, XXXVII also *Christian Astrology*, Lily, Chpt. 7, The eighth House; Chpt 16A, 16B). They provided the model for the femme-fatale. Scorpio is a sign of extremes; extreme love or, if jilted, extreme hatred. Love that ends in tragedy is often referred to as Scorpionic (as seen in Romeo and Juliet where love is turned against itself as suicide). The symbol for Scorpio (sigil) is a phallic symbol just as the sigil for Virgo is a yonic symbol.

Shakespeare makes veiled references to his use of this sign as when Lady Macbeth pleads *"unsex me here"* (1.5.41) and when Macbeth complains *"O! full of scorpions is my mind"* (3.2.36).

William Lilly observed that Scorpio signified *"fear and anguish of Mind"*. Lady Macbeth manifests these qualities only when Macbeth begins to leave her on her own. It is then that she begins to unravel; absence begins to fill her world (5.1.4-8).

Since his majesty went into the field, I have seen her rise from her bed, throw her nightgown upon her, unlock her closet, take forth paper, fold it, write upon't, read it, afterwards seal it, and again return to bed; yet all this while in a most fast sleep.

His absence has allowed her time to reflect, she has a chance to improve her soul. The metaphor of enlightenment is symbolized by her having a light by her side continuously. Reflection upon her behavior has manifest itself as a fear of darkness both in her soul and in the world (5.1.21)

she has light by her continually; tis her command.

The fear of a scorpionic suicide is also clear as the doctor issues commands (5.1.72-74)

Look after her;

Remove from her the means of all annoyance,

And still keep eyes upon her.

Why We Love Macbeth

When we first hear of Macbeth we are put in awe of his strength and courage. We are alerted to his resolve and the fact that he gets the job done regardless of adversity. We also love him because he is vulnerable, he has weaknesses, he has a conscience. He speaks to us of our humanity. He is clearly an earthling, he loves life, dirt, the feeling of being alive, he will not give it up, he will not go peaceably into the hereafter, this world must be ripped from him.

His courage is frightful as he strides from crime to crime even though his very soul is screaming out. It is this triumphant nature that separates him from every other character in the play. He faces his fears over and over again but never backs down. Through the play's dialogue we are allowed to feel his fears more than any of the other characters and yet he never retreats, though fearful he heads straight into the fray. All other characters initially flee when faced with adversity, Malcolm and Donalbain (sons of King Duncan) flee even before being accused of a crime, Fleance (son of Banquo) flees when his father is attacked, Macduff flees to England when he becomes fearful of Macbeth's eminent attack leaving his family unprotected, a family that clearly feels abandoned and views his leaving as an act of cowardice (4.2.8-12)

> He loves us not;
>
> ...for the poor wren,
>
> The most diminitive of birds, will fight,
>
> Her young ones in her nest, against the owl.
>
> All is the fear, and nothing is the love.

With Macbeth we can say the opposite, all is the love and nothing is the fear. He does anything and everything he feels Lady Macbeth requires of him. He is unaware that he abandons her while he goes about trying to secure their safe future. He is unaware and because of her secretive nature she never tells him. They love and support one another, they suffer together. Even in Macbeth's most inhuman state at the end of the play he is still admirable because he fights out of love; love for life. He will not be a victim to the Fates, he does not care if he is vulnerable, his fears still mean nothing to him, he is David against the universal Goliath (5.5.51-52)

> Blow, wind! Come, wrack!
>
> At least we'll die with harness on our back.

Yet it is this very courage that in the end is his enemy for as it is written in the *Meno* (88b):

"courage, for example, when it is not wisdom but like a kind of recklessness: when a man is reckless without understanding, he is harmed".

Even though he is an antihero, his refusal to bow down, even to God, is somehow admirable, he is more like Christ in his final scenes than he is Satan. As Macbeth's fortunes fade you can almost hear echoes of Christ's plea (Matt.27.46)

"My God, my God, why hast thou forsaken me".

Logic: The Real Villain

Returning to the initial argument that *Macbeth* was Shakespeare's response to the threat posed by the Ramist logic system, I would like to illustrate how Logic is portrayed in the play.

Macbeth, though manifestly evil, comes off almost Christ-like whereas Lady Macbeth comes off as manipulative and genuinely evil. If there is any villain in the piece it is her even though she never physically hurts anyone and is always one step removed from the violence. It is her ability to manipulate others and to cold heartedly plan evil that makes her one of Shakespeare's best villains. I do not think this is an accident. Shakespeare has purposely chosen Logic to be her weapon and Logic is the real villain in this work.

Lady Macbeth employs her higher rational mind and an evolving system of morality to allow her to manipulate others and minimize the horror of her crimes. She is what we today would refer to as a 'spin doctor'. She uses logic to both justify and trivialize. She is the 'office manager' that coolly, logically goes about her task. She plans and assigns roles. She's the Mastermind (1.5.66-68)

> *He that's coming*
> *Must be provided for; and you shall put*
> *This night's great business into my dispatch.*

She uses logic to persuade; she uses logic to imply that it is hypocritical, nay, dishonest not to act on one's desires; relying on the fact that everyone knows dishonesty is a sin (1.7.39-41)

> *Art thou afeard*
> *To be the same in thine own act and valor,*

As thou art in desire?

She has found a way to turn vices into virtues (foul is fair) and her tool is not witchcraft but logic. Her logic also detaches her from the crime (2.2.52-53)

> *The sleeping, and the dead,*
> *Are but as pictures.*

Or (2.2.66-67)

> *A little water clears us of the deed*
> *How easy is it then!*

Or (3.2.12)

> *what's done is done.*

Shakespeare is reminding us that the imageless Ramist logic systems are our undoing. That logic can be used to commit and justify the most horrific acts. That they can be used to make Foul into Fair and Fair into Foul.

Shakespeare is telling us that God speaks to us through images. That our vivid imaginations are the best part of us just as they are the best part of Macbeth and Lady Macbeth.

For just as Logic allowed Lady Macbeth to commit the crimes it is through her Imagination that God exacts punishment for these same crimes. In act 5 Lady Macbeth begins to pay the price for her abuses on Reason; now she too is haunted by images like the spot that will not wash away (5.1.33). God's punishment is through images emblazoned on her mind. This is the form that justice takes shape in; afterall the soul's language of communication is through phantasms.

Shakespeare does not argue with the Ramists by using logic, he argues with them through the imagery of his play; the vivid, black and red, bloody, dark, thunderous, witch infested, ghost haunted, violent story of *Macbeth*.

Conclusion

What becomes clear from this discussion is that within the play *Macbeth* images/visions were seen as good, moral and assisting the Will of God.

Logic was depicted as a manipulative force with the potential of doing great evil.

The play itself is a mnemonic work filled with violence, action, and unusual characters. It is however a fundamentally moral work and a cautionary tale. It proves Shakespeare's point that if imagery is put to creative use it can engage the public, entertain, and serve God. *Macbeth* is manifestly a defense of the Imagination in a society that was putting it under threat.

Footnotes

[1]   King Duncan and Macbeth were grandsons of King Malcolm II (1005-1034).   They were the offspring of Beatrice and Doada, respectively, the only daughters of King Malcolm II. Lady Macbeth's name was Gruoch and she was the granddaughter of King Kenneth III (997-1005). It could be argued that Macbeth should have been King after Malcolm II or at least shared the throne with Duncan. He was of royal lineage by both blood and marriage. When Duncan proclaimed his son as prince (and not Macbeth) this was a very provocative action for it meant that Duncan intended to take sole control over the Royal Line rather than alternate it with either Macbeth or Macbeth's offspring.

[2]   In France on August 24, 1572 a chaotic blood bath occurred in which thousands of defenseless French Protestants were killed by organized Catholics representing the State; it was referred to as the massacre of St. Bartholomew.

[3]   The obsession with memory training also had to do with the law of correspondence; like communicates with like. As your mind became more like God's Mind then you would be able to better access the Divine Mind to learn God's will and the secrets of creation.

Hermetica Libellus XI (ii) 20b

"If then you do not make yourself equal to God, you cannot apprehend God; for like is known by like. Leap clear of all that is corporeal, and make yourself grow to a like expanse with that greatness which is beyond measure; rise above all time, and become eternal; then you will apprehend God. Think that for you too nothing is impossible; deem that you too are immortal, and that you are able to grasp all things in your thought, to know every craft and every science"

[4]   The Hermetic magus saw the physical world as a pale reflection of the real thing or more precisely the physical world was a shadow cast by the real celestial ideals that were illuminated by the divine light from the Celestial Sphere. To see beyond this physical world they depended not just on dreams and visions they also depended on mathematics to help reveal this true nature within the object.

Pythagoras was educated among the Egyptians and Chaldeans and his search for wisdom required the liberation of the mind from the body. He achieved this through mathematics. He felt mathematics could bridge the gap between the material world and that of the celestial ideals. Pythagoras praised the Demiurge as the *"Number of numbers"* and felt that the mathematization of the structures of reality could lead to understanding of the true principals present in the ideal. This led to the Pythagorean principal that *"all is likened unto number"*. He felt that the fifth element or quintessence that defined the celestial world was in fact mathematics.

[5]   Philip Sidney was also engaged in this debate; he wrote his *Defense of Poesie* in the 1580s to passionately defend the value of poetry and *"art in general"* against criticisms of the most radical Protestants who wished to limit the use of language to just didactic and religious purposes (*Giordano Bruno and Renaissance Science* by Hilary Gatti, Chapter 12, p.224).

Bibliography

1) *Macbeth*, W. Shakespeare, Edited by Kenneth Muir, Methuen and Co. Ltd. 1951, Reprinted by Thomson for The Arden Shakespeare, Third Series, 2002.

2) *Shakespearean Tragedy,* A.C. Bradley, MacMillan and Co. Ltd., 1964.

3) *The Art of Memory,* F. A. Yates, Routledge and Kegan Paul, 1966, reprinted by Pimlico, 1999.

4) *The Rosicrucian Enlightenment,* Francis A. Yates, Routledge and Kegan Paul, 1972.

5) *Shakespeare's England, Life in Elizabethan and Jacobean Times,* R.E. Pritchard, Sutton Publishing Ltd., 1999.

6) *The Elizabethan World Picture,* E.M.W. Tillyard, Vintage, 1964.

7) *The Book of Scottish Names,* Iain Zaczek, McArthur and Co., 2001.

8) *Holinshed's Chronicle, As used in Shakespeare's Plays*, R. Holinshed, Edited by A. and J. Nicoll, publ. J. M. Dent and Sons Ltd., 1969.

9) *Giordano Bruno and Renaissance Science,* H. Gatti, Cornell University Press, 1999.

10) *From Caveman to Chemist: Circumstances and Achievements,* H.W. Salzberg, American Chemical Society, Washington, D.C., 1991.

11) *The New Astrology, The Art and Science of the Stars,* N. Campion and S. Eddy, Trafalgar Square Publishing, 1999.

12) *Tetrabiblos,* Ptolemy, C., Edited and translated by F.E. Robbins, Harvard University Press, 1980.

13) *Christian Astrology,* William Lilly, London, 1647. Reprinted by Astrology Classics, 2004.

14) *Three Books of Occult Philosophy*, Agrippa, translated by James Freake, edited by Donald Tyson, Llewellyn Publications, 2004.

15) *Five Dialogues,* Plato, translated by G.M.A. Grube, Hackett Publ. Co., 1981.

16) *Hermetica: The Ancient Greek and Latin Writings Which Contain Religious Or Philosophic Teachings Ascribed To Hermes Trismegistus*, Trismegistus, Hermes, Edited and translated by Walter Scott, Vol. 1, Boston, Shambhala Publications Inc., 1993.

17) *Hermetica*, Trimegistus, Hermes, translated by Brian P. Copenhaver, Cambridge University Press, 2000.

18) *The Eclogues, Georgics and Aeneid of Virgil*, Virgil, translated by C. Day Lewis, Oxford University Press, 1974.

19) *Telling Lies: clues to deceit in the marketplace, politics, and marriage,* Paul Ekman, Norton, 1985.

Abstract for *The Merchant of Venice*
The Character of Cabala

This essay proposes that the characters and story engine for *The Merchant of Venice* both came from the Jewish mystical practice of Cabala. The characters in the play embody the Sefirot. The interdependence of the characters and the Cabalistic desire to achieve balance drives the story towards a happy ending.

The play's economic backdrop is put into perspective by comparing it with both Adam Smith's ideas on the economy and the overall metaphor of Cabala.

The Character of Cabala

Introduction

The Spanish Expulsion of the Jews in 1492 led to a mass migration back towards the east. The Ottoman Empire (Turkey) was more tolerant of the Jews than was the West. Many exiles also found a home in Italy. A large Jewish community grew up in Venice and became a center of Hebrew learning and publishing. Of the northern Protestant countries Holland was the most accepting of the Jewish refugees. In Amsterdam it was possible to live openly as a Jew, to establish schools and synagogues. In England, officially there were no Jews; they had been expelled in 1290 by Edward I. Unofficially, some Jews were present. The increase in trade and commerce, for which they acted as agents, would have necessitated their presence. Jewish refugees from the Spanish Expulsion were also present in England as murranos (Christianized Jews that had accepted or were forced to accept baptism) but they were required to conceal their old religion and live as Christians.

Although Jewish practices were censured in England acceptable versions of Cabala (Christian Cabala) became widely known. Pico della Mirandola (1463-1494) founded Christian Cabala in Florence, shortly before the Expulsion of 1492. He adapted the techniques of the Spanish Jews (Sephardic) to Christianity. He convinced the Catholic Church that Cabala could be used to confirm the truth of Christianity and the role of Christ as the Messiah. Reuchlin, a disciple of Pico's, published *De arte cabalistica* in 1517. The most famous Italian Cabalist was Francesco Giorgi and he published his *De harmonia mundi* in 1525 (Pico's *Heptaplus* published in 1489 was one of Giorgi's chief sources).

While England as a whole still did not look favorably on the Jews the Elizabethan court did [1] as did the rising Puritan population which transferred their respect for the Old Testament into a respect for

77

the Jews as well [2]. This respect seemed to be shared by Shakespeare [3] and his writing of the *Merchant of Venice* (1598) was an homage to Jewish wisdom, a cabalist compliment to the community.

The Character of Cabala

By blending the ideas of Cabala with the plot of Ser Giovanni's *Il Pecorone* (the first story of the fourth day) printed in Italian (1558), Shakespeare produced a comedy housed within a totally Jewish philosophical framework. By understanding Cabala we understand the framework and we understand the intent of Shakespeare. This allows a clearer interpretation of the work both for directors and actors; it also provides audiences with a means to interpret the play. To learn more about Cabala I would like to recommend Kim Zetter's book *Simple Kabbalah*. It provides an excellent overview of ideas I deal with only briefly and is intended for a general audience. I would also like to recommend Daniel Banes' book *The Provocative Merchant of Venice*; in it he outlines the relationship between the Sefirot of Cabala and the characters in *The Merchant of Venice*. His work is also summarized in Chapter 12 of Francis Yates' book *The Occult Philosophy in the Elizabethan Age*. The analysis that follows differs from Banes' point of view but owes a debt to him.

Cabala (Kabbalah) refers to the 'traditional knowledge' Moses received in addition to the Torah or The Law. This 'traditional knowledge' was the secret language of God hidden in the narrative of the Torah. Apocryphally, when Moses wrote down the Torah he made 13 hand-scribed copies, one for each of the judges of the 12 tribes and one copy to be kept with the tablets of the Ten Commandments housed in the Ark of the Covenant. When Moses passed down the Cabala it was only by word of mouth. It provided a way of finding coded messages within the text, in essence, it was the key to a very elaborate code. This code provided insight into the forces that created and maintain the universe. This code was made up of the 10 numbers and 22 letters (the 32 paths of wisdom) of the Hebrew alphabet. The numbers represent the forces involved and the letters how these forces are interconnected and balanced thereby binding all creation together. The 10 forces are the 10 names of God or the 10 Sefirot (3 represent hidden forces, 7 represent manifest forces). Shakespeare has personified these forces and turned them into major characters in the play. In the following text I define these forces and suggest the character which best embodies the traits. The 10 forces and 22 paths make up the 'Tree of Life'.

A) The Hidden Forces

1) Keter

Because God is everywhere S/He had to create a space where S/He did not exist in order to create something distinct from Herself. The process of creating a space, a vacuum, a nothingness represents the act of contraction. Keter is the darkness, the nothingness, the hunger, the desire.

2) Hochma

It was into this nothingness that God breathed the letters of His name. The act itself mimics breathing; God first empties a space and then fills it with Her breath. Hochma is felt to represent the thought that follows desire. Words are being put in place, imaginary images constructed, schemes are forming.

3) Binah

From the energy poured into the vacuum Binah becomes the 'Mother' of the lower Sefirot. It is like a white light pouring into the darkness and then being refracted into the 7 distinct colors. Binah represents the action to be taken after thought has occurred. Binah is the plan.

In the play, Bassanio is the personification of these hidden forces. He is Keter, the hunger, the desire. He confesses that he is nothing, in fact, less than nothing (3.2.256-262)

Rating myself at nothing, you shall see

How much I was a braggart, - when I told you

My state was nothing, I should there have told you

That I was worse than nothing; for indeed

I have engag'd myself to a dear friend,

Engag'd my friend to his mere enemy

To feed my means.

He has no wealth (1.1.122-123)

'tis not unknown to you Antonio

How much I have disabled mine estate.

Only debt upon debt (1.1.146-147)

I owe you much, and (like a willful youth)

That which I owe is lost.

He only has the desire to become wealthy and it is this desire that starts the play. He schemes to court a lady, Portia, but must borrow the money to do it. This he plans to get from Antonio. This plan is laid out in (1.1.161-185).

By these actions Bassanio shows he's not just Keter but Hochma and Binah as well; for he is not just the emptiness (the desire) but also the scheme and the plan. He is all the hidden forces that must be put in place before action can be taken. He's going to get the ball rolling; out of his desires comes the play, the world inhabited by the rest of the characters. Bassanio portrays the three hidden forces from which the created world (the play) arises.

B) The Manifest Forces

These next seven Sefirot are the engines behind the system. They accomplish the physical work that was intellectually planned out.

On their own they each represent a strong unbalanced force but in the 'Tree of Life' balance is achieved by setting the Sefirot up in groups of three (two in opposition, one at equilibrium). This balance is also reflected in the sexes; the right side of the Tree is seen as masculine, the Left, feminine and the middle, both.

4) Hesed

Hesed represents unmitigated compassion. On a human level it finds expression in charity and the nurturing of others. In its extreme form it can represent a kind of obsessiveness, smothering, or indulgence that breeds a sense of entitlement in others through the absence of any discipline. In the play these characteristics are embodied in Antonio, the long suffering friend of Bassanio and the entire city. He gives without asking anything in return (1.3.11)

Antonio is a good man

also (1.3.39)

He lends out money gratis

and again (3.3.22-23)

I oft deliver'd from his forfeitures
Many that have at times made moan to me.

Antonio wants to be seen doing good (3.4.35-36)

pray God Bassanio come
To see me pay his debt, and then I care not.

Antonio has the patient long-suffering spirit of a mother (4.1.10-12)

I do oppose
My patience to his fury, and am arm'd
To suffer with a quietness of spirit.

5) Gevurah

Gevurah is the opposite of Hesed. Gevurah represents greed, discipline, the law, limits, and boundaries. In its extreme case it's oppressive and tyrannical, lacking any compassion. It can be embodied in everything from an overly disciplinarian parent to a fascist police state. In this drama it is Shylock, representing tradition and the uncompromising letter of the law (4.1.103)

I stand for judgment.

Or more precisely (4.1.142)

I stand here for law.

He in fact hungers for the law (4.1.202)

I crave the law.

He hungers for law and order (3.1.60)

if you wrong us shall we not revenge?

6) Tiferet

This Sefira is known as 'beauty' in the sense of balance and harmony. It is the balance between giving and receiving. It is the symbol of justice. It is Portia, physically beautiful and the one who dispenses justice in the play. She fulfills all the requirements of Tiferet, she is both masculine (when disguised as a lawyer) and feminine; she is justice (blind and objective) (4.1.170)

Which is the merchant here? And which the Jew?

She is also mercy; see her speech (4.1.180-201). It begins with:

The quality of mercy is not strain'd

It droppeth as the gentle rain from heaven…

She is also a Christian who is a Jew (4.1.219)

A Daniel come to judgment: yea a Daniel!

This idea that she represents both religions arises from a couple of allusions; the first occurs when her lawyer persona is described as a Daniel in reference to the Old Testament story of Susannah and the Elders where a youth (Daniel) convicts the Elders with their own words. The second is in the symbology of the caskets. When the princes are given their choice of caskets it is really a choice among the 3 great religions, the Prince of Morocco (a Muslim) chooses gold, the symbol of the Sun; the Prince of Aragon (a Spanish Christian) chooses silver, the symbol of the Moon and Christianity (the 3 dark days around the new moon correspond to the days of the resurrection); and Bassanio chooses the lead, the symbol of Saturn and (according to Giorgi) the Jews. Banes notes its allusion to the Old Testament, Proverbs 8:10-11

"Receive my instruction, and not silver; and knowledge rather than choice gold.

For wisdom is better than rubies; and all the things that may be desired are not to be compared to it."

The choice of lead is the choice of instruction, knowledge and wisdom. In short it is to choose divine law, the Torah. The choice shows Bassanio has changed, the Prodigal is no more, and by choosing the lead casket he has chosen divine wisdom and Portia.

When Portia resolves the case between Shylock and Antonio both selfishness and violence are rejected and a partnership is forged. The notes in John Russell Browns' Arden Edition of *The Merchant of Venice*, p. 119 note 379 support this interpretation by specifying that Antonio would be put in trust of Shylock's estate but the interest would still go to Shylock, in essence they could become partners; Antonio the venture capitalist, Shylock the money-man. Balance would be in keeping with the role of Tiferet and the theme of the play.

7) Netzach

Netzach refers to domination and confidence. At their best they are the qualities of a parent or protector. Qualities like leadership (knowing when to take action), maturity, endurance, and independence. At their worst they can be extreme and crush the spirit of those they should nurture. These qualities are required for progress or change (confidence in one's abilities to meet challenges, skill and maturity that can rise above one's fears). Graciano seems to possess these qualities although in an extreme form as he is described as too wild, too rude, too bold, too liberal, and frankly just too extreme overall and he is cautioned to control himself as he offends people (2.2.171-179). It is a criticism that he takes to heart and agrees to adopt a more conservative demeanor (2.2.180-188) thereby embodying the ability/maturity to change.

8) Hod

Hod is the opposite of confidence and finds its expression more in vulnerability, complacency, fear of change, stasis, and acceptance. Hod is the child to Netzach's parent, the servant to Netzach's master, the laborer to the boss. In this play Jessica is the child. Along with the good aspects of childlike behaviour come the bad, those of immaturity, thoughtlessness, and rashness. Shylock tries to control his child by prescribing too many rules (2.5.28-36)

Hear you me Jessica,
Lock up my doors, and when you hear the drum
And the vile squealing of the wry-neck'd fife
Clamber not you up to the casement then
Nor thrust your head into the public street
To gaze on Christian fools with varnish'd faces:
But stop my house's ears, I mean my casements,
Let not the sound of shallow fopp'ry enter
My sober house.

This can only lead to rebellion (5.1.14-17)

In such a night
Did Jessica steal from the wealthy Jew,
And with an unthrift love did run from Venice,
As far as Belmont.

9) Yesod

This is the balance point between the adult and the child, confidence and vulnerability, independence and dependence, complacency and change. It is the balance everyone must find when growing up. It is a quality manifest in respect for others. Yesod is symbolic of the union between male and female. Lorenzo is Yesod. He is the only character to actually consummate his marriage and he defines harmony, respect, and thoughtfulness with his soul-mate Jessica (2.4.19-20)

> *...tell gentle Jessica*
> *I will not fail her.*

This idea of partnership is emphasized in their commitment to one another (3.4.36)

> *I shall obey you in all fair commands.*

Nothing demonstrates their love and equality better than the banter they share in the dialogue that begins *"In such a night..."* (5.1.1-24) and no scene expresses their love and harmony better than when they stare together at the vault of heaven in (5.1.54-65). Yesod is the foundation of a good marriage, a happy family, and a balanced life.

10) Malkhut

In the 'Tree of Life' Malkhut represents the roots, for it is through the roots the tree takes nourishment, in humans it represents our senses for it is through our senses that we take in the information that allows us to make sound judgments.

All the other Sefirot contain a quality that performs a function, Malkhut does not; it represents the last day of creation, the day of rest, it is the sum total of the work done by all the other Sefirot just as the Sabbath is the sum total of the week.

Because it receives its light from all the other Sefirot it is like the Moon with no light of its own.

In the play Act 5 is Malkhut. It is not a character but a summation. The main action of the play is over but Act 5 is still essential, it is full of sensual description, it is full of Moon imagery, it is full of acts of love.

When Lorenzo and Jessica are playing a game of one-upmanship by adding to the phrase *"In such a night"*, they are telling stories of love, sometimes obsessive love, and of couples that later suffered tragedy or betrayal. This is a preamble before Bassanio's and Gratiano's betrayals are discussed. This section of the play is a reprise on the idea of mercy. Bassanio and Gratiano have both broken the vows they made to protect their rings, but in all honesty they swear that they did not give the rings to women, that they are innocent (5.1.208-210)

> Por. *I'll die for't but some woman had the ring!*
> Bass. *No by my honour madam, by my soul*
> *No woman had it.*

But we know they, in fact, did give the rings to women albeit ones dressed as men. So they are guilty by the letter of the law even though innocent in spirit. It shows that mercy and forgiveness are required by all no matter how guiltless we may see ourselves.

Malkhut is the point where one world joins to the next. In Cabala there are 4 worlds, 3 above the physical world I have just described; Malkhut of the Third world is joined to Keter of this Fourth world, the world we occupy, and the Malkhut of our world joins to the world of the microcosm found within ourselves producing an ever diminishing and yet connected 'Tree of Life'. Everything is connected, everything has the spark of the divine in it. Our actions in this world produce echoes not just on earth but in the spiritual worlds as well. Energy is constantly pulsing from one world to the next trying to restore the divine balance.

Malkhut, Yesod, and Tiferet represent the 3 main points of balance and harmony in the 'Tree of Life'. Malkhut is the Moon, Tiferet is the Sun, and Yesod is Marriage. Their union is the Alchemical Wedding. Their union represents a world in harmony, where conflicts are resolved, and where balance is restored. It represents the reuniting of all those who are exiled or estranged, the prodigal returned. It is the ideal marriage and the happy family. It is the Happy Ending.

Adam Smith as the Merchant of Venice

It's not called *The Merchant of Venice* for nothing; economic philosophy permeates the work. To see this it helps to apply some of the ideas of Adam Smith to the analysis of the play.

Adam Smith is generally thought of as the 'father of economics' but he saw himself as a moral philosopher [4]. Unlike Plato and Aristotle he did not believe that the job of Reason was to master our Emotions but rather he felt Reason was slave to the Emotions. Reason's job was to figure out how to get what the passions Desired.

He understood that Desire was central to any economic system. It was the Want, the Yearning, that was to be the engine required to drive the machine. He felt that in order to obtain the pleasures of wealth, people were willing to put up with all kinds of toil and anxiety. In fact, he believed it was enough if we could just imagine ourselves as rich and famous and that this 'inner image' alone could spur our efforts and focus our energy toward what could be an elusive goal. He created a system at the heart of which was the fundamental deception 'that we could have it all'; a myth that anybody could achieve wealth and fame if they just worked hard enough.

A system based on self-gratification could easily fall into anarchy so in order to create a stable system efforts had to be taken to prevent any one member from hurting or disturbing the happiness of another. This system offers a form of Liberty, the freedom to pursue one's own self interests, but this Liberty is held in check by a counterbalancing principal, that of Authority, or the power to punish those whose self interests disturb that of another's or whose self interests threaten the long–term interests of the community.

This balance between an individual's needs and society's needs can over time be internalized as 'the voice of conscience', the voice that judges our behaviour. This judging-self cannot be deceived, it knows when we are really honest, generous, or trustworthy, it lets us know if we are fit for society.

Before proceeding too far in examining Adam Smith's views let us return to *The Merchant of Venice*. This is a tale of commerce, many deals are made and contracts signed (loan contracts, marriage contracts) and many different types of commercial personalities are depicted [5]. Much of the wording and phrasing in the play comes from the business world [6]. The similarities to Adam Smith's system are striking: Bassanio is Desire, he wants wealth, he wants Portia, he wants it all, it is his desires that start the action in the play; Antonio is Liberty, he is free enterprise, he assumes the risk of Bassanio's pursuit of happiness and it is he who will answer to Shylock who in turn represents Authority and its awful virtues of discipline, self-restraint, moral rectitude and righteous anger. Shylock represents the forces that act when rules are broken; he is tradition and the Law. Portia represents the "internalized conscience" or the honest judge that cannot be deceived and who determines the balance point between unbridled indulgence and harsh discipline. She is the balance point, the point of equity, along which societies develop.

Adam Smith's system created a way in which needs (real or imagined) could be fulfilled by trading with others, so in essence, he took a system created for self gratification and made it into a way of reaching out to others. Working as a team people became more efficient at making, selling, advertising and improving a product. This inevitably led to specialization in all aspects of production, the consequence of which is that individuals caught up in the process found their interests had become narrowed, less was demanded of their whole person, they became the cogs in the wheels, the economic working class, the assembly line factory workers. They suffered from too much discipline and were offered little room to expand their minds or spirits. Under such conditions apathy could set in and qualities like integrity, loyalty, and leadership would be lost, the very qualities required to maintain excellence in workmanship. Adam Smith felt the solution to this problem was in Education. He proposed a system of education that would teach everyone to read, write, and calculate, knowing that through education the spirit would be restored, imagination would flourish and the system would have the potential to renew itself from its widest possible roots and not just be driven from the elite. Everyone would have the tools and be given the opportunity to rise through the system.

In terms of *The Merchant of Venice* the overly disciplined, marginalized individual that is treated like a child is Jessica. Little is expected of her and Shylock has her symbolically locked in a prison, all the qualities that would make her a good daughter are drained from her until she finally breaks free into the arms of Lorenzo where her spirit and intellect become a match for his.

Education was not the only solution, however, Smith also proposed the formation of citizen militias. He hoped that militias would preserve the traditions of physical courage, self sacrifice, discipline, and confidence in one's own physical prowess. He also felt it would re-establish the idea that Liberty had to be defended and that it could be lost to either tyranny or monopoly.

In *The Merchant of Venice* these parental qualities of self defense and education are embodied in Gratiano and Lorenzo. Gratiano, the overconfident friend and body guard of Bassanio, represents the security that comes from physical empowerment; the healthy body that allows the mind to achieve its goals. Lorenzo, the loving helpmate to Jessica, represents the development of the mind and imagination through gnosis or knowledge. It creates respect for oneself and the world and allows one to be united with the Divine.

Adam Smith's work was produced over a hundred years after *The Merchant of Venice* was written. It is unlikely that *The Merchant of Venice* influenced Adam Smith but it is possible that both works could have shared a common source and that source could have been the Cabala.

In both Cabala and Adam Smith's economy a system of opposing tensions is produced along with a complex web of interconnected interests. One of the secrets of Alchemy is that all the world is seen as if in a state of dynamic equilibrium; it is this dynamism that allows societies to grow and this balance that makes them stable. An active system of checks and balances, dynamic equilibrium, is what makes nature stable, it was also the idea enshrined in the Cabala and mimicked in Adam Smith's economy.

Usury and The Deuteronomic Double Standard

It was a scripture from Deuteronomy that set Christian doctrine apart from the Jewish Law. This argument is presented in Donna Kish-Goodling's article "Using *The Merchant of Venice* in Teaching Monetary Economics".

Deuteronomy 23:19-20

"You shall not lend upon interest to your brother, interest on money, interest on victuals, interest on anything that is lent for interest. To a foreigner you may lend upon interest, but to your brother you shall not lend upon interest..."

(New Oxford Bible, Revised Standard Edition).

Because all Jews are descendents from Jacob, they are all brothers and cannot charge each other interest, but they can charge interest to foreigners or non-Jews, i.e., Christians. However, Christians regard all men to be their brothers, as all are descended from Adam, this means Christians are prohibited from lending money to anyone, since all are regarded as their brothers.

This tradition allowed Jews to become money lenders without the fear of excommunication that hung over the heads of any Christian entering this vocation. As economies of Europe grew during the Middle Ages the need for capital became increasingly important so much so that many governments subtly forced Jews into the role of money lender by prohibiting them from taking any other kind of work. In this way they protected their growing economies by providing access to capital and they safeguarded the souls of their Christian citizens from excommunication.

Levels of Meaning

Believers in Cabala understand that there are four layers of meanings to be found in the stories of the Torah. The first layer is the literal, or physical story, what you see is what you get; the second layer is the metaphorical story, the story stands for something else, a transfer of meaning occurs from one thing to another (it gives us an image with which to think), this technique is often used to express emotional concepts not easily verbalized. The next level of meaning is the allegorical, some subject is addressed under the guise of another, and often this is a symbolic or intellectual puzzle. The final meaning is esoteric referring to a spiritual or secret truth. For instance there is a story that starts *"Three rabbis walk into a orchard..."* The literal meaning is referred to as <u>peshat</u>; the metaphorical, <u>remez</u>; the allegorical, <u>drash</u>; and the esoteric, <u>sod</u>. The first letters of these words make prds or pardes (the vowels are not included in Hebrew) the word for orchard. As you can see their walk into the orchard was just the beginning of a spiritual journey of reflection and intellectual effort to uncover hidden spiritual truths.

The Merchant of Venice employs several Jewish metaphors in the service of its Cabalistic framework. These can be seen in the character arcs of the major figures.

1) Jessica's Arc: Her story is best summed up in the metaphor of the Exodus, just as Moses led his people out of oppression and into liberty so does Lorenzo help Jessica escape her oppressive father.

2) Antonio's Arc: He is Job, the righteous sufferer, never cursing or lashing out against God or those who persecute him.

3) Bassanio's Arc: He is the Prodigal son who squanders his wealth but returns to find enlightenment and forgiveness.

4) Portia's Arc: She is the embodiment of the Flood story; the second chance given to humanity. Hers is the story of God's mercy.

5) Shylock's Arc: Perhaps he is best seen as Abraham, a man capable of killing his own offspring until he is stopped by an angel representing God's mercy.

6) Shylock and Antonio's relationship: Several other biblical stories surround and enlighten our understanding of Shylock and Antonio's relationship and one of these is the idea of Yom Kippur (the Day of Atonement) where two sacrifices are made, the first to atone for the sins of the priest the second to atone for the sins of the people. On Antonio's judgment day he is to be sacrificed only to find himself saved when it becomes apparent that Shylock must face a similar fate; two sacrifices, two sets of sins atoned for by the mercy of God.

7) More on Shylock and Antonio: The other metaphor surrounding Shylock and Antonio is the story of Jacob and Laban. Banes points out that this story is best understood from Shylock's point of view as interpreted in *The Zohar* (a Cabalistic work). Shylock sees himself as Jacob, an honest hard working man whose efforts bring his employer,

Laban, a surplus profit of thousands of ewes, lambs, and goats. For his effort Laban grudgingly gave Jacob only one percent of the profits and even this pittance was regarded as thievery by Laban's family. The success of Laban's enterprise depended upon Jacob's efforts but Laban saw success as his rightful due no matter how little he personally exerted himself. Shylock sees himself as Jacob, his money as Jacob's efforts. When he funds venture capitalists like Antonio he feels justifiably upset when these same people behave like Laban and think the profit is only theirs to enjoy and refuse to pay even a moiety of those profits to those that contributed to their success and even accuse those same people of thievery. This is the source of Shylock's resentment.

If we were to look for the four levels of meaning in *The Merchant of Venice* we might come up with the following set of interpretations.

1) Physical: the play itself, the story as presented.

2) Metaphorical/Emotional: It's a metaphor for stories in the Old Testament; the characters personifying stories from the Torah and Cabala.

3) Allegorical/Intellectual: It's an allegory of the economy as outlined using economic principals derived from but not exclusive to Adam Smith.

4) Esoteric/Spiritual: The Cabalistic framework of the play and its secret of harmony and balance and interdependence. This spiritual message is the key to interpreting the play,

Conclusion

The Cabala holds the secret to the play, not only is it the source for the characters in the play but it is the engine for the play itself. Everything is moving toward balance. All the characters are being forced to empathize with 'the other'. Jessica chooses to marry and become a Christian; Bassanio chooses to marry Portia, who is really the embodiment of Jewish wisdom; females choose to adopt male personas (Jessica dresses as a boy during her elopement, Portia and Nerrisa as male lawyers); Antonio chooses to take on Bassanio's debt; and Shylock chooses Antonio's fate, that of being judged by the letter of the Law.

Not only are the characters taught to empathize with one another but they also receive help from each other. Portia gets help from her dead father through the 'shell game' he devises in order to protect her from any undesirable suitors; Jessica gets help from Lorenzo in order to flee a bad family situation; Bassanio gets help first from Antonio in the form of a loan and then is helped by Portia his wife and friend; Antonio gets help from Portia in her lawyer persona, Balthazar; and Shylock in the end gets help from both the Judge and Antonio as they pardon his life, renounce his fine, and impose a partnership or balance to his life, that may include a better relationship with his daughter Jessica.

No character is presented as wholly good or bad but they all are taught to empathize and assist one another. As they bring balance to themselves they bring peace to the world.

Footnotes

[1]   There is an apocryphal story that relates to the year 1593 that tells of a Jewish brother and sister who left Portugal (their parents killed in the Inquisition) to find refuge in Amsterdam. Their ship was captured by the English and brought in to port. The story goes on to relate how Queen Elizabeth was charmed by the sister, became pals, and were often seen together about London. Elizabeth was said to have encouraged them to stay but they expressed the wish to practice their religion openly so decided to continue their journey to Amsterdam. This story was probably the modern equivalent of 'launching a trial balloon' to test public reaction. The story is covered in more detail in Francis Yates' *The Occult Philosophy in the Elizabethan Age*, Chapter 10, p.132.

[2]   The Puritan tolerance of the Jews led to strong Parliamentary support and allowed Charles II to permit Jews to openly practice their religion with virtually no opposition to the idea (Yates, ibid., Chapter 18, p. 213).

[3]   Shakespeare probably wrote the "Ill May Day" scene in *Sir Thomas Moore* which dealt with the poor treatment of strangers among another nation, relating to the anti-alien riots of 1588, 1593 and 1595 in London (The Arden Edition of *The Merchant of Venice*, edited by John Russell Brown, Preface, xxv).

[4]   He credits David Hume's *A Treatise of Human Nature* as forming the basis to his own book *The Wealth of Nations*.

[5]   There are several classes and types of wealth depicted in the play; Antonio represents the venture capitalist, the new money as it were;

Portia, an heiress, is old money or inherited money; Shylock is a symbol of the developing banking system essentially funding venture schemes; Launcelot represents labor and its power as he searches out better working conditions; Jessica represents the dark side of generating capital by theft; finally Bassanio, the gambler, the gigolo, is the public always wanting more and in the process fueling the whole system.

[6]   When it comes to dialogue Portia uses business terms in many of her speeches:

(3.2.10)   *Before you venture for me*

(3.2.18-20)   *O these naughty times*
      Put bars between the owners and their rights
      And so though yours, not yours,

(4.1.411)   *He is well paid that is well satisfied*

(3.2.312)   *Since you are dear bought, I will love you dear.*

Bibliography

1) *The Merchant of Venice,* W. Shakespeare, Edited by John Russell Brown, first published by Methuen and Co. Ltd. 1965, Reprinted by The Arden Shakespeare, Third Series, 2000.

2) *Simple Kabbalah,* K. Zetter, Published by Castle Books in cooperation with Conari Press, 2002.

3) *The Origin of the Kabbalah,* Gershom Scholem, Princeton University Press, 1990.

4) *The Occult Philosophy in the Elizabethan Age,* Frances Yates, Routledge and Kegan Paul, 1979.

5) *The Rosicrucian Enlightenment,* Frances Yates, Routledge and Kegan Paul, 1972.

6) *The Art of Memory,* Frances Yates, Routledge and Kegan Paul, 1966.

7) *The Provocative Merchant of Venice,* Daniel Banes, Malcolm House Publications, 1975.

8) *The Queen's Conjurer The Science and Magic of Dr. John Dee, Adviser to Queen Elizabeth I,* Benjamin Woolley, Henry Holt and Co., New York, 2001.

9) *Using The Merchant of Venice in Teaching Monetary Economics,* Donna M. Kish-Goodling, Journal of Economic Education, (Fall), p. 330-339, 1998.

10) *How The Scots Invented the Modern World,* Arthur Herman, Three Rivers Press. New York, 2001.

Abstract for *The Winter's Tale*
White Magic in *The Winter's Tale*

This essay on *The Winter's Tale* argues that Shakespeare enfolded Pico della Mirandola's oration *On the Dignity of Man* into his play. Pico's work not only provided Shakespeare with his major characters but it also supplied him with the understanding he needed to create the magic required in the play.

White Magic in *The Winter's Tale*

Introduction

The Winter's Tale is an ode to Nature. Her images fill its pages as does the magic of Her workings. Magic, more precisely natural magic, is the key to a deeper understanding of the play and its characters. This key laying open Shakespeare's secrets is to be found in the writings of Pico della Mirandola [1].

Giovanni Pico della Mirandola (1463-1494) spent most of his career trying to discover the unity that existed between different sacred theologies and Christian revelation (*On the Dignity of Man* by Pico della Mirandola, translated by Charles Glenn Wallis, Paul J.W. Miller and Douglas Carmichael, Hackett Publ. Co. Inc., 1998, p. 23)
"I have wished to bring into view the things taught not merely according to one doctrine...but things taught according to every sort of doctrine".

Pico manifested a tolerant eclecticism that was much appreciated by those who played a role in the English Renaissance. This essay will show his work, *On the Dignity of Man,* (a short work of only 34 pages in the Wallis translation) had a major influence on Shakespeare's work *The Winter's Tale.*

The Winter's Tale tells of the possession of a King by the spirit of jealousy, and of the unjust acts he perpetrates on his newly born daughter and falsely accused wife. His greatest injustice, however, is committed against Apollo, the Sun god. His act of defiance against Apollo, the Life Force of Nature, results in his son's and wife's deaths, the loss of his daughter, and the King's sixteen year penance.

The magic of resurrection makes up the rest of the play and the type of magic involved is the White Magic described by Pico della Mirandolla in his oration, *On the Dignity of Man.*

"A great wonder, Asclepius, is man" cries Pico at the beginning of his oration. It is an allusion to the *Asclepius*, a work contained in the *Hermetica*. The quotation is of the famous passage on man (*Hermetica, Asclepius*, (6), p. 69, as translated by B.P. Copenhaver)

"Because of this, Asclepius, a human being is a great wonder, a living thing to be worshipped and honored for he changes his nature into a god's, as if he were a god".

This is the setup for Pico's oration and also for Shakespeare's play. It is an examination of how to change our nature. The *Asclepius* goes on to discuss how humans can both touch the heavens with their minds and the earth with their bodies and how being in this unique position makes them the envy of creation. The work then explains how to bring statues of the gods to life using natural magic. This act of animation plays no small part in the plot of *The Winter's Tale* or in Pico's oration *On the Dignity of Man* but it is Pico's understanding of the magic required that Shakespeare uses to give life to his characters and a unity to his work.

Pico's Concepts Create Characters

Pico felt the root of man's excellence and dignity lay in the fact that humans were the makers of their own natures (*On the Dignity of Man*, Pico della Mirandola, p. 5)

"Thou...art the molder and maker of thyself; thou mayest sculpt thyself into whatever shape thou dost prefer".

And

"At man's birth the Father placed in him every sort of seed and sprouts of every kind of life. The seeds that each man cultivates will grow and bear their fruit in him".

Pico's work is, like Shakespeare's, replete with references to nature, full of plantings, seeds and sprouts. Pico's work also sets the stage for many of Shakespeare's characters; for instance, Leontes, the jealous brute, can be seen as the product of self-indulgence (ibid., p.5) [2].

"If he cultivates...the seeds of sensation, he will grow into a brute."

Early in the play Leontes is possessed by the 'spirit of jealousy'. He then goes on to feed this self-indulgent vice. His early possession functions as a bookend to the last scene in the play where the statue of Hermione (the clay body) is possessed by her spirit. In both cases a material body seems to be taken over by forces outside that body, in both cases these forces must be encouraged to grow, and in both cases the unreal becomes the real. If we are the clay garden, then we can choose to nurture either the seeds of evil or the seeds of goodness. This is the point that Pico makes and that Shakespeare mimics.

Pico's work not only suggests how characters develop but also speaks to some of the fluidity seen in their identities. When he states (ibid., p. 5)

"Who does not wonder at this chameleon which we are?"

he foreshadows the type of shape shifting that goes on in the play; Autolycus who is a former servant to Prince Florizel becomes a thief, a musician, a salesman, and by the end of the play perhaps a servant to the Prince once again. Even though Autolycus is the most flexible character in the play each character undergoes identity shifts; King Polixenes poses as a commoner, Prince Florizel as a shepherd, Perdita is a shepherdess who becomes a Princess, and her father, the shepherd, becomes a gentleman. No one's identity is static; a King becomes a tyrant and a Queen a whore.

Pico's work showed a strong belief in personal growth, self determination and will power. He felt that all humans had the power to become what they wanted to be, that we were not the victims of Fate. In this way his work was openly emancipating (ibid., p. 6,7) *"man is an animal of diverse, multiform, and destructible nature...born in this state so that we may be what we will to be".*

We see this determination of will expressed by Florizel's character (4.4.465)

> *I am but sorry, not afeard; delay'd, But nothing alter'd: what I was, I am.*

This idea of self determination undermines the rigid class structure that is apparent in Green's *Pandosto* and Longus's *Daphnis and Chloe* (both works that influenced Shakespeare; see, *The Winter's Tale*, The Arden Shakespeare, preface xxvii, xxxiii, and Appendix IV).

Shakespeare's Kings and Gentlemen are the same under the sun as the shepherds. This is an important point in a play whose supreme ruler is Apollo, the Sun god (4.4.445)

> *the self same sun that shines upon his court*
> *Hides not his visage from our cottage, but*
> *Looks on alike.*

Shakespeare also openly mocks the idea of what it means to be a gentleman in the dialogue between Autolycus, the clown, and the shepherd (5.2.136-138)

> Aut. *I know you are now, sir, a gentleman born.*
> Clo. *Ay, and have been so anytime these four hours.*
> Shp. *And so have I, boy.*

I'm sure Shakespeare's break with the status quo was nothing new; as a playwright and poet, he would have experienced more social mobility than most in his society and this must have had an influence on his point of view. Seeing people or imagining people of all classes and writing about them in a believable manner would have necessitated an egalitarian attitude and a recognition that we are all subject to the same emotions and battles in our lives.

Insight into human behaviour was something Shakespeare would have been looking for in his research and it was something Pico's work supplied. Pico felt all persons were subject to an internal civil war (ibid., p. 10)

"Job the theologian: he signifies to us that two natures are planted in our souls: by the one nature we are lifted upwards to the heavens, and by the other, shoved downward to the lower world".

Pico also felt that hope was available to the conflicted in the form of moral philosophy (ibid., p. 11)

"moral philosophy will still those wars in us…if our man will seek a truce with the enemy, he will subdue the uncurbed forays of the multiple brute, the quarrellings of the lion, and the feelings of wrath".

For Pico moral philosophy was not just a Christian term but also applied to the cult of Apollo. The same cult Hermione turns to for help when she is accused of infidelity. It was the place to turn to when you desired to turn mere hope into a more practical form of relief (3.2.115)

I do refer me to the Oracle:

Apollo be my judge!

Pico understands the three Delphic precepts on moral philosophy and expands upon them (ibid., p. 14-15); briefly they are: everything in moderation, know yourself, and through this self knowledge recognize God. Pico understands the role that Natural philosophy can play in our lives (ibid., p. 11)

"Natural philosophy will calm the strifes and discords of opinion, which shake the unquiet soul up and down, pull her apart, and mangle her. But natural philosophy will bring calm in such a way as to command us to remember…our nature is born of war, and therefore is called a struggle".

This comment to *"remember our nature"* was contained within the Delphic precept *"to know yourself"*; it required of the adept not only

103

an understanding of their personal strengths and weaknesses but also an understanding of all of Nature since we are a part of that Nature. Natural philosophy was a term that meant understanding the whole natural world; both the science of who we are and the psychology. We had to know ourselves to succeed in the struggle. To employ our virtues in the service of God and to avoid our vices.

Pico, in this quotation, has not only instructed our troubled selves in how to obtain some kind of relief but has also defined the role of Shakespeare's Paulina. She moderates the very troubled Leontes (the lion) by reminding him of his evil nature. She effectively becomes Leontes' conscience, always bringing up the past so that he will not forget who he was and the part he played in betraying his wife and friend. She is his perpetual reminder of his sinful nature so that he can become better than he was (5.1.15-18)

> Paul. ...she you kill'd
>
> Would be unparallel'd
>
> Leon. I think so. Kill'd!
>
> She I kill'd! I did so: but thou strik'st me
>
> Sorely, to say I did.

Pico goes on to point out that Natural Philosophy (Paulina) can remind us of our failings and teach us who we are but that she is limited in her ability to heal, limited in her ability to provide us with relief (ibid., p. 11-12)

"...in natural philosophy true quiet and lasting peace cannot offer themselves to us, and that this is the office and prerogative of their mistress, most holy theology. Theology herself will show the way to that peace and be our companion and guide... "Come unto me, and I will give unto you peace which the world and nature cannot give unto you!"...let us fly...into the embrace of our most blessed mother and enjoy the longed for peace: the most holy peace, the indivisible bond, the

friendship which is one soul... (to) become absolutely one. This is the friendship which... is the end of all philosophy".

If Paulina is a personification of Natural Philosophy then Hermione, her mistress, is the personification of Theology. It is only through Grace, the gift of Hermione, that Leontes will find peace, a peace he has been unable to earn through his long years of penance.

The three female leads in *The Winter's Tale* are characters beyond reproach and for that reason it will come as no surprise that Perdita represents the soul. She is Leontes' "lost soul". Her recovery marks his recovery. In many ways their fates are linked. Her marriage makes his marriage possible. Both marriages symbolize the soul's incorporation into the Divine.

Pico describes this idea of marriage (ibid., p. 12)
"...after she (the soul) has, through moral and dialectics, cast off her meanness and has adorned herself with manifold philosophy as with a princely garment, and has crowned with garlands of theology the summits of the gates, the King of Glory may descend, and, coming with the Father, may make his residence in her...forgetful of herself, she will long to die in herself that she may live in her bridegroom".

Pico tells us that through education and self knowledge we can cast off our brutish natures, our meanness. And that by embracing Natural philosophy and Theology we can make ourselves acceptable to become a part of God. This is the ascent of the soul. The soul's incorporation with God becomes the marriage to God.

Perdita's love for Florizel and their marriage is the emotional equivalent of what we are to feel for Leontes when Hermione, through an act of Grace, accepts him into the embrace of most holy peace; a peace he has not felt for sixteen years.

Leontes' journey of becoming, of changing his nature was not an easy one. He needed to learn moderation. He needed to acquire self knowledge and finally he had to recognize and accept the miraculous nature of God.

The Sun God Apollo

Sun worship and the role of Apollo are as central to *The Winter's Tale* as they are to Pico's work *On the Dignity of Man*. Knight and Hoeniger (*The Crown of Life* and *The Meaning of The Winter's Tale*) do a very good job of demonstrating how Nature plays a role in almost every scene of *The Winter's Tale* but what they attribute to Nature I feel would be more appropriately assigned to Apollo. Apollo is the god of *The Winter's Tale*. Apollo is a Sun god, the deity that provides the light, heat, and energy necessary for Nature to accomplish her work. Apollo was responsible for day and night, the seasons, and time in general. He was the god that brought hidden things to light. The play cleverly wraps itself around Apollo's attributes, from the oracle scene through to the introduction by Time of the pastoral and musical scenes. It's Apollo's role as a pastoral god, and god of music that gives these scenes a resonance and unity with the rest of the play. Even the last scene of the play is centered around Apollo's abilities, as god of medicine, to bring the dead back to life. It is Apollo and his retinue of muses, the original deities of spring, that in fact permeates every aspect of the play.

The attributes of Apollo are expanded on in Yates's book *The Art of Memory* (Chpt. 6) and together with her appended chart of Camillo's Memory Theatre provide a more complete understanding of the revival of Sun worship. The *New Larousse Encyclopedia of Mythology* also offers a supporting view of Apollo's character, see p.109-119.

The play begins in winter (a time when the sun's strength is at its weakest) and reaches one of its most dramatic points when Leontes (a representative of earthly political power) decides to defy Apollo by

106

ignoring his Delphic Oracles. His disobedience to the Sun god is nothing short of the rejection of the Life force. He is punished for this by the death of both Mamillius (his son) and Hermione (his wife) as well as by the loss of his daughter and only heir, Perdita.

This tragedy begs comparison to the quintessential winter's tale of Persephone, the young girl who is abducted by Pluto and taken to the underworld and whose safe return was required before winter could end. It is a mother/daughter story that functions as a generational allegory. James Frazer (*The Golden Bough*), in his analysis of the myth, pointed out that Persephone was the seed sown in autumn, hidden in the earth during the barren winter and who blossomed forth with the return of spring. Her mother, Demeter, is the personification of the ripe crop of the year and Persephone, the seed crop taken from it. Likewise Perdita is born during winter and planted on the shores of Bohemia. The connection of Hermione with Perdita is primal; but in the case of *The Winter's Tale* it is expanded to include her father, Leontes. Until Perdita returns he too is locked in a world of remorse and unending winter. It is the enormity of these losses that finally shock him back to a proper state of mind (3.2.146)

> *Apollo's angry and the heavens themselves*
> *Do strike at my injustice.*

For the first time he begins to appreciate the consequences of his actions (3.2.154)

> *Apollo, pardon*
> *My great profaneness 'gainst thine Oracle!*

The Magic of Redemption and the Rites of Spring

Leontes' acknowledgement of the sin he committed against Apollo and his need for redemption begins his journey of awakening. It is a journey that finds resonance in Pico's description of what we as humans must do once we have come to "*know ourselves*" and recognized our weaknesses; after we have learnt moderation, we then must go on to recognize and understand God (ibid., p. 15)

"*But after we have...relieved ourselves of the appetite for overflowing sensual pleasures and ...trimmed...the sharp pricks of anger...only then may we begin to take part in the aforementioned sacred mysteries of Bacchus...whose father and leader is rightly said to be the Sun. At last, he will advise us to feed the cock, that is, to nourish the divine part of our soul with knowledge of divine things...This is the cock at the sight of which the lion, that is, every earthly power, feels fear and awe. This is that cock to which intelligence was given, as we read in Job. At the crowing of this cock, erring man returns to his senses. In the morning dawn this cock daily crows in harmony with the morning stars praising God*".

But what are these sacred mysteries of Bacchus we are to begin to take part in? Pico goes on to explain that they are in fact, the rites of spring, the secrets of creation (ibid., p. 14)

"*Bacchus the leader of the muses, in his own mysteries, that is, in the visible signs of nature, will show the invisible things of God to us as we philosophize*".

Discovering how nature worked, how God worked invisibly in nature, was a big part of understanding God; it was also a big part of what was called natural or white magic and what would later evolve into the natural sciences. Much of Renaissance science straddled the line between science and religion, frankly, because no other means of enquiry was possible. The Churches controlled all the avenues of higher education. The universities were run by the Churches and clergy made up its body of instructors. Religion permeated everything; even the heretics were all trained by the Church. Pico, himself, was trained in canon law.

Natural magic was tolerated (up to a point) by the Church but demonic magic was strictly forbidden. The distinction was simple; demonic magic required the use of demons. Pico refers to the two types as *"the first type"* (demonic) and *"the second type"* (natural) in his oration.

"I have proposed theorems about magic, too, where in I have signified that magic is twofold. The first sort is put together by the work and authorship of demons" (ibid. p. 26);

"the first magic makes man subject to and delivered over to the powers of wickedness" (ibid., p. 28);

"the second is full of the deepest mysteries and includes the most profound and hidden contemplation of things, and finally, the knowledge of all nature. The second, among the virtues sown by the kindness of God and planted in the world, as if calling them out from darkness into light, does not so much make wonders as carefully serve nature which makes them" (ibid., p. 28);

"(This second magic) discloses in public the wonders lying hidden in the recesses of the world...And as the farmer marries elm to vine, so the magician marries earth to heaven, that is, lower things to the qualities and virtues of higher things. Hence the first magic appears as monstrous and harmful as the second, divine and salutary. And especially because the first magic delivers man over to the enemies of God...this second magic arouses that admiration at the works of God which so prepares that charity, faith, and hope most surely follow. For nothing impels more toward religion and the worship of God than assiduous contemplation of the wonders of God. When we shall have well explored these wonders by means of this natural magic we are speaking of, we shall be inspired more ardently to the worship and love of the maker" (ibid., p. 28,29).

So understanding God through natural magic not only alerts us to the wonders of God but prepares us for charity, faith and hope, the tools we all need in our redemption. Not only is Pico's discussion of magic appropriate to Leontes' needs but it is also very close to the discussion Shakespeare has written between Polixenes and Perdita over the streak'd gillyvors (4.4.92-97)

> *You see, sweet maid, we marry*
> *A gentler scion to the wildest stock,*
> *And make conceive a bark of baser kind*
> *By bud of nobler race. This is an art*
> *Which does mend nature - change it rather - but*
> *The art itself is nature.*

I believe this dialogue goes on to highlight the distinction between the two types of magic Pico described; the first soul destroying because it draws our attention away from God, the second soul enlightening because it directs our attention to God [4].

The two 'possessions' in the play also highlight this same distinction. Leontes becomes the example of what happens when a man is possessed by a demon (jealousy, a self-indulgent vice) and the subsequent harm that comes into the created world as a result. The possession of Hermione's statue becomes an example of the second type of magic, the kind devoid of evil, unselfish and beneficial, possession akin to possession by the Spirit of God (5.3.110)

> *If this be magic let it be an art*
> *Lawful as eating.*

It was an 'art', however, that some could still find objection to (5.3.96)

> *those that think it is unlawful business*
> *I am about, let them depart.*

Pico refers to the first type of magic as being a bastard, without anyone claiming parentage, whereas the second, he proclaims, has illustrious and proud parents (ibid., p. 27)

"the first is the most fraudulent of arts, the second is firm, faithful and solid. Whoever cultivated the first always dissimulated it, because it would be in ignominy and disgrace to the author. From the second comes the highest splendor and glory of letters, desired in ancient times and almost always since then...Pythagoras, Empedocles, Democritus, Plato, traveled across seas to learn the second. When they came back, they preached it and held it chief among their esoteric doctrines. The first can be proved by no arguments nor certain founders; the second, honored as it were by most illustrious parents, has two principal founders: Xalmosis...and Zoroaster".

This thought echoes in Polixenes' defense of the *"art which does mend nature"*; he sees it as an art that is in harmony with nature (4.4.98)

> *Then make your garden rich in gillyvors,*
> *And do not call them bastards.*

So the *"bastards"* in this case would be the authors and practitioners of the first type of demonic magic, magic that no one wishes to claim as their own. Polixenes is claiming that the flowers were produced in partnership with Nature, by understanding Her principles and not in violation of them. In a subtle way Shakespeare is preparing the way for the statue animation scene. He wants it to be understood as an example of this second kind of good magic. This attitude is shared by Pico in his strong defense of the magic practiced in the *Asclepius*.

Pico's Breakthrough

For Pico the act of drawing down spirits into statues of the gods was an acceptable form of magic for he felt he had made a breakthrough no one else had made. By using Cabala he could guarantee that no evil demons could participate in his magic. Transitive magic, that requiring forces outside one's own body, was always regarded with suspicion because even with the best intensions it was felt you could still accidentally attract a bad demon. With Pico's understanding of Cabala he found a way to ensure this could not happen. The guarantee came in the form of Hebrew. For the Cabalist, Hebrew is not just a language but 'The Language of God'; the letters are not just an alphabet but describe the forces God used in the creation of the world. So to write a word in Hebrew was not just to create a symbol associated with the object; it was actually to define and describe how to make that object, i.e. to invoke the forces God used to create it. Because of this 'power of God in the word' it meant if you wrote an angel's name in Hebrew it not only described the angel but it was capable of creating the angel, no misinterpretation was possible, the desired angel would be contacted. This was Pico's great contribution to Western magic and why his work introducing and defending Cabala to the Christian world had a significant impact. It made magic acceptable or at least defendable against attacks from the Church.

When one reads the magic and philosophies of Ficino, Pico della Mirandola, Agrippa, etc., it becomes difficult to understand what they really believed because so much of their writing is either coded or just cryptic, rendered that way in order to obscure. The one thing we can be sure of is that they were looking for ways to justify their research to an increasingly authoritarian Church. Even investigations into questions which we would regard as pure science were looked upon with suspicion so it was essential to find ways to broaden the discussion. Thomas Aquinas had found a way to justify Aristotle's writings, Pico della Mirandola found a way to justify the study of Cabala; I think more than anything these people wanted to find new ways to investigate the world and not be restricted by the limits set out in the Old and New Testaments.

Ways of introducing texts from other cultures, ways of exploring new ideas, philosophies, something to shake up the stagnant logic that was holding the world in the dark ages, this was their self-appointed task, and they had to do this while still pacifying the more conservative, fundamentalist elements in the Church [5].

How to Bring a Statue to Life

The animation scene in Shakespeare's *The Winter's Tale* follows the prescription in the *Asclepius* (*Hermetica*, Asclepius 24, 37, 38). D.P. Walker provides a very clear understanding of magic as practiced by Pico and his friend and colleague Ficino in his book *Spiritual and Demonic Magic.*

One of the central metaphors in magic came to us from Pythagoras and has to do with music and harmonics. Walker explores these ideas in his chapter "Ficino and Music". Here he explains the concept of 'spiritus'; that spiritus was seen as an intermediary between the soul and the body. The soul, coming from God, had to be insulated from contact with the body, which was tainted by original sin. The spiritus was an insulator and communicator between the perfect soul and the imperfect body. The body was seen as a clay vessel, the soul belonged to God, and the spiritus allowed for separation and communication between the two.

Spiritus was to the microcosm of the individual what the Spiritus Mundi (the cosmic spirit) was to the Macrocosm of the Universe. The Spiritus Mundi operated between God (The Paternal Mind) and the physical universe (Kosmos). It insulated God from the creation but allowed for communication. The Spiritus Mundi flowed through the entire universe and could flow through an individual's spiritus as well. Just as a vibrating string will make another (tuned to the same note) vibrate so too the heavenly spirit could resonate within the individual, and this individual could be tuned (so to speak) to better receive this cosmic influence.

Tuning the individual's spiritus could be accomplished in many ways but first we must recognize that humans were seen as matter; lumps of animate clay (not really much more than the clay sculpture of Hermione). Humans were considered to be part of the sublunar world hence composed of the four elements and subject to their properties. Fire, Air, Water, and Earth were represented by the four humors of the body Choler, Blood, Phlegm, and Melancholy respectively. The four elements were also represented in the five senses (Agrippa's *Three Books on Occult Philosophy*, Book 1, Chpt. LXI). The eyes were said to have an affinity for light and therefore represented Fire; the ears had an affinity for sound and music and therefore represented Air; the Nostrils' association with smell tied them to both Air and Water while taste was representative of just Water; lastly touch was associated with Earth. These associations meant that all the humors and all the senses, in fact, the whole individual could be accessed through the appropriate manipulation of the four elements. It meant that if we were ill physically or spiritually, if one of our humors were out of balance, we could appropriately correct the imbalance by ridding ourselves of any excess or by attracting a compensating benefic force, thereby restoring health.

The material world and all of Nature was affected by the influxes of the Spiritus Mundi. This cosmic spirit can be viewed much as white light, that when passing through a prism, is broken into its component parts producing the spectrum of the rainbow with its seven different colours. In the case of the Spiritus Mundi it was broken into its component parts by passing through the seven Celestial spheres. Because of this each sphere or planet was responsible for reflecting an aspect of the Spiritus Mundi into the material world. This meant each planet possessed a unique set of gifts, qualities, and moral character that could be called upon to help an individual whose humors were out of balance. By making the individual more in tune to the influences of a specific planet it was possible to make them more receptive to its healing forces. For example, an excess of Melancholy (an attribute of the planet Saturn) could often be healed by the benefic effects of influxes from Venus (Love) and Jupiter (Joviality).

The ceremonies involved with tuning an individual to the appropriate influxes did not involve making the planetary gods "do anything" but rather they just involved making the individual's spiritus more receptive to these natural influxes by bringing them into harmony with its forces. By intensifying the planetary influences upon the individual through resonance it was believed that it would help heal them by making up for any imbalance they were suffering from.

Music and song were used in this operation. Song was a product of the mind, imagination, and emotions and when it along with music was transmitted through the air it stirred the entire listener; the lyrics reached the mind and the music stirred the senses and emotions.

Music was produced by action and since actions had a moral character so music was seen as possessing a moral character. By playing certain 'moral music' one could purify the air in a space and make it more sanctified for the performance of other ceremonies. Music was seen as a type of living air that could animate a space. Music, as an aerial spirit, acted directly on the ear of the listener and his/her spiritus thereby raising the moral character of those in attendance and providing them with a type of musical psycho-therapy.

To correct any imbalances in the humors or to address deficiencies in a particular type of influx required extensive knowledge of the natural world and a classification system for all its properties. It also involved the purification of substances in the natural world in order to enhance these properties and bring them into closer alignment with their platonic ideals (i.e. uniting the lower world with the Ideas that governed them in the higher world so as to maximize their potential) [6].

To heal the individual required healing their spirit and to heal the spirit required that spirit to resonate with the healing forces of the universe. This meant flooding the humors and senses with healing energies that were in harmony with the deficient planetary influx. A planetary 'vitamin pill' as it were. To do this one had to be diligent in capturing and focusing these influxes by respecting which minerals, plants, animals, odors, libations, lights, hymns, and music were appropriate for the planet in question and to carry out the ceremony at a time when the planet was in a favorable astrological position; for example to harmonize with influxes from the Sun one might sing Orphic hymns (Orpheus was son to Apollo) to tune the air, bathe the space in sunlight, fill the air with the smell of incense (in this case frankincense was seen as solar), drink wine (again seen as a concentration of the sun's energy) and perform the ceremony at a particular time [7] on a Sunday. Lists of stones, minerals, plants, drinks, fabrics etc. appropriate to each planet are widely available and can also be found in Agrippa's *Three Books of Occult Philosophy*.

By surrounding yourself or a statue with items tuned to the planet's influxes allowed the space, the individual, the statue, to resonate with that planet's celestial music thereby allowing those celestial influxes to be amplified for either use in healing or for storage in the statue or talisman.

The ceremonies were similar to a Catholic mass only in the mass the end achieved would be the transubstantiation of the host; in natural magic the role of host would be played by an appropriately chosen talisman, statue, or an individual in need of healing.

Lazarelli, in his book *Crater Hermetis* (1505), gives advice to King Ferdinand of Aragon, his disciple

"Apply here all the strength of your soul. Beseech, admire, praise, contemplate the divinity. For thus you will be properly disposed for the great secret of god-making mystery...attend then with the whole emotional force of your mind, while I sing this hymn of contemplation" (*Spiritual and Demonic Magic*, D. P. Walker, p. 65).

When one looks at *The Winter's Tale,* the animation of Hermione's statue follows the same principles that are set out in the *Asclepius.* Paulina makes sure Leontes sees the statue with a penitent heart; she focuses his attention on the statue as if using his grief and love to infuse it with life, praise is heaped upon Hermione, they kneel before her, the air vibrates, and music is used to finally awaken her. For the scene to be moving you must believe she has been dead and that this is no trick but a true act of beneficent magic achieved by tuning the space and the statue for the return of Hermione's soul. The inanimate has called to the animate; the clay has been made to resonate with the spirit. Hermione is reanimated and reunited with her lost daughter and penitent husband. The older generation is left to make amends while the younger generation has the hope and blessings necessary to begin their new lives.

Conclusion

The Winter's Tale is a story from beginning to end about the worship of Apollo and Nature and the cost paid by the next generation if those who came before do not live by its judgments. Pico's oration has been seamlessly folded into Shakespeare's work providing him with the characters and magic necessary to create his story of penance and redemption. It is a story that contains within it an understanding of and appreciation for natural magic. It is a story about our changeable natures and how there is a seed of hope in this inconstant flaw. We all have the ability to change and to change for the better.

It is a story about our search for our lost soul. This theme is repeated three times. Hermione's lost soul is returned to its clay vessel when the statue is brought to life. Leontes lost soul is returned when Hermione forgives him. Lastly Perdita's return marks the end of winter. She reunites the family and allows for a future. Their lost heiress has returned and her return brings hope to a hopeless situation. She reanimates the family.

The story is bitter sweet. We, as an audience, can delight and see hope in the characters' futures but we are aware of what they have lost to the past. Time has taken away what they have wasted. Nothing in the past can ever change. The play makes us feel and understand that all we have is the future and that is where we must focus our efforts.

Footnotes

[1]   Pico's philosophy was widely disseminated, and his work was both directly and indirectly influential in England. In 1570 John Dee reported in his Mathematical Preface to Euclid's *Elements of Geometry* that Pico's *Conclusiones* were readily available in England (see Mebane, p. 38).

[2]   Northrop Frye points out in his essay, (*On Shakespeare, Shakespeare's Romances: The Winter's Tale*, p.162) that Leontes has nothing in the way of evidence against his wife but that he smells, feels and tastes his situation. The senses were always associated with our lower selves, the beast within, his dependence on these senses shows how instinctive he has become and how cut off he is from his rational self.

[3]   See Francis Yates, *The Art of Memory*, Chapter 6: The Memory Theatre of Giulio Camillo, p.144.

[4]   Perdita's argument with Polixenes appears to be a discussion over the appropriate uses of 'art' (meaning the technologies of humans). The discussion is very close to Pico's on the two types of magic; the one type that corrupts the individual and the world (demonic) and the other type that turns our attention to God (good magic). Perdita sees Polixenes as a corrupt man who only corrupts through his 'art'. He creates ostentatious flowers that divert man's attention from God rather than to God. The flowers draw attention to the human skill exercised by intervening with nature, the flowers become a symbol of man's hubris, they seem to mock those flowers created by God alone. She sees the

unadorned world as a means to help focus on God for our needs, she does not wish to be distracted from God. Hoeniger feels she represents the heavenly Jerusalem that God created, it does not need improving, it is sufficient in and of itself. Polixenes, on the other hand, represents the Fallen Adam creating the earthly paradise of Babylon full of sensual pleasures (alcohol, gambling, gluttony, prostitution). The product of his 'arts' drag people down away from heaven, his 'arts' titillate and must become more and more stimulating to the senses over time. They are a distraction from God not a way to God. They do not disagree that all human abilities come from God or that all 'art' comes from God they only disagree as to whether the 'art' is used to focus attention on God or away from Him (toward sensual earthly pleasures). Perdita is a simple girl and she prefers simple, pure, unadorned nature while Polixenes can no longer appreciate the simple pleasures and so cannot appreciate Perdita. His objection to her marriage to his son is not inconsistent with this position for she is not the product of sophistication.

Pico makes this same argument about magic; does its use bring the practitioner closer to God, help others, heal nature, create harmony, help move the world towards the ideal or is it used for selfish purposes to increase sensual pleasure and drive the operator further away from God. This is the distinction between the second and first kinds of magic Pico refers to, one heals while the other corrupts.

[5]   The English Renaissance was fighting for its life during Shakespeare's time. Those studying Nature were under constant threat of being labeled witches. John Dee was given free reign under Elizabeth I only to be charged with practicing 'black magic' during the reign of James I. The Church felt the world was miraculous and that trying to understand God's workings was a waste of time because God was unknowable as would be His world. The advances made by Paracelsus

(1493-1541) in regards to purifying medicines and taking a more systematic approach to illnesses was still regarded with suspicion and would not take root for more than a hundred years. Shakespeare's hope placed on natural magic truly was not misplaced; it was the only game in town.

The Winter's Tale can be seen as an allegory about how fundamentalism, the Jealous God of the Old Testament, was being made manifest in both Catholicism and Protestantism, and that these faiths were holding the world in a stasis. These myopic religions were holding back the new emerging science (Natural Magic in Shakespeare's day) and any hope for progress or understanding of the world. Science's strengths were to be found in uncertainty and questioning while Religion always valued certainty and acceptance. The religion promoted in this play was a belief in Nature. That to understand Nature was to understand the world and ourselves. Shakespeare's play suggests that he saw the Jealous God of the Old Testament in much the same way as he saw the jealous King Leontes, as a tyrant locking us into an unchanging world devoid of enlightenment. A Dark Age of endless Winter.

[6]   This was all a prelude to the more stringent classification strategies that would be employed by science but this was still the early days of enlightenment and the goals were different. Very few compounds were pure so purification was an essential first step in both magic and science. This was the role played by alchemy. By purifying a substance one could often make it more like its pure Ideal, more like what God intended it to be. By taking impure substances and purifying them the first steps were being made in both magic and science.

[7]   Each hour of the day was assigned to a planetary god. This assignment of hours also produced the names for the days of the week.

121

To see how this worked begin with Saturday; it was named for Saturn so the first hour of that day (12am-1am) was assigned to Saturn. The next hour (1am-2am) was assigned to Jupiter and so on over the 24 hour day. The order the planets were assigned to the hours corresponded to the Ptolemaic order i.e. Saturn, Jupiter, Mars, Sun, Venus, Mercury, and finally the Moon. If you follow this pattern assigning each hour to a planet continuously you will find that the first hour of the next day is assigned to the Sun hence Sunday. Maintaining the order keep assigning hours to planets until you reach the first hour of the next day which will be the Moon hence Monday. You keep this process going till you reach the end of the cycle; finding the first hour of the eighth day to again be assigned to Saturn. This assigning of times of the day to planets meant that there was an appropriate hour to perform ceremonies to specific gods but that these times would change throughout the days of the week (see Agrippa, *Three Books of Occult Philosophy*, Book II, Chapter XXXIV).

Bibliography

1) *The Winter's Tale*, W. Shakespeare, J.H.P. Pafford Editor, The Arden Shakespeare, Thomas Nelson and Sons Ltd., Third Series, 1999.

2) *The Crown of Life; Great Creating Nature: An Essay on The Winter's Tale*, Wilson G Knight,. p. 76-128, Methuen and Co. Ltd. London, 1958.

3) *The Meaning of The Winter's Tale*, F.D. Hoeniger, University of Toronto Quarterly, Vol. XX, no.1, Oct., p.11-26, 1950.

4) *On The Dignity Of Man,* Pico della Mirandolla, translated by Charles Glenn Wallis, Paul J.W. Miller, and Douglas Carmichael, Hackett Publishing Co. Inc., 1998.

5) *Spiritual and Demonic Magic: From Ficino to Campanella*, D.P. Walker, The Pennsylvania State University Press, 2000.

6) *Renaissance Magic and the Return of the Golden Age, The Occult Tradition and Marlowe, Jonson, and Shakespeare*, John S. Mebane, University of Nebraska Press, 1989.

7) *Pico della Mirandola's Encounter with Jewish Mysticism*, Chaim Wirszubski, Harvard University Press, 1989.

8) *Hermetica*, Hermes Trismegistus, translated by Brian P. Copenhaver, Cambridge University Press, 1992.

9) *Three Books of Occult Philosophy*, H.C. Agrippa, translated by James Freake, edited by Donald Tyson, Llewellyn Publications, 2004.

10) *The Art of Memory,* F.A. Yates, Routledge and Kegan Paul, 1966.

11) *On Shakespeare,* Northrop Frye, Fitzhenry and Whiteside Ltd.,1986.

12) *New Larousse Encyclopedia of Mythology,* The Hamlyn Publishing Group Ltd., 1982.

13) *Shakespeare's Imagery: and What it Tell us*, Caroline F.E. Spurgeon, Cambridge University Press, 2005.

Abstract for *A Midsummer Night's Dream*
Hekate Weaves *A Midsummer Night's Dream*

The role of Hekate in *A Midsummer Night's Dream* has generally been limited to a few footnotes referencing classical literature and alluding to her association with the moon. This essay demonstrates that by understanding the role that Hekate played from the Hellenistic period (323 BCE) onward she should be considered as the keystone metaphor operating in *A Midsummer Night's Dream*.

Shakespeare draws our attention to Hekate through his repetitive use of the word "*Moon*" and by setting the time of the play during the traditional 'Hekate supper'. The Moon plays a central role not just as to when the play takes place but also in coordinating and synchronizing the actions of all the groups in the play. This interconnectedness of the groups acts as a metaphor for the interconnectedness of all creation and highlights Hekate's greater role as the Cosmic Soul.

Hekate Weaves *A Midsummer Night's Dream*

Introduction

The role of Hekate in *A Midsummer Night's Dream* has generally been limited to a few footnotes referencing classical literature and alluding to her association with the moon (three-formed Hekate, bright orb of heaven, glory of the night, great goddess of the woods; all from Seneca's *Phaedra*) or to cosmic disorder (referencing the floods and unnatural weather as found in Seneca's *Medea*) or in reference to her as a guide to demons. This essay shows that by understanding the role Hekate played from the Hellenistic period (323 BCE) onward, she should be considered as the keystone metaphor operating in *A Midsummer Night's Dream*. To appreciate Hekate as she was understood in *The Chaldean Oracles* I would recommend reading *Hekate Soteira* by Sarah Iles Johnston. She provides a rigorous well researched background to 'all things Hekate'.

The Moon, Shakespeare and Hekate

The Moon behaves like a character in *A Midsummer Night's Dream*. It affects the action that takes place and its watery nature helps establish a mood for potential change.

The action in the play takes place during the three dark days of the Moon. This is the time the Moon takes to transition from the old sickle Moon of the previous lunar month to the new Moon of the next. This transition from old Moon to new Moon marked a metamorphosis or change. In this play the change wrought is seen in Titania, Bottom and the couples that flee into the woods.

The Moon is rich in symbolic character and has been personified under various names such as Lucina, Luna, Selene, Cynthia, Artemis, Diana, Latona, Noctiluca, Proserpina, and Hekate. When Hippolyta compares the new crescent Moon to a silver bow (1.1.9-10) the image is not only characteristic of herself, an Amazon huntress, but is also symbolic of the Moon goddess Diana.

The word "*Moon*" occurs 28 times in the play. This is no accident as Shakespeare uses many other expressions to allude to the Moon without using this specific word. He has chosen to use the word 28 times. This is a clear reference to the 28 days in a lunar month. It also is a clear indication that the Moon plays a major role in his conception of the play.

The first key role played by the Moon is in setting the time frame and coordinating and synchronizing the action of play. By Theseus's speech (1.1.1-3) and Hippolyta's reply (1.1.9-11) we know when the wedding will take place, we know the fairies' timetable is set to that of the weddings, we know Lysander and Hermia plan to elope during the evening of the dark Moon before the wedding, we know Helena plans to lure Demetrius into the woods to foil their elopement, and we know the artisans plan to rehearse their play before the wedding in these same woods.

The second key role played by the Moon, is that it is associated with the three main characters in the play. Triple Hekate was a common expression for the Moon (5.1.370); it generally referred to the three dark days of metamorphosis, these days were sometimes personified with Salene standing for the old Moon, Hekate for the dark Moon, and Artemis (Diana, the virgin huntress) as the new Moon. It also represented the three domains of Hekate; Hekate representing the underworld of Hades, Diana the earth, and Luna the heavens. "Triple Hekate's team" in this play refers to the 3 "H's" of our play; Hippolyta, Hermia, and Helena. It is no coincidence that the three female leads all have names beginning with the letter "H". This is a clear reference to the Moon and triple Hekate.

The Goddess Hekate

Hekate of the Hellenistic period (after Alexander the Great 356-323 BCE) was a kinder gentler goddess with greatly expanded but related powers to the Hekate known to classicists as the patroness of witches.

Her change in status occurred prior to the 2nd century. Her expanded role was part of a fundamental understanding expressed in *The Chaldean Oracles*. *The Chaldean Oracles* were well known during the reign of Marcus Aurelius (161-180 CE) and her new identity and expanded role remained intact from that date onwards. This essay will demonstrate that Shakespeare must have been acquainted with Hellenistic Hekate and probably with *The Chaldean Oracles* since this is the Hekate we see operating as a backdrop to his play.

Hellenistic Hekate was portrayed in a very Platonic way as the Cosmic Soul responsible for ensouling both the cosmos and the individuals that were within it [1]. She stood on the border between the Intelligible and Sensible Worlds acting as both a barrier (boundary) and link (transmitter) between them. This role is well documented in the works of Porphyry (232-305), Iamblichus (250-325), Proclus (412-485), Damascius (6th century), and Psellus (11th century), and were incorporated into Ficino's (1433-1499) works. It is also a role in which modern scholars like W. Kroll, H. Lewy, R.T. Wallis, J. Dillon and M. Tardieu are all in agreement.

Hekate was 'The Boundary Goddess'. She stood between Paternal Intellect and the Demiurge to make up the Trinity of Creation. The amorphous, indefinable Paternal Intellect of the Intelligible World would emit Ideas that Hekate (the Cosmic Soul/Spiritus Mundi) would receive, measure, limit, and then pass on to the Demiurge of the Sensible World who would turn these Ideas into matter i.e. the material, physical, created world. The Demiurge is the god of physical creation. Hekate was the boundary between the created material cosmos (The Sensible World) and the Ideas that governed them (The Intelligible World). She separated them but also linked them. For everything that was created she provided the link to the Ideas that informed its creation. She was the goddess alchemists contacted in order to find out how to perfect matter, how to bring it closer to its Ideal form.

Hekate was also believed to be the source of dreams. As an intermediary between the Divine and human worlds she was responsible for any messages sent between these worlds. Prayers from the human world to the Divine and visions and dreams from the Divine to the human world.

Fundamentally Hekate was a liminal goddess, a goddess that helped individuals cross boundaries (points of transition) [2]. These could be boundaries of an everyday nature, or extraordinary boundaries that one crosses only once in a life time; those between life and death (embodiment and dissolution).

In the play *A Midsummer Night's Dream* we are dealing first of all with a Dream whose source was considered to be Hekate. Then we are dealing with a world of boundaries, such as those between City and Country; Civilization and Wilderness; Order and Chaos; Day and Night; Reason and Passion; Reality and Dreams.

Hekate is the goddess of boundaries. *A Midsummer Night's Dream* is Hekate's play, it takes place in Hekate's domain (the woods), at Hekate's time (the dark night between old moon and new moon). The more we can learn about Hekate the more we can learn about the play and Shakespeare's intent.

Hekate and the Soul

Just as Hekate was part of the creative Trinity consisting of the Paternal Intellect (that which emits Ideas), Hekate (who transmits Ideas), and the Demiurge (who turns Ideas into matter) so too was Hekate the divinity that ensouled the Cosmos and all that was in it. Her ensouling chains (that linked matter to the Ideas that gave rise to them) became part of everything and were <u>woven</u> throughout the physical world, binding everything together. Hekate, like Bottom, is a weaver.

"For all around the hollows of the cartilage of [Hekate's] right flank,
The abundant liquid of the Primal Soul gushes unceasingly,
Completely ensouling the light, the fire, the aether, and the Cosmoi"
(Oracle fr. 51).

Hekate was also seen as the source of an individual's soul, for as Socrates argues in *Philebus* (30 a ff.), if our bodies are to be seen as part of the cosmos, then logically, our souls must be part of the Cosmic Soul.

Hekate connected the Divine with the material but also maintained the boundary between them. This connection between all things and the Divine is what made magic possible, in theory [3]. This is why Hekate, even after her makeover, was still the goddess of magicians and witches. The connection between all things was Eros, love was the glue that held the cosmos together. Eros, as Plato understood it, was a turning towards the Divine. It was the first primeval force that helped turn chaos into order. It was the desire to be linked with God, with the ideals from which all creation came. In order to understand Hekate's web one must understand Eros; in order to understand Magic one must understand Eros, for Eros is magic.

Ficino's Theory of Love and Magic

A Midsummer Night's Dream is a play about love and it takes place partly in a world of magic. The two ideas were connected with each other for both Shakespeare and Ficino. Ficino wrote *A Commentary on Plato's Symposium on Love* (1482) (sometimes referred to as *De amore*). It was a work that became widely popular throughout Europe (including England) during the Renaissance. Ficino took Aristotle's ideas on physiology and applied them to Plato's ideas to come up with his commentary on love. His ideas became common currency influencing many writers including Shakespeare and Giordano Bruno.

For Ficino love was the unconscious aspiration to the transcendental. Everything was united in its desire to ascend to God. He defined love as a desire to return to the cause, to recover the more perfect being from which all creatures had degenerated in the process of being created; essentially a return to their Platonic Ideal. It was a force, a drive that detached us from the material world.

To begin let's examine Ficino's ideas of love and put them into the context of Shakespeare's play. Then let's examine Ficino's ideas of magic and see how these fit into the magical world of *A Midsummer Night's Dream* and our conception of Hekate.

It was believed that the Soul came directly from God (the Paternal Intellect). In order to preserve its sanctity it was isolated from direct contact with the physical body. The Soul was wrapped in the Spirit (or pneuma) and was then placed in the body. The Spirit allowed communication between the body and the Soul. Without the Spirit the body and Soul would be completely unaware of each other. The Soul would have no aperture through which to see the world and the body, being only a collection of elements, would have no life and so would disintegrate into its components (dust to dust).

The Spirit is referred to by different names but its role as intermediary between the body and soul is constant regardless of name. This is true for the Soul as well, which can be referred to as Mind but again the one constant is that it is the part which comes from and returns to the Paternal Mind (God). It is always insulated from any direct contact with the hylic (material) world.

The Soul communicates 'life' (vital activities) to the body through the Spirit; the body communicates information about the world through the Spirit to the Soul.

The body communicates information from its five senses to the Spirit which translates these messages into phantasms that are perceptible to the Soul. The Soul can only grasp information in the form of phantasms. Phantasms are the language of the Soul just as words are the language of the body. This is why Aristotle said that "*to think was to speculate with images*", images were the language of the soul (mind). Phantasms had primacy over Words just as the Soul had primacy over the Body.

The Spirit is like a two way mirror. It takes information from the body, turns it into phantasms that it then projects onto its surface for the Soul to see. The Soul, in turn, communicates information to the body by phantasms projected onto this same Spirit mirror.

Ficino, *Commentary on Plato's Symposium on Love*, (VI.6)

"*Certainly three things seem to be in us: the soul, the spirit, and the body. The soul and the body, which are by nature very different from each other are joined by means of the spirit, which is a certain very thin and clear vapor produced by the heat of the heart from the thinnest part of the blood. Spread from there through all parts of the body. It also receives through the organs of the senses images of external bodies, images which cannot be imprinted directly on the soul because incorporeal substance, which is higher than bodies, cannot be formed by them through the receiving of images. But the soul, being present to the spirit everywhere, easily sees the images of bodies shining in it, as if in a mirror, and through those judges the bodies. And this cognition is called by the Platonists sensation. While looking at these, by a power of its own, it conceives within itself images like them but much purer still. This kind of conceiving we call imagination or fantasy. Images conceived here are stored in memory. By these the eye of the soul is often aroused to contemplate the universal Ideas of things which it contains in itself. And for this reason at the same time that the soul is perceiving a certain man in sensation, and conceiving him in the imagination, it can contemplate, by means of the intellect, the reason and definition common to all men through its innate Idea of humanity; and what it has contemplated, it preserves."*

Ficino felt the Soul had a strong memory but that the senses did not. The senses had to constantly see and touch what they desired in order to be comforted.

Ficino, ibid., (VI.6)

"But the eye and the spirit, which, like mirrors, can receive images of a body only in its presence, and lose them when it is absent, need the continuous presence of a beautiful body in order to shine continuously with its illumination, and be comforted and pleased."

This idea resonates in *A Midsummer Night's Dream* (2.1.213) when Helena speaks of her passion for Demetrius

And I am sick when I look not on you.

Ficino was of the same opinion as Plato and Galen with regards to the act of seeing. He felt *'the internal fire'* is externalized through the eyes along with the thin blood of the engendered spirit.

This idea is common to both casting the 'evil eye' and 'falling in love'. It was felt that when someone looked at another person, their emitted spirit (pneumatic ray) penetrated through the other's eyes and entered their spiritual organism. Once in their spiritual system it could cause a disturbance in their heart, the generator of spirit, that could create a flutter or could even damage the heart.

Ficino's theory of the externalization of love through the eyes created the image (in French literature through the 16th century) of a woman as one who wounds her lover's heart. It gave rise to terms like *"this beautiful murderess"*, *"my warrior"* and *"my beautiful mankiller"*. This understanding is also reflected in Shakespeare's play when Demetrius speaks of the damage he will do and what will be done to him when he finds Lysander and Hermia (2.1.190)

> *The one I'll slay, the other slayeth me.*

Love arrows for Ficino were not just a metaphor and the love they generated had a drawing power.

Ficino, ibid., (VI.2)

"A man's appearance, which is often beautiful to see...can send a ray of its splendor through the eyes of those who see him and into their soul. Drawn by this spark as if by a kind of hook, the soul hastens towards the drawer."

This same understanding is reflected in Helena's pleas to Demetrius (2.1.195-198)

> *You draw me, you hard-hearted adamant –*
> *But yet you draw not iron, for my heart*
> *Is true as steel. Leave you your power to draw,*
> *And I shall have no power to follow you.*

Recognizing Ficino's strong reliance on 'eyes' as part of the mechanism by which love operates, it is not surprising that the word appears more frequently in *A Midsummer Night's Dream* than in any other of Shakespeare's plays. For example in reference to Hermia (2.2.90-91)

> *For she hath blessed and attractive eyes.*
> *How came her eyes so bright?*

To the modern day reader this seems merely to be an idle

compliment but for Shakespeare and Ficino much more was intended.

Ficino, ibid., (VI.10)

"...the ray of beauty...has the power to be reflected back to what it came from, and it draws the lover with it...it shines out, especially through the eyes, the transparent windows of the soul."

Ficino, ibid., (VII.4)

"...the spirit...shines out more copiously through the eyes since they themselves are transparent and the most shining of all the parts.

...And it is said that the deified Augustus had eyes so bright and shining that when he stared at someone very hard, he forced him to lower his eyes, as if before the glow of the sun."

 Earlier it was mentioned that love could lead to problems of the heart but it could also affect the blood and the spirit in other ways. By understanding Ficino we can discover how the mechanics of love can lead to these problems. We can also understand some of the concerns expressed in the play such as when Oberon sends Puck to find Helena because he is worried for her health (3.2.94-97)

> *About the wood go swifter than the wind,*
> *And Helena of Athens look thou find;*
> *All fancy-sick she is, and pale of cheer*
> *With sighs of love, that costs the fresh blood dear.*

Ficino, ibid., (VI.9)

"Moreover, wherever the continuous attention of the soul is carried, there also fly the spirits, which are the chariots, or instruments of the soul. The spirits are produced in the heart from the thinnest part of the blood. The lover's soul is carried toward the image of the beloved planted in his imagination, and thence towards the beloved himself. To the same place are also drawn the lover's spirits. Flying out there, they are continuously dissipated. Therefore there is a need for a constant source of pure blood to replace the consumed spirits, since the thinner

and clearer parts of the blood are used up every day in replacing the spirits. On that account, when the pure and clear blood is dissipated, there remains only the impure, thick, dry and black. Hence the body dries out and grows squalid, and hence lovers become melancholics."

Also, Ficino, ibid., (VII.4)

"For this reason the blood in a young man is thin, clear, warm, and sweet...Why am I saying these things? Certainly in order that you may understand that the spirits at this age are thin and clear, warm and sweet."

Although anemia and melancholy can result from unrequited love, obsessive love or doting can produce even worse consequences since it involves an altering of one's phantasms to the point that they no longer reflect reality.

The Soul is between two worlds, the Ideal World of Real Truths and the material world of sensory truths. In the process of sensory knowing the sensual input is translated into phantasms that are reflected in the mirror of the Spirit so that the Soul may learn about the world. The Soul is also privy to phantasms of Real Truths that come down to it from the Intelligible World. These too can be reflected into the Spiritual mirror to offer insights of the Divine to the individual in the physical realm.

Obsessive love or doting produces a negative feedback loop in the fixated victim. The lover becomes fixated on his beloved. He spends much time looking on her. The phantasm of her produced in the Spiritual mirror is communicated to the Soul who in turn has access to the world of Ideal Forms. These Ideals are fed back into the phantasm making the beloved even more desirable to the lover. He spends more time looking, longing, contemplating, and thinking about her through her phantasm which is an idealized version of her. It gets to the point that the phantasm monopolizes the Spiritual mirror to such a degree that the lover thinks of nothing else.

Ficino, ibid., (VI.5)

"...the image...penetrating through the eyes into the soul of the other, matches and corresponds completely with a certain identical image which was formed in...its inner nature from its creation. The soul thus stricken recognizes the image before it as something which is its own...The soul then puts the visual image beside its own interior image, and if anything is lacking in the former...the soul restores it by reforming it. Then the soul loves that reformed image as its own work. This is how it happens that lovers are so deceived that they think the beloved more beautiful than he is. For in the course of time they do not see the beloved in the real image of him received through the senses, but in an image already reformed by the lover's soul, in the likeness of its own innate idea, an image which is more beautiful than the body itself."

This obsessive love operates to the detriment of the lover who is weakened over time. Such obsession can result in death if the beloved does not accept the offer of love. If accepted then the beloved creates a more realistic phantasm of themselves in their lover as their relationship continues over a period of time. Eventually the lover's Spiritual mirror releases the idealized phantasm and the obsession is broken.

In *A Midsummer Night's Dream* several characters are afflicted by obsessive love or doting. The first is Hermia, who is described in (1.1.108-110) by a concerned Lysander

> *...and she, sweet lady, dotes,*
>
> *Devoutly dotes, dotes in idolatry,*
>
> *Upon this spotted and inconstant man.*

Lysander himself is accused by Egeus of bewitching his daughter. This employs the same mechanisms as those involved in doting, mainly the creation of an unrealistic phantasy in the lover (1.1.27,32,36)

> *This* (Lysander) *hath bewitch'd the bosom of my child.*
>
> *...And stolen the impression of her fantasy*
>
> *...With cunning hath thou filch'd my daughter's heart.*

This problem of altered perception produced by doting is shown in its most extreme case in Titania, who is made to dote upon an Ass. She confesses to this aberration in her own words (4.1.44)

> *O how I love thee! How I dote on thee!*

Puck comments on this ability of love to alter perceptions (1.1.232-235)

> *Things base and vile, holding no quantity*
>
> *Love can transpose to form and dignity:*
>
> *Love looks not with the eyes, but with the mind,*
>
> *And therefore is wing'd Cupid painted blind.*

This possession of another's inner phantasy can lead to resentment and even hatred if discovered through self reflection or if it becomes otherwise revealed.

Ficino, ibid., (VI.10)

"Love cannot exist without hate. Who would not hate one who took his soul away from him."

Because love lies so close to hate the extreme swings we see in Lysander, even though induced by magic, can be understood as coming from a genuine place. Ficino felt love also possessed other properties that could lead to confusion.

Ficino, ibid., (VI.10)

"Besides this, she (Diotima [4]) calls Love a sophist and a magician. A sophist Plato defines, in the dialogue "Sophist", as an ambitious and crafty debater who, by the subtleties of sophistries, shows us the false for the true, and forces those who dispute with him to contradict themselves

in their speeches. This lovers as well as beloveds endure at some time or other."

Lysander animates this claim in (2.2.110-121) where he rejects his love for Hermia in order to embrace a new found love for Helena. Reason serves his Desire and not the other way round. Helena tries to make this clear to him (3.2.134-135)

> Lys. *I had no judgment when to her I swore.*
>
> Hel. *Nor none, in my mind, now you give her o'er.*

In this play Reason has very little to do with love. The play suggests that the choices people make are almost entirely inexplicable. What the Soul yearns for is what the Soul gets [5]. The body seems like a helpless captive to the whole event. Bottom summarizes in (3.1.138-139)

> *And yet, to say the truth, reason and love*
>
> *Keep little company together nowadays.*

In the Platonic theology of the school of Proclus, love was conceived as a cosmic force in which all creation participated; falling and rising, emanating from and reverting to the One. Love was what united the Cosmos.

Hekate, Eros and Magic

Theurgy was a type of magic that grew out of *The Chaldean Oracles*. Theurgy is a term that was not known prior to the Oracles. This is not all that surprising since the Oracles were believed to be written by Julian 'The Theurgist' son of Julian 'The Chaldean'.

Theurgy was a means of improving and purifying the Soul. It was a form of 'white' or beneficent magic practiced in order to cause the Soul's ascension and unification with the Divine through ritual. Alchemists used similar ideas to provide the basis for improving and purifying the material world. Even though the type of magic involved in each is identical they served different purposes and so are sometimes defined differently. 'Vertical Theurgy' was that which explored the links between the Soul and the Divine whereas 'Horizontal Theurgy' was that which explored the links between an individual and the material world.

Seeking to unite your mind with the Divine Mind was the way to purify your Soul. It was achieved primarily through actions, contemplation, prayer and by making your mind as much like the Divine Mind as possible. Although this is generally a meditative activity it could involve the use of talismans and daemon guides. It could, of course, only proceed with Hekate's involvement and cooperation. She controlled all communication between the Divine and Material worlds. The individual's job was to become the receptive vessel tuned to receive Divine input; the gods were in control of the entire proceeding including which symbola (material object like a plant, stone, metal, incense, word or sound) could be used to make contact with them.

The result of Divine contact would be in the form of phantasms since this is the language of the Soul. Receiving these phantasms would result in an 'ecstatic vision' that somehow must be communicated to the world through words. In *A Midsummer Night's Dream* Bottom is faced with this problem and he decides that the best way to communicate what he has 'seen' is to have Quince write a song about it (4.1.213-214).

Ficino felt that both magic and love shared a dependence on the Spirit's ability to receive and modify phantasms as well as an aspiration for improvement. For Ficino, Eros = Magic. Eros was the aspiration to ascend to the Divine, to be like the Divine; Magic's role was to bring the material world into harmony with the Divine Ideals that governed them. The Macrocosm was to be mimicked in the microcosm. Creation of the Cosmos was to be mimicked by procreation in the world. Human love was an aspect of Divine Love. Love and Magic were part and parcel of the same desire.

Ficino, ibid., (VI.10)

"But why do we think that Love is a magician? Because the whole power of magic consists in love. The work of magic is the attraction of one thing by another because of a certain affinity of nature. But the parts of this world, like the parts of a single animal, all deriving from a single author, are joined to each other by the communion of a single nature."

"...From this common relationship is born a common love; from love, a common attraction. And this is the true magic.

...Therefore the works of magic are the works of nature, but art is its handmaiden. For where anything is lacking in a natural relationship, art supplies it through vapors, numbers, figures, and qualities at the proper times.

...The ancients attributed this art to daemons because daemons understand what is the inter-relation of natural things, what is appropriate to each, and how the harmony of things, if it is lacking anywhere, can be restored.

...Therefore no one can doubt that love is a magician, since the whole power of magic consists in love, and the work of love is fulfilled by bewitchments, incantations, and enchantments."

In *A Midsummer Night's Dream* when Egeus comes before Theseus it is witchcraft that Lysander is accused of (1.1.26-38)(my underlining)

> *And, my gracious Duke,*
>
> *This hath bewitch'd the bosom of my child.*
>
> *Thou, thou, Lysander, thou hast given her rhymes,*
>
> *And interchang'd love-tokens with my child:*
>
> *Thou hast by moonlight at her window sung*
>
> *With faining voice verses of feigning love,*
>
> *And stol'n the impression of her fantasy*

With bracelets of thy hair, rings, gauds, conceits,

Knacks, trifles, nosegays, sweetmeats (messengers

Of strong prevailment in unharden'd youth):

<u>*With cunning*</u> *hast thou filch'd my daughter's heart*

Turn'd her obedience (which is due to me)

To stubborn harshness.

Egeus speaks of Lysander bewitching his daughter using songs (incantations) and love tokens (bewitchments) to create a false impression of himself which he has fixated on her spirit, the source of phantasy, by cunning means. Lysander has used this magic to lead her away (enchant her). Ficino's words come alive in this verse. The line between love and magic has become blurred as early as Act 1 Scene 1.

It is in Act 2 that we are truly introduced to the fairy world. A conversation between Puck and a fairy relays the information about the conflict between King Oberon and Queen Titania over a changeling mortal boy. This unresolved conflict, in turn, is wreaking havoc with the weather.

Shakespeare's sources become apparent when Oberon conspires with Puck to "*torment*" the Queen for this injury she inflicted on his pride. He plans to drug her and make her fall in love with something unpleasant (2.1.177-182)

I'll watch Titania when she is asleep,

And drop the liquor of it in her eyes:

The next thing then she waking looks upon

(Be it on lion, bear, or wolf, or bull,

On meddling monkey, or on busy ape)

She shall pursue it with the soul of love.

And again (2.2.33)

Wake when some vile thing is near.

This plan and subsequent events in the play owe much to Apuleius and his book *Metamorphoses* (sometimes referred to as *The Golden Ass*). Apuleius was born around 125 C.E. and was a lawyer, writer, and priest in the Cult of Isis; his book is a collection of connected short stories that revolve around a man who has been magically transformed into an Ass. The insights he receives while in this condition lead to his eventual enlightenment and return to human form.

Oberon's plan corresponds directly to a plan hatched by Venus in (*Metamorphoses* IV, 30-31). Apuleius' story involves Venus, Psyche (Greek for Soul), and Cupid. Venus has grown jealous of Psyche's beauty and requests her son Cupid to strike Psyche with a passion for the meanest, poorest, most sickly man in the whole world. This plot is repeated with Oberon standing in for Venus and Puck for Cupid.

When one examines *A Midsummer Night's Dream* it is apparent that Puck is playing Cupid throughout this play. He is the playful boy who doles out the love potion blindly. When he defines Cupid (3.2.440-441) he is defining himself

Cupid is a knavish lad

Thus to make poor females mad!

The connection between Bottom and Apuleius' story of a man changed into an Ass will be discussed later but right now let's focus on the world of the fairies.

When Oberon speaks to Puck he reverentially recalls seeing a mermaid on the back of a dolphin (2.1.149-154)

Since once I sat upon a promontory,

And heard a mermaid on a dolphin's back

Uttering such dulcet and harmonious breath

That the rude sea grew civil at her song

And certain stars shot madly from their spheres

To hear the sea-maids music.

This image, I believe, comes from the legend of Amphitrite (daughter of Oceanus and Nereus) and her arranged marriage to Poseidon. At first she fled but Poseidon sent a dolphin to bring her back [6]. Amphitrite became the feminine personification of the sea. Giordano Bruno in his *Heroic Furors* sees Amphitrite as even more than this; he saw her as the equivalent of the Paternal Mind. Bruno believed Diana to be the daughter of Amphitrite

"...for the monad that is the divinity (Amphitrite) produces this other monad (Diana), which is nature, the universe, the world, where she contemplates herself and is reflected, like the sun in the moon" (Couliano; *Eros and Magic in the Renaissance*, p. 80).

For Bruno, Amphitrite played the role of the Sun (the Intelligible World), and Diana played the role of the Moon (the Material or Sensory World). Amphitrite is the source of Love. All turn to her and listen to her song. She is the ultimate Siren. She is the harmony of the spheres. Shakespeare's description confirms Bruno's influence.

Oberon goes on to describe how he saw Cupid between the moon and earth (2.1.155-157)

> *That very time I saw (but thou couldst not),*
> *Flying between the cold moon and the earth,*
> *Cupid all arm'd.*

Hekate's daemons in *The Chaldean Oracles* were imagined to dwell between heaven and earth in the sublunar region. Plutarch wrote of the mediating nature of daemons and cited Plato when referring to them as a race that conveyed prayers and petitions of men to the gods, and that brought oracles and gifts of the gods to men. These daemons could be bad or good; in later philosophical systems the good daemons became known as angels and those intent on deceiving humans retained the name daemon.

These later systems were intent on ridding Hekate (the Cosmic Soul) from her older undesirable and even threatening traits, including her role as mistress of bad daemons. This was done through the ideas contained in Middle Platonic Philosophy. Later Platonists posited a double Soul; the upper half remained connected to the Intelligible world (the rational soul) and the lower half could come into contact with the material world (the irrational soul).

Hekate became subject to this division. Hekate retained her role of Cosmic Soul, transmitter of the Divine, ensouling web of the Cosmos and Physis became her irrational soul, her connected counterpart. Physis looked after the Material world (the physical operation of the universe). Physis was not evil, simply tainted by contact with the material world.

This division of Hekate into Hekate and Physis meant the good daemons (angels) functioned as ferrymen for Hekate and her previous earthly entourage of spirits that could not cross over now became assigned to Physis. These were the disembodied souls that were trapped between the upper world and Hades, often associated with phantasms, bad dreams, and apparitions and that were known to wander the crossroads. Physis took responsibility for these daemons as well as those responsible for the operation of the physical world. The power wielded by these daemons came from the material world, possibly the earth itself. This is why they were consulted by alchemists; they had extensive knowledge of how the physical world operated and how to bring it into alignment with its ideals.

This preamble is given to provide background to understanding Puck's warning and Oberon's assertion in (3.2.378-388)

Puck. *My fairy lord; this must be done with haste,*

For night's swift dragons cut the clouds full fast;

And yonder shines Aurora's harbinger,

At whose approach, ghosts wandering here and there

Troop home to churchyards. Damned spirits all,

That in cross-ways and floods have burial,

Already to their wormy beds are gone,

For fear lest day should look their shames upon:

They willfully themselves exil'd from light,

And must for aye consort with black-brow'd night.

Obe. *But we are spirits of another sort.*

Oberon is clearly separating himself from the wandering spirits of Physis' entourage and putting himself either among her daemons responsible for the day to day operation of the physical world or in Hekate's camp.

A Midsummer Night's Dream seems to have an unspoken understanding of the concept of Platonic Soul-Mates. This is why Oberon feels morally obliged to match Helena with her desire, Demetrius. It matters to him which mortals are paired up; it is not simply a question of pairing them up. This is also true of Oberon and Titania. They represent the Hekate-Physis union in the microcosm of the fairy world. Oberon is the rational component and Titania the more worldly. Two parts of one soul.

The text of *A Midsummer Night's Dream* bears this out. Titania is clearly identified with worldly operations but Oberon seems somehow aloof from the operation of the material world, this he always performs through Puck. Titania is directly linked to worldly occurrences. She is clearly a *"spirit of the elements"*, when she and her fairies *"dance to the wind"* is interrupted by Oberon, it causes the wind to suck up the sea and dump it on the land causing flooding (2.1.86-92)

To dance our ringlets to the whistling wind,

But with thy brawls thou has disturb'd our sport.

Therefore the winds, sipping to us in vain,

As in revenge have suck'd up from the sea

Contagious fogs; which, falling in the land,

Hath every pelting river made so proud

That they have overborne their continents.

Northrop Frye in his book *On Shakespeare* points out that Titania also appears to be a possessive and entangling spirit, one that binds others to herself and to her woods (3.1.145-146)

Out of this wood do not desire to go:

Thou shalt remain here, whether thou wilt or no.

This behaviour may have something to do with the fight between Titania and Oberon over the custody of the changeling boy. Oberon throughout the play shows himself to be a moral character, empathetic and acting in others' best interests. He only appears petty, vindictive and jealous with regards to the boy and in his actions towards Titania.

It could be that Oberon is a version of the *"Jealous God"* of the Old Testament or it could be he is acting out of love for both Titania and the changeling. Titania's version of events, looking after her friend's child, certainly seems like a duty of honour; but Titania is an entangling spirit and in fact could be holding the boy against his will or even worse could be holding him against Nature's will. It wouldn't be the first time that a doting Mother has ensnared a child and become overprotective to the point of doing harm. If this were so, consider also the harm Titania is doing to herself. She is a spirit who has transferred her affection to the material world and who is not giving due observance, i.e. love, to the spiritual world.

Ficino wrote *De amore* with the purpose to *"summon the lost lovers of earthly beauty to return to the love of immortal beauty"*. This could be Oberon's task; by making Titania fall in love with an Ass he is demonstrating to her that she is focusing her love downwards on the bestial world rather than upward toward the Intellectual realm.
Ficino, ibid., (VI.8) (my underlining)

"Thus every love begins with sight. But the love of the contemplative man <u>ascends</u> from sight to intellect. That of the voluptuous man <u>descends</u> from sight to touch.
The love of the contemplative man is called <u>divine</u>...
That of the voluptuous man, <u>bestial</u>."

Needless to say, Oberon's actions do make Titania a victim of bestial love. In regards to the earlier proposal, that Titania might be interfering in the natural order of things, let us reflect on what was considered to be the natural passing of a mortal according to Plutarch. It was referred to as the double release of the soul. First the Soul was separated from the body in the *"realm of Demeter"* i.e. the Earth; then the Soul was separated from the Mind in the *"realm of Persephone"* i.e. the Moon. The Mind then returned to its source *"The Paternal Mind"* in the Intellectual realm. So each part of the human returns from whence it came; body back to the elements, soul/spirit back to the moon, and mind back to God.

Titania is an entangling spirit but it may be time for the boy to pass to the next realm or merely break free of her apron strings; for both their welfare this must be allowed to occur. With these ideas in mind Oberon may very well be the moral, well intentioned voice of reason he appears to be in the rest of the play.

Returning to the idea of phantasms let's look at Oberon's weapon of choice, the flower, love-in-idleness. According to Dent's article this refers to a flower, a pansy, which Shakespeare used in other plays (*Hamlet* (4.5.174-175) *"And there is pansies, that's for thoughts"*) and whose meaning is in keeping with its French origin, pensée; a thought or a flower. We also know Aristotle believed that to think *"was to speculate with phantasms"*. Thinking involved accessing data that was stored as phantasms; this is what reason meditated upon.

So Oberon's magic involved the lover's imaginations, their phantasms. This is in keeping with Ficino's as well as Bruno's views on magic; that magic involved phantasms which constituted the language of the soul.

Imagination in the Elizabethan Age

Imagination in the Elizabethan Age was looked upon with great suspicion. W. Rossky's article *Imagination in the English Renaissance: Psychology and Poetic* explores views that were prevalent at the time. To briefly summarize, he points out that Elizabethan society regarded the imagination/phantasy (words they used interchangeably) as a key faculty in the hierarchy of our Understanding. All Sensory information was pooled in the Common Sense and from there the condensed information went to The Phantasy where it was converted into images that the higher faculties could think upon. Because it was the gateway to Reasoning it was critical that it be reliable; to quote a concerned writer of the time *"Reason could only be as accurate as the images presented to it."*

A large segment of society (Puritans in particular) held the Phantasy in disrepute. They felt it to be a falsifying faculty corrupted by its close association to the Senses. Since the Senses were tied to the flesh they suffered under the sins of the flesh. Phantasy, being closely associated with the Common Sense, could also be attracted to things of the sensual world, things the body enjoyed. The Phantasy, they feared, could be corrupted by the body's desires and passions.

Worse still, the Phantasy was seen as an 'active faculty' capable of building on the information given it. It could abstract information in any number of ways. The Phantasy was, in short, a liar.

The Phantasy could, or more specifically, its images could stimulate emotions. These emotions could override Reason and lead to irrational behaviour. In *A Midsummer Night's Dream* we can see an example of this when the Players' imaginations are led astray by the passion of fear and Puck's encouragement (3.2.27-28)

> *Their sense thus weak, lost with their fears thus strong,*
> *Made senseless things begin to do them wrong.*

The conservative element of the population felt that if objects were accurately presented, then reaction to them would be proportional and adequate but if the images were exaggerated then so would the passionate response and the result would defy Reason. This idea of *'objects accurately presented'* draws us back to *A Midsummer Night's Dream* and the play within the play.

Much of the humour of this embedded play (5.1) comes from the players going out of their way to accurately present themselves. Pyramus points out to the audience that he is not Pyramus but an actor awaiting his cues. The lion points out that he is not a lion but Snug the joiner so there is nothing to fear. Shakespeare is slamming the conservative element in his society by showing what a play might look like if one adhered to such ideals.

Arguments had to be made to defend the Phantasy and works of an imaginative nature. Philip Sidney's *The Defense of Poetry* (written in the 1580s) is one such work. In it the Phantasy is shown to be capable of conjuring possible futures that are necessary for planning, inventing, and to devise any new thing.

Arguments to dismiss the idea that the Phantasy was in league against Reason were made by demonstrating that one could use images to arouse the emotions and passions in *'good causes'* for *'good results'* to help people *'do what they should'*.

Poets argued that you could tell more truths by lying, by showing nature in its more ideal form, and that by doing so they were showing the world the way God intended it and not in its corrupted worldly state.

Poets argued that their feigning was not haphazard, but deliberate and purposeful therefore moral and rational. Their Phantasy was under the control of their Reason. Poetic imagination was good imagination. They created verisimilitudes that imitated real life for the purpose of instruction; they moved the passions with the intent to reveal a higher truth than was possible in this world. This is why the poet was superior to the historian because they could mold their images to secure the proper emotional and moral response to the information presented.

Their strong imagery was defended by the doctrine of *'persuasion to do good'*. Good imagination becomes controlled imagination.

The players do a bad job of enacting *Pyramus and Thisbe* but do a great job enacting these concepts. They are the opposite of deliberate, purposeful poets constructing images to fine tune the passions. They are poets of the other sort. The haphazard kind.

They do not accomplish their purpose of performing a tragedy but rather turn it into a comedy. They also fail to appreciate the role the audience's imagination plays in becoming caught up in the *'safe terror'* of the stage. Dent's article demonstrates how the players think their audience is both over- and under- imaginative. For instance Quince is worried that the lion should not roar too terribly lest it frighten the ladies (1.2.70-72). Bottom's solution to this is to roar *"as gently as any suckling dove"* (1.2.77). So to avoid the threat of over-imagination they accurately present themselves as actors and not as the characters thereby preventing any harm coming to the audience from their exaggerated response. At the same time remedies are also created to assist the audience with their lack of imagination by creating two characters, where none were required, those of Moonshine and Wall.

The players have failed in controlling any of the passions appropriate to the play; and its moral lesson against '*impetuous action*' has gone unnoticed.

On the other hand, they have done no harm. They protected their audience from fear and helped them use their imaginations when they felt it was safe to do so. They also succeeded in releasing one great passion, joy.

The '*players scene*' is certainly to provide comic relief but it serves a serious function in demonstrating the power that could be released by the deliberate and purposeful exercise of the imagination. Even Theseus, who dismisses the imagination as a trickster, is shown to employ it to intuit the good intensions of those incapable of expressing them. He shows that his imagination helps him to see beyond the veil of the material world to see this intent in others (5.1.104-105)

> *...tongue-tied simplicity*
>
> *In least – speaks most.*

He also understands how theatre works as a safe haven to experience emotionally charged events at a safe distance (5.1.208-209)

> *The best in this kind are but shadows; and the*
>
> *Worst are no worse, if imagination amend them.*

Oberon is really the character in the play that employs phantasms to accomplish moral goals. Theseus's problems disappear because of Oberon's imaginative intervention. Oberon's imaginative interference helps to perfect Theseus's world. The couples find happiness because Oberon has manipulated the phantasmic apparatus of Demetrius. Magic has been accomplished through Imagination. Lives have been transformed for the better. The happy ending is a result of Oberon's Phantasmical interference.

Bottom is at the Bottom of it All

In the Elizabethan Age we are looking at a world, a cosmos really, that was arranged as a hierarchy extending from God through the physical world to the humblest form of inanimate matter. Every level evolved from the level above it in a descending hierarchy growing increasingly distant from God. Every creature desired to rise above its level and ascend back to God. For Platonists this desire to return to the source was called Love and the quality in the source which attracted this desire was called Beauty.

All the universe, falling and rising – emanating from and reverting to – The One. This is the dynamic equilibrium of existence; change being the only constant.

Bottom is, of course, another name for Ass. In the play he and his fellows are at the bottom of the social hierarchy depicted. Of his fellows he is the only one to become a beast so he is, in fact, the lowest creature in the play. But it is from the bottom that we all must rise, and Bottom can claim witness to this ascent better than anyone.

Bottom has seen behind the curtain of our existence. He is the mechanical who has seen the mechanicals that operate our world. He is sole witness to the fairies (the operational daemons of our world).

Bottom is also our link to a world of abstract magical thought that was available to Shakespeare. There are several '*Ass*' related references that are significant to understanding Bottom and this play. The first of these works is by Apuleius and is called *Metamorphoses* or *The Golden Ass*. Interestingly Apuleius was also believed to be (at least by Lactantius) the translator of the *Asclepius*, the Hermetic text that related information about how to magically bring a statue to life (a theme Shakespeare explored in *The Winter's Tale*). The other Ass related works of significance are by Giordano Bruno. He wrote a trilogy between 1584 and 1585 while in England. They are:

The Expulsion of the Triumphant Beast (*Lo spaccio della bestia trionfante*)

The Cabala of the Pegasean Horse (*La cabala del cavallo Pegaseo*) and annexed to this document was

The Cyllenic Ass (*Assino cillenico*)

and finally

The Heroic Furors (*De gli eroici furori*).

These works lay out much of Bruno's philosophy of the Ass. The theme of the works is change. In *The Expulsion...*, Bruno points out that ignorance is the preparatory condition for receiving wisdom. According to cabalistic revelation the ass or assinity is the symbol of wisdom. This makes Bottom our prime candidate for being privy to any Divine wisdom that is to be offered in *A Midsummer Night's Dream*.

In Bruno's work *Cabala*, his character Onorio is turned into an ass and in *Furors*, Acteon's metamorphosis into a stag is presented. In the *Triumphant Beast* he speaks of the lesson Capricorn taught the gods; the lesson of transforming themselves into beasts (this trick allowed them to win in the fight against Python and defeat the Titans; it was also the reason Capricorn was revered and placed among the stars).

Bruno saw that Divinity could descend, in a certain manner, to become part of Nature and so he felt humans could ascend to Divinity through this same Nature. Nature was nothing other than '*God in things*'. The ladder of Nature provided the way for the gods to descend and a way for humans to ascend. The Divine Idea that generated the material object rested in each object and could be understood and worshipped as a way to reach back to the Divine Mind.

For Bruno there was one Divinity, found in all things. In his story of Actaeon (*Giordano Bruno and the Philosophy of the Ass*, p. 88 for Ordine's translation from the *Eroici*) he explains one of his central metaphors; while Actaeon is out stag hunting with his dogs he comes across Diana, bathing. Diana turns Actaeon into a stag who is, in turn, attacked by his own dogs. For Bruno the story of Actaeon is one of self enlightenment. As Bruno interprets the story, Actaeon through his thoughts (the dogs) is seeking to understand Nature (the stag). In his search he accidentally comes across naked Diana (the secrets behind Nature's operations). To see naked Diana is to see beauty, the Divine ideas behind things. It is not possible to look upon the Sun (the world of Intelligible Ideas) but it is possible to see the Sun reflected in the Moon - Diana - Nature. It is like seeing the soul through the opacity of matter, the divine within. This is an epiphany that one cannot turn away from or unlearn. Actaeon now sees the truth, that he himself is a part of Nature, a part of the Divine so he becomes nature (the stag). He knows he is part of the Divinity and that he no longer has to search for the Divinity outside of himself. His thoughts turn inward (he is consumed by the dogs). He is now dead to the material world because he now lives in the intellectual world with the gods. As he contemplates the divinity within himself he learns to harmonize with it, adding to its song.

This explains why Bruno felt the *'beast in man'* was an important revelation but let's look explicitly at his understanding of the Ass.

The Ass was important to Bruno; it was a symbol of fecundity, fertility, and regeneration, it was also seen as one of the spirits of the waters, and was considered a symbol of knowledge. All these readings of this symbol easily fit within the theme of *A Midsummer Night's Dream*. Shakespeare's choice of an Ass head for Bottom was not inappropriate or ill considered. Titania is being honest when she says of Ass-headed Bottom (3.1.142)

Thou art as wise as thou art beautiful.

Nuccio Ordine explores in detail Bruno's ideas in his book *Giordano Bruno and the Philosophy of the Ass*; so I will only briefly touch on those ideas I feel most pertinent to understanding *A Midsummer's Night's Dream*.

The Ass is most familiarly seen as a symbol of humility and hard toil, but because of its large ears was also seen as being privy to the secrets in the invisible world (beyond the sense of sight). The Ass was sacred to Isis and is well known as the beast that carried Christ. Because of its divine and beastial nature the ass was a nice stand-in for humans who also possess this dual nature.

For Bruno work and toil represented the only possibility for the development of knowledge and with it civilization and culture. Bruno felt there were two kinds of Asses; Positive Asses, that through hard work, humility, knowledge, and action could achieve change and thereby exercise control over the Wheel of Fortune and that there were Negative Asses that through dogmatism, arrogance, intransigence, and ignorance persist in an idleness brought on by a belief in the myth of the Golden Age (the return of Christ and Paradise on Earth). These Negative Asses would watch their fingers become hoofs as they became incapable of ever picking the fruit from the tree of knowledge.

Of all the characters in *A Midsummer Night's Dream*, Bottom as the Ass-Man embodies the certainty of metamorphosis; he has changed and hopefully will change again, to be reborn.

Bottom has seen the fairy world, the operational daemons of the physical realm, he knows there is more to our existence than just the visible material world. Behind his comic image is a profound truth (4.2.28)

I am to discourse wonders.

But Bottom's wonders escape him, he has not the tools to make his vision tangible. We learn from Philostrate that Bottom and the other players "*have never labour'd in their minds till now*" (5.1.73). This is undoubtedly why Bottom hoped to employ Quince to help write a ballad of his dream.

Bruno understood the effort required to grow in wisdom; that a dialogue was required between contemplation and application (*Giordano Bruno and the Philosophy of the Ass*, p.40 or *The Expulsion of the Triumphant Beast*, Third Dialogue: First Part, Imerti transl. p.205-206).

"And for this reason Providence has decided that man be occupied in activity thanks to his hands and in contemplation thanks to his intellect, in such a way that he never contemplates without acting and never acts without contemplating...In this way, the more and more humanity distances itself from the condition of animals thanks to their urgent and pressing activities, the closer they come to the divine being."

Bruno understood that culture is built from hard work, that it must grow and always change. There is nothing static in Bruno's conception of culture only that it should operate to the betterment of the community.

Bottom recognizes his experience to have been '*spiritual*' and he attempts to quote or integrate the Bible into his thoughts (4.1.209-215)

> *The eye of*
> *man hath not heard, the ear of man hath not seen,*
> *man's hand is not able to taste, his tongue to*
> *conceive, nor his heart to report, what my dream was.*
> *I will get Peter Quince, to write a ballad of this*
> *dream: it shall be called 'Bottom's Dream', because*
> *It hath no bottom.*

Consider the Biblical allusion (1557, Geneva New Testament, 1 Corinthians ii. 9-10).

9. But we preache as it is written, Things which eye hath not seen, & ear hath not heard, neither have entered into mans mind, which things God hath prepared for those that love him.

10. But God hath opened them unto us by his Spirit, for the Spirit searcheth all things, yea, the bottom of Gods secrets.

Those that share the '*spirit of God*' share the '*secrets of God*'. Bruno would agree whole-heartedly with this statement, but he would make it more universal, knowing all creation shares in the Cosmic Soul. Bottom has glimpsed into this world, he knows a secret, but unfortunately it is escaping his ability to communicate it.

Harmony for Bottom's Ballad

Phantasy or Imagination is at the core of the play. It is at the core of Love. Love defies Reason but it does not defy the Soul. The Soul recognizes its mate or at least what it lacks and needs in another. The Soul communicates by phantasms that function beyond mere words (a picture is worth a thousand words). Magic too communicates through our interconnected Spirits through the vast Cosmos to the Divine. It too communicates through images and phantasms. Magic can improve our souls by bringing our minds and bodies into conformity with or into harmony with the Divine Mind. Magic can improve our world by bringing objects into closer conformity with the Ideas that govern them. Love can bring the beloved and lover also into closer conformity with each other and the ideals governing each of their souls. Using phantasms we '*make and match*' our world to that of the Divines'. Through phantasms we show the Divine our world and the Divine through prophesy reveals truths necessary to us in order for us to re-make our world. The dialectic continues until we are harmonized into the Divine. This operation is one Theseus recognizes (5.1.12-13)

> *The poet's eye, in a fine frenzy rolling,*
> *Doth glance from heaven to earth, from earth to heaven.*

159

Harmony should not be misunderstood to mean '*sameness*'. Valeriano in his *Hieroglyphica* explains (*Giordano Bruno and The Philosophy of the Ass,* p. 21-22).

"*In fact, each of the lyre's strings emits its own sound; deep, sharp, medium, or clear, each has its own particular sound. But harmony can be neither discerned nor recognized unless one adds the art of playing the lyre. The modulation and the sweetness of the various sounds are revealed when he who holds the lyre makes each string resonate...In the same way...if a wise intellect rules over them, then the spirit discerns what is dissonant and what is consonant.*"

The tuning of ourselves to each other and to the Divine can only proceed through action. All are in motion. Change is constant. Intelligence and Action (playing) are required to produce harmony. The lyre does not play itself nor does our world get better by waiting for an apocalypse.

Bottom is correct in wishing to write a song about his experience; music can add an emotional component to help the words rationalize the phantasm experience. Even as he says this his dream is leaving him, he is forgetting.

This brings me to the last Ass-related story pertinent to *A Midsummer Night's Dream*. Again it comes from Bruno and is in his book *Cabala*. It is the story of Onorio. His story reveals how the human soul is no different than that of an ass's or any other living being [7]. At the basis of all life is the same "*material body*" and the same "*spiritual matter*". Onorio died on earth as an ass, he transmigrated into human bodies and upon death returned to heaven each time as the Pegasean Ass (*Giordano Bruno and the Philosophy of the Ass*, Chapter 5, p.35-37). Onorio remembers the experience because, in heaven, he only pretends to drink from the Lethe (the river of forgetfulness). By doing so he keeps the memory of his different lives intact.

This story is important in understanding what Bottom has almost said. He has alluded to 1 Corinthians ii. 9–10 but to appreciate what has been inferred let's continue the quotation to verses 11 and 12 .

11   For what man knoweth the things of a man, save the spirit of a man, which is in him? Even so the things of God knoweth no man, but the Spirit of God.

12   Now we have received not the Spirit of the world, but the Spirit, which is of God, that we might know the things that are given to us of God.

Essentially the quotation says that to know God and the things of God you need to share the Spirit of God. This is what Onorio in Bruno's tale has discovered; that all life is connected and all life shares the Spirit of God. This is the secret that lies within ourselves that we are a part of nature, a part of the cosmos, the knowledge that all creation is connected and that God lies within.

Bottom, like Onorio, has crossed the boundary into the daemon world and he has felt the love and acceptance offered there. Bottom is born again when he returns to this world but unlike Onorio he has drunk from the water of forgetfulness. Bottom grapples with his memories. He knows he had a religious experience. He matches his experience with things he has learned from the Bible but even while doing so he is forgetting. He falls from epiphany to confusion. He knows he knows but he is no longer sure what he knew.

Bottom is a weaver. He has joined together characters and locations from disparate plots to create one coherent play. Hekate is regarded as the Weaver of the Cosmos. She connects everything to the Idea that governs it. She weaves in place the lines of communication from the Divine to the material world. Hekate began our play and Hekate is called to end it.

Hekate, among all the divinities, had a close and almost exclusive connection with dogs. Hounds always preceded Hekate's arrival. Let me quote Virgil, *Aeneid*, Book VI, ll. 257.

"And a baying of the hounds was heard through the half-light: the goddess was coming, Hekate."

In *A Midsummer Night's Dream* the sound of the hounds (4.1.105) marks the end of Act 4, the end of the dream portion of the play. A boundary must now be crossed as the characters move from the woods back to civilization and the rule of reason. The chaos of love is behind them, the order of marriage and devotion is ahead as the play proceeds to Shakespeare's defense of a well trained imagination.

Conclusion

So how much of the subtext did Shakespeare want us to understand or take away from the play?

Shakespeare's allusion to Hekate and *"triple Hekate's team"* (Hippolyta, Hermia, and Helena) is made purposeful through his strong use of the word *"Moon"*, and by setting the time of the play during the traditional '*Hekate supper*'. He wants us to connect his play with concepts concerning Hekate. He wants us to understand her role as the Cosmic Soul and to sense the interconnectedness of all creation through the interconnectedness of his characters.

This is the point of Bottom's Dream. It's a reprise of these ideas. It speaks of the interconnectedness of the human spirit with God's Spirit. In many ways the lovers reinforce this understanding. Their characters are left ill-defined while their interconnectedness is stressed by having one standing in for the other at various times [8]. It is not always entirely clear who loves who and how the matches will end.

Bottom embodies this concept. Bottom is Everyman. At the beginning of the play (1.2.11-103) he offers to play not just Pyramus but

Thisbe and the lion too. He is all sexes and all creatures. This is made even more apparent in Bottom's metamorphosis to an Ass. Bottom seamlessly drifts from being a human to an Ass with no apparent change to his character. The man and the beast are the same; both share his nature and thereby show their interconnectedness.

The world itself also reveals an interconnectedness to that of the fairies' world as their feud has its repercussions in our weather.

Hekate is the Weaver of this vast tapestry of the Cosmos and Bottom, the weaver, reveals the secret of our interconnectedness to us. Bottom connects all worlds and characters together; he forms part of the players' company, he shows up in the Lovers' woods, he finds himself beloved of the Queen of the fairies and finally he performs in Athens before the King. He is the thread that ties the various parts of the play together.

When Shakespeare presents us with the lovers he does so by employing Ficino's theory of Love which was identical to his theory of Magic. Shakespeare then takes these lovers and abandons them in the magical woods of the fairies. So for both Shakespeare and Ficino Love and Magic are intimately connected.

In the last act Shakespeare mounts a defense of the imagination (and in fact magic) by showing us its healing power; that even the worst can be made into the best, *"if imagination amend them"*.

Shakespeare has woven a play out of a theory of love and magic; shown us how we are interconnected with each other and the universe, and offered us a way to improve ourselves and the world through our imaginations. A major accomplishment for a mere dream.

Footnotes

[1]   I prefer the term Spiritus Mundi for Hekate rather than Cosmic Soul. The problem one encounters in much literature of this period is the drifting definitions of Soul, Spirit, and Mind. Sometimes Soul and Spirit or Soul and Mind are used interchangeably.   Usually the context makes things clear.

In general there are three parts to an individual. The body is the material part, generally regarded as unclean; next is the Spirit (but can be called the Irrational Soul or even Soul). Its job is to insulate the pure part that comes from the Divine from any contact with the Material world. Lastly we have the pure bit that comes from God (the Paternal Mind) and returns to God after death. This can be referred to as the Soul or Mind. The three parts are standard: a material part, an insulator, and a pure part from God.

In terms of understanding the magic of Shakespeare's day, I feel it is important to maintain the macrocosm-microcosm symmetry. The insulator or boundary separating the material from the divine always comes from Hekate (the boundary goddess), so by using the term Spiritus Mundi for her it is easy to see that our Spirit comes from and returns to Hekate and that it is connected to all other spirits. This term also makes clear that our Mind (soul) is part of and returns to the Paternal Mind. The term helps to maintain the logic of the body-spirit-mind trinity.

[2]   Hekate was the goddess of liminal places. She was called on to assist passage through thresholds, crossroads, and other such boundaries. Boundaries belonged to no one; because of this dissociation, crossroads became the realm of ghosts and those dispelled from society.

'Hekate Suppers' were taken to crossroads each month at the time of the new moon; that is, on the night the old month ended and the new one began (the dark night). This was the time to supplicate Hekate.

[3]   Sympathy (Harmony, Eros) was the natural force underlying and giving unity to the Cosmos that connected the Intelligible world to the Sensible world. It was what made magic possible. Searching for this underlying unity, examining nature to find sympathetic connections, links between things, constituted much of the work done by magicians. This was a search for connections that could be exploited in order to create worldly magic. The role played by the Cosmic Soul or Spiritus Mundi in connecting objects to ideas meant that the world was rationally ordered and understandable. This is a tremendous help as a 'basic assumption' to make about the universe. It marks one of the first steps needed in order to gain any control over your world.

[4]   Diotima was a prophetess who taught Socrates about Love.

[5]   In Plato love can be seen as a yearning for the Divine and beauty is a term that characterizes how much an individual matches the Divine Idea (it should not be confused with physical beauty). When a soul recognizes beauty it recognizes the "*aspect of the Divine*" in another. It yearns for this if it is lacking in that aspect itself or is not as good a representation of it. Soul-mates complete each other by offering something the other soul is missing or needs an improved copy of.

Diotima called Love a daemon because it occupies the middle ground. What she meant by this was that soul-mates see something they desire in the other soul, something they need to more closely match their Divine Ideal, Love is the meeting place between two desires; the middle ground.

We do not desire that which we completely possess or that which we completely lack. Again desire occupies that middle ground. See Ficino, ibid., (VI.7) and (VI.2).

[6]   It is important to note that the Mermaid is on the back of a dolphin. This distinguishes her from other Sirens. Sirens often were symbols of *"desire that brings destruction"*. Here, because of the dolphin, we have a symbol of Amphitrite – Love – the Source of Desire; what Plato referred to as the first turning towards God. This is love in its best possible form, that which draws us towards God. This is not sensual desire that draws us away from God but just the opposite. She is intellectual desire that draws us to the Intelligible world. The stars (angels) being attracted to her reveals the purity of this symbol. This symbol links Shakespeare to Ficino and Bruno. See Ficino, ibid., VI.7, *On the birth of Love*; and see I.P. Couliano, *Eros and Magic in the Renaissance*, p. 79-80; also *New Larousse Encyclopedia of Mythology*, Greek Mythology, Amphitrite, p. 133.

[7]   The same could be said in *A Midsummer Night's Dream* where pains are taken to show there is no difference between the lion and Snug, the joiner.

[8]   Unlike the characters in many of Shakespeare's plays the characters in *A Midsummer Night's Dream* are merely types devoid of much depth or even individuality. He does not develop them so much as use them in his story telling.

Hermia (short, dark, fierce, willful) is contrasted against Helena (tall, blonde, gentle, obsessive). The two are presented as different characters and yet they see themselves as interchangeable or at least as close as twin sisters (3.2.198-214) possessing a single voice and mind.

This allows Shakespeare to make his point that two such physically different types could actually be treated interchangeably in the play; Lysander first loves Hermia, then loves Helena (while under a spell) finally to return to his love of Hermia; Demetrius first loves Helena, then loves Hermia, finally to love Helena once again (with Oberon's help). I believe Shakespeare, with the goal of revealing our fundamental interconnectedness, is using two physically different types to show that they are, in many ways, the same. It is a sameness that Helena prayed for in (1.1.191) where she states she would offer the world to be translated into Hermia.

Shakespeare also reveals this unity between Lysander and Demetrius. Both appear as interchangeable characters. Both love Hermia. Both are made to love Helena. Both return to their first loves of Hermia and Helena respectively. Both treat the woman they reject dreadfully. Both are willing to physically remove their competition. There is very little to distinguish the two characters at any given time apart from the object of their affection.

Again it is their *interchangeableness* that Shakespeare is after. These characters, like all of us, like all creation are woven together. We are all interchangeable, our souls come from one source, we are all part of one whole.

Bibliography

1) *A Midsummer Night's Dream*, William Shakespeare, edited by Harold F. Brooks, The Arden Shakespeare, Thomson Learning, Third Series, 2002.

2) *Hekate Soteira: A Study of Hekate's Role in the Chaldean Oracles and Related Literature*, Sarah Iles Johnston, Scholars Press, The American Philological Association, 1990.

3) *The Expulsion of the Triumphant Beast*, Giordano Bruno, translated by Arthur D. Imerti, University of Nebraska Press, 2004.

4) *Giordano Bruno and the Philosophy of the Ass*, Nuccio Ordine, translated by Henryk Baranski and Arielle Saiber, Yale University Press, 1996.

5) *Metamorphoses* (Books I-VI), Apuleius, translated by J. Arthur Hanson, Harvard University Press, 2001.

6) *Metamorphoses* (Books VII-XI), Apuleius, translated by J. Arthur Hanson, Harvard University Press, 2001.

7) *Commentary on Plato's Symposium on Love*, Marsilio Ficino, translated by Sears Jayne, Spring Publication, Dallas, Texas, 1985.

8) *Psychanodia I: A Survey of the Evidence Concerning the Ascension of the Soul and its Relevance*, Ioan Petru Culianu, E. J. Brill, Leiden, 1983.

9) *Eros and Magic in the Renaissance*, Ioan P. Culianu, transl. by Margaret Cook, The University of Chicago Press, 1987.

10) *On Shakespeare*, Northrop Frye, edited by Robert Sandler, Fitzhenry and Whiteside Ltd., 1986.

11) *Imagination in the English Renaissance: Psychology and Poetic*, William Rossky, Studies in the Renaissance, Vol. 5 (1958), p. 49-73.

12) *Imagination in A Midsummer Night's Dream*, R.W. Dent, Shakespeare Quarterly, Vol. 15, No. 2 (spring, 1964) p. 115-129.

13) *Sir Philip Sidney An Apology for Poetry and Astrophil and Stella: Texts and Contexts,* Sir Philip Sidney, edited by Peter C. Herman, San Diego State University, College Publ., 2001.

14) *The Eclogues, Georgics and Aeneid of Virgil*, translated by C. Day Lewis, Oxford University Press, 1974.

15) *New Larousse Encyclopedia of Mythology*, translated by Richard Aldington and Delano Ames, Hamlyn Publishing Group, 1982.

Abstract for *King Lear*
King Lear and the Blinding of Cupid

King Lear is an apocalyptic drama that contains within it the seeds of hope. The tale is one of moral education but not of Lear or Gloucester but of Edgar, a representative of the next generation.

This nihilistic drama, where even love is used as a weapon, finds its hope in Moral Philosophy and in its rules for governing our passions.

King Lear and the Blinding of Cupid

That Dark Place

The world presented in *King Lear* is a world free from the machinations of the gods. They don't appear to participate in the affairs of humans. It is a world of actions and consequences. People choose to be either compassionate or unkind towards others. How they treat others often affects how they are treated in return. There appears to be no higher power operating in the play than simple cause and effect.

The world of *King Lear* is an apocalyptic one. The world of Revelation. Violence rules in this land of the beast (4.2.50-51)

Humanity must perforce prey on itself,

Like monsters of the deep.

Innocence and weakness have little chance here for this is the world "*red in tooth and claw*" [1] where survival belongs to the fittest (5.3.31-33)

Know thou this, that men

Are as the time is; to be tender-minded

Does not become a sword.

If ever the world was a prison this was the time. It is a world as painful to leave as it is to enter with only suffering in between (5.2.9-10)

Men must endure

Their going hence even as their coming hither.

When Lear cries to the heavens to strike down and destroy the world (3.2.1-9) it is as one selfish person cursing a world of selfish people. He is neither righteous nor a prophet but his despair is real. Lear wishes to disengage with the world when he calls for its destruction "*strike flat the thick rotundity o'the world*" because he does not care for anyone in it. Just like the stormy weather the Celestial influences only seem to add to his grief and isolation by offering only ill omens (1.2.103-

171

109) about the stability of relationships in this harsh wilderness.

Civilization is but a veneer on the surface of this barbarism. It is teetering on a cliff and can easily be lost. Lear's world is filled with animal images so one gets the sense that this is the early world just shaking off its beginnings from Chaos and that humans are barely distinguishable from the animals they share the world with.

King Lear is no Dream

An understanding of *King Lear* is greatly assisted by an understanding of *A Midsummer Night's Dream*. They are poised at the opposite poles of a circle; one a tragedy the other a comedy.

Both plays are about Love. One thesis the other antithesis. *A Midsummer Night's Dream* is about selfless love that results in marriage and creates community while *King Lear* is about selfish love that is all-consuming and therefore brings about isolation and destruction. In *A Midsummer Night's Dream* love leads to marriage; in *King Lear* love is an obstacle to marriage. In *A Midsummer Night's Dream*, Theseus is a wise ruler; in *King Lear*, Lear is a fool. In *A Midsummer Night's Dream* the gods assist the humans; in *King Lear* they are either absent or allow the torture of humans.

Of all the plays Shakespeare wrote the word "*eye*" is used most frequently in *A Midsummer Night's Dream* followed closely by *King Lear*. In *A Midsummer Night's Dream* the gods anoint the lovers' eyes whereas in *King Lear* the gods allow eyes to be plucked out. It is interesting to see the adjectives and context attached to the word "*eye*" in both plays. In *A Midsummer Night's Dream* eyes that are light, bright, and attractive become heavy, fierce, and scornful in *King Lear*. We are at opposite poles of the circle. In the following table is a partial list showing the adjectives used in each play. Even though incomplete it still gives a true sense of the differences between the plays.

A Midsummer Night's Dream		King Lear	
my eye your eye	1.1.188	soliciting eye	1.1.233
anoint his eyes	2.1.261	washed eyes	1.1.270
attractive eyes	2.2.90	eyes may pierce	1.4.341
eyes so bright	2.2.91	heavy eyes	2.2.169
watery eye	3.1.191	scornful eyes	2.2.355
apple of his eye	3.2.104	eyes are fierce	2.2.361
eyes of light	3.2.188	eyeless rage	3.1.8
the poets eye	5.1.12	eye of anguish	4.4.14

Lessons we have learned in *A Midsummer Night's Dream* will apply in *King Lear* but they will be employed in an opposing manner. Instead of the interconnected web that joins the characters together in *A Midsummer Night's Dream* we have isolated individuals in *King Lear*.

Marriage in *King Lear*

Lynda Boose, in her article *"The Father and the Bride in Shakespeare"*, provides valuable insight into the way marriage is presented in *King Lear*. It is in clear opposition to the happy marriages that occur in *A Midsummer Night's Dream*.

The healthy effect that marriage brings to a family is that it divides, recombines, and regenerates that family by extending and redistributing its wealth. Lear, in spite of overtures made along these lines, has no interest in giving up any of his daughters or any wealth. Lear subverts the process by claiming all his daughters' love. He wishes to retain his daughters' love even over the love they have for their husbands. Lear wishes to 'give away' and 'retain' everything. His wish is to (1.3.18-19)

> *manage those authorities*
> *That he hath given away*

and this is the source of his tragedy.

His convoluted logic is best expressed in his dealings with Cordelia. By giving her away in marriage he hopes to keep her. If she proclaims her love for him over that of a husband he keeps his cardinal standing in her heart. If she does not, she loses her dowry (one third the kingdom) and becomes unmarriageable and again Lear retains his primacy in her life.

His logic is circular, he will only give her her dowry if she publicly confesses a pledge that would nullify the pledge given in marriage. If she will not *"love him all"*, she will mar her fortune and loose any chance to be separated from him. By disinheriting Cordelia, Lear is not casting her away but is, in fact, preventing her from going.

The role of marriage in society was partially to redistribute the wealth one family accumulated *"distribution to undo excess"* (4.1.73) but Lear is not going to allow this to occur. He is not going to let his daughter go and found a new family. In a traditional marriage the priest poses the question *"Who giveth this woman to be married unto this man?"* The bride stands at the altar between her father and her husband-to-be owing to each a different kind of love; this Cordelia outlines in her speech (1.1.95-104). Marriage normally ends the father's role in his daughter's life.

Shakespeare subverts this ceremony in *King Lear*. Instead of the priest posing the question *"Do you take this woman?"* It is Lear who poses the question (1.1.203-206)

> *Sir, will you, with those infirmities she owes,*
> *Unfriended, new adopted to our hate,*
> *Dowered with our curse and strangered with our oath,*

174

Take her or leave her?

Lear defames the character of the bride to make her unacceptable to the proposed matches. His motive is to retain her by rejecting her. Burgundy rejects Cordelia but France unexpectedly accepts her despite more mudslinging from Lear (1.1.208-214).

Lear wishes to subvert the linear pattern of progression – his daughters receive dowries, take on husbands, create new families, and in the process both divest and create new wealth. He tries to replace it with a circular pattern of retention centered on himself. Lear wishes to retain both his daughters' love and the use of their dowries.

The text makes this clear in several ways. First we have the public proclamation of their love for him (a proclamation he believes). Second, when we see Goneril and Regan complaining about Lear and his gluttonous knights (1.4.232-237) it is apparent that Lear and his men are eating their way through his daughters' kingdoms and treating them like his own. Lear sees this as his right to live off their dowries. Third when we see Lear curse his daughters with sterility (1.4.268-273) we are aware that this is a desperate attempt to prevent any growth from occurring and any chance of his being displaced in their affections. He is trying to halt natural progression. Finally, after Lear has thrown a tantrum and in essence run away from home we see that he has crowned himself with weeds (4.4.3-4). Weeds that stop the growth of other plants. Lear has declared himself the 'King of Arrested Development'.

Returning once more to *A Midsummer Night's Dream* it is apparent how Lear in this last role stands in stark contrast to Oberon, King of the Fairies, whose role is to assist Nature and whose job, as a fertility god, is to bless the marriage bed and its issue (MND, 5.1.389-392).

Lear's retentive passions deny his children their rite of passage. He will not allow detachment to occur because he subverts the marriage ritual.

Lear is a father that devours his own paternity to become the 'child-again' of his daughters. This is revealed in his plan to rest in Cordelia's *"kind nursery"* (1.1.124). Lear's planned-for sin is dependency rather than incest as he sets about making his daughters his mothers.

This selfish behaviour is reminiscent of that of Saturn's who devoured his own children lest they succeed him. Both wish to maintain control and are willing to sacrifice their own children's futures in order to accomplish their goal. Lear and his devouring knights are an apt metaphor for these Saturnine tendencies.

Lear's Character

Lear's character is defined both by his fortune and by his nature. His fortune seems to be tied to Saturn. Saturn, because he was father to all the gods, was considered to represent parental authority and because of its slow orbit was also considered the planet of old age. Saturn's association with old age meant he was often depicted as the Grim Reaper, the herald of Death. In the play, Lear's age not only heralds his own death but he is instrumental in bringing about the deaths of all his children.

Classical astrologers saw the planet as the 'Greater Malefic' or 'Greater Infortune' and texts listed its dire consequences. When Saturn was in ill-aspect it could make short the lives of the young, indicate the loss of money for the rich, or be a sign of coming disgrace for the powerful (*Tetrabiblos II*, 8, p.179-180; *Tetrabiblos III*, 13, p.340-341; *Christian Astrology*, Chpt. 8, p. 57, Chpt 108, p.539; *The New Astrology*, p. 179-181).

When the soul ascended back to the stars, Saturn was the last gateway before enlightenment and represented the greatest spiritual test of all, the renunciation of all physical possessions. This is the situation Lear has tried to avoid but is finally forced into when his daughters take everything from him.

Saturn defined Lear's fortune but his character seems to be linked to his choleric nature. This is recognized by his daughters as they lament about the *"unruly waywardness that infirm and choleric years bring with them"* (1.1.299-300). They recognize that too much choler has been his problem all his life; *"The best and soundest of his time hath been but rash"* (1.1.296). A choleric person was said to be hot tempered, rash, combative, and thoughtless (*Three Books of Occult Philosophy*, Appendix IV, The Humors, p.731) although they also possessed some redeeming features like being bold, brave and active.

Lear's daughters also recognize his immaturity; Lear has never really grown up. Regan comments on this (1.1.294-295)

'Tis the infirmity of his age, yet he hath ever but
slenderly known himself.

Tillyard (*The Elizabethan World View*, p.72-73) comments on this passage in the context of education. Not to know yourself meant you resembled the beasts for the angels knew themselves but the beasts did not. To know yourself was the gateway to virtue [2]. Lear is impulsive, thoughtless, and rash; he has spent his life living like a beast in an oppressive world. Lear has developed bad habits and he has no intention of giving up anything he considers to be his. If Lear is to save himself, to become more than just a beast, he must begin by understanding himself and the world around him.

The Daughters' Characters

Goneril, Regan, and Cordelia are all daddy's girls. They all possess aspects of his egotism, selfishness, and ruthlessness. They come into conflict with Lear because they are so much like him. In a winner takes all world they each plan to win, only their methods differ.

In order to understand Lear's daughters and much about the story's engine it is necessary to examine another source, *The Iliad* [3].

Two stories relating to *The Iliad* are of central importance in *King Lear*. The first story is the 'Judgment of Paris' (*Larousse Encyclopedia of Mythology*, Greek Mythology, The Judgment of Paris, p. 131). This is the story where Paris is asked to judge who is the fairest from among the three goddesses Hera, Athena, and Aphrodite. Paris chooses Aphrodite. Aphrodite rewards Paris by allowing a romance to grow between him and Helen, the most beautiful woman in the world but also the wife of Menelaus. Hera and Athena never forgave Paris for the wound he delivered to their pride and avenged themselves on his country and his people by destroying them in the Trojan War.

A second story arises out of this war. Aphrodite, on occasion, would participate in the battles to help defend her Trojans. One day she came to the aid of her son Aeneas. She was recognized on the battlefield by Diomedes, one of the Argives, and he knew her to be a divinity lacking in courage so he attacked and wounded her.

She fled the battlefield retreating to Olympus and complained to Zeus. Zeus smiled at her, and dismissing her powers told her to leave matters of war up to others and that she should attend only to the sweet tasks of love (*The Iliad*, Book 5, ll. 370-381, 396-399, 490-494).

From these two tales it is possible to glean some information pertinent to Shakespeare's telling of *King Lear*. First Shakespeare has inverted the 'Judgment of Paris'. Rather than Paris telling the goddesses who is the fairest it is the three daughters telling Lear how much they love him.

The daughters can easily be assigned roles appropriate to the goddesses. Just as Paris had judged Athena to have a severe beauty, Hera a sophisticated beauty, and Aphrodite to have an approachable seductive beauty so too can we see similar qualities in Shakespeare's characters.

Goneril represents the severe, somewhat emasculating Athena, goddess of military strategy. She is described by Oswald as the better soldier (4.5.4)

your sister (Goneril) *is the better soldier.*

Regan represents the gossamer goddess of the air, Hera, who presided over all phases of feminine existence and was regarded as the ideal wife (2.2.359-363)

No, Regan, thou shalt never have my curse.

Thy tender-hafted nature shall not give

Thee o'er to harshness. Her (Goneril) *eyes are*

fierce, but thine

Do comfort and not burn.

Regan is more delicate than Goneril, more finely dressed, possessing a haughty beauty (2.2.456-459)

Thou art a lady,

Why, nature needs not what thou gorgeous wear'st

Which scarcely keeps thee warm

but Regan is disciplined and curtails Lear's demands (2.2.481) like a good mother

For his particular, I'll receive him gladly,

But not one follower.

Cordelia represents Aphrodite, the chosen one, the one ill-equipped for battle but the one that Lear has always loved. She, like Aphrodite, possesses no bitterness and easily forgives the 'old man' his affronts.

The second tale relating to Zeus's dismissal of Aphrodite's powers bears remarkably on the tale of *King Lear*. For in *King Lear* it is the 'confession of love' that sets up the central conflict and the resultant tragedy. It is also of some note that everyone who dies in *King Lear* dies in a love- related tragedy. Love rather than being the sweet diversion from war becomes central to it. Beyond any doubt *King Lear* is a love story and in it <u>love is the weapon of choice</u>.

Love is withheld and sparingly given out. It is so seldom seen that it is often fatal to the observer. Gloucester dies of joy when treated to it (5.3.195-198)

> *But his flawed heart*
> *Alack, too weak the conflict to support,*
> *'Twixt two extremes of passion, joy, grief,*
> *Burst smilingly.*

When one looks at the other deaths in the play they all relate in some way to love. Love is sought by all and fatal to all. Edmund, a much neglected son, desperately sought love himself and consoled himself upon his dying with the knowledge that he was loved (5.3.238)

> *Yet Edmund was beloved.*

He was killed by the avenging hand of Gloucester's loving son, Edgar. Regan and Goneril both sought Edmund's love but were driven to acts of jealousy, murder and suicide by it (5.3. 239)

> *The one the other poisoned for my sake*
> *And after slew herself.*

Cornwall died when attacked by a loving and devoted servant of Gloucester's (3.7.71-98). Cordelia dies in an act of love, doing her father's business (4.4.23-24). Finally Lear dies of a broken heart after his failure to save Cordelia.

So, like *A Midsummer Night's Dream* love is the central story engine motivating all the characters and driving the action in the play. But unlike *A Midsummer Night's Dream* love is used as a weapon in *King Lear*. Instead of uniting lovers and bringing together soul-mates love is used to divide and conquer.

Character Arcs

Most of the characters in the play show very little development. For the most part their motives are fixed and their behaviour remains unchanged. Edmund, Goneril and Regan are all self seeking and are drawn to each other through the shared goals of a common enemy. Only as the prize is within sight does division arise. There is no softening in their positions; evil is never displaced by pity. As a group they are the archetypes of selfishness.

Kent and Cordelia also show very little change to their initial character motivation. Both are loyal servants, unselfish, and speak truth even to their own disadvantage. Cordelia does wish to distance herself from Lear by lessening the parental ties but both she and Kent acknowledge a bond of duty they owe to Lear. This is as true at the beginning of the play as it is at the end. In this sense they are selfless characters.

Gloucester and Lear go through similar circumstances. Both are fools, both are betrayed by their children, both are stripped of all personal fortunes. In addition Gloucester is stripped of his eyesight and Lear of his identity.

Gloucester responds to his new life first with despair (4.1.38-39) then with endurance (4.6.75-76)

> *Henceforth I'll bear*
> *Affliction till it do cry out itself.*

He begins to understand how the world works now that he has been removed from it. He, like Cupid, sees it feelingly.

When Edgar finally reveals himself to Gloucester, Gloucester dies of joy. His heart bursts *"smilingly"* (5.3.197). Gloucester is set free knowing he was forgiven and loved.

Lear's journey mimics Gloucester's. He is reduced to nothing, *"Now thou art an O without a figure"* (1.4.183) and begins to see his own weaknesses *"You heavens, give me that patience, patience I need!"* (2.2.460), he begins to see himself for what he is *"A poor, infirm, weak and despised old man"* (3.2.20). In this position he starts to relate to the suffering of others *"I have one part in my heart That's sorry yet for thee"* (3.2.72-73). His experiences allow him to relate to the poor and he prays for the *"poor naked wretches"* (3.4.28-36) realizing he has *"ta'en too little care of this"* problem in his kingdom.

Lear's ongoing enlightenment allows him to see flattery for what it is: lies (4.6.96-104). He realizes that the ears can be as easily fooled as the eyes (4.6.160-163)

> *Through tattered clothes great vices do appear;*
> *Robes and furred gowns hide all. Plate sin with gold,*
> *And the strong lance of justice hurtless breaks.*

He knows the world is full of hypocrisy but this only deepens his cynicism. He sees great thieves hang little thieves (4.6.159) and no longer cares *"which is the justice, and which is the thief"* (4.6.149).

Lear has gone through an ordeal and has gained insight but it does not change him. He understands he has not done enough for the least fortunate, he understands the falseness of flattery, and he sees the hypocrisy of those in authority but his response to it is very similar to Edmund's, he plans to level the playing field. From now on there will be no crimes. In Lear's new kingdom adultery will not be a crime (4.6.110-112)

> *Thou shalt not die – die for adultery? No!*
> *The wren goes to't and the small gilded fly*
> *Does lecher in my sight. Let copulation thrive.*

In Lear's new kingdom the other hypocrisies he's seen (4.6.146-166) he shall also ignore (4.6.164)

> *None does offend, none, I say none. I'll able 'em.*

Lear speaks of enabling them, empowering them all. Lear

concludes that none offends because all do. As far as he is concerned sinners and criminals can go on sinning (see note 4.6.164, *King Lear*, edited by R.A. Foakes, The Arden Shakespeare, 3rd series). He is opening the doors of all the prisons. Humans are beasts in his eyes so should have free range to do as they please.

Lear's chance at an epiphany passes him by, he remains the animal he always was. He remains self centered and childish. He wants what he always wanted; power, control and revenge against those that offend him (4.6.182-183)

> *And when I have stolen upon these son-in-laws*
> *Then kill, kill, kill, kill, kill, kill, kill!*

He cannot yet see himself (his nature) as the cause of his tragedy. He still views himself as a victim *"more sinned against than sinning"* (3.2.59).

Once Lear is taken into Cordelia's care he begins to know himself yet again. He has a second chance at an epiphany (4.7.60; 63)

> *I am a very foolish, fond old man*
> *I fear I am not in my perfect mind.*

He acknowledges the harm he has done her (4.7.72; 74)

> *If you have poison for me, I will drink it.*
> *You have some cause.*

But then with Lear's speech beginning *"Come, let's away to prison..."* (5.3.8-18) he escapes into a fantasy where he and Cordelia live out a happy life removed from the cares of the world. They become buddies watching the 'theatre of life' from afar; watching the powerful and ambitious come and go and gossiping about the goings on. It is a retentive fantasy not unlike his retentive need which started the tragedy. This is yet another retrograde movement for Lear. Again he disengages and abandons Cordelia and the world.

Cordelia's death finally snaps him out of this delusion. He will reap what he has sown. He recognizes *"She's dead as earth"* (5.3.258). Nothing could be more final. What is done cannot be undone. Lear has come full circle but is still the man he was. He, like Gloucester, knows he is forgiven and that he was loved but he will not die smilingly.

Edgar is the last character and has much in common with both Lear and Gloucester. He too is a fool or naive at the beginning of the play. He is forced to adopt a new persona and shifts from being a foolish man to the guise of 'poor Tom' a *"man brought near to beast"* (2.2.180). Edgar, like Lear, disappears *"Edgar I nothing am"* (2.2.192) and 'poor Tom' begins his education to become a wise King. His education mirrors both Gloucester's and Lear's as he picks up the virtues he needs.

Edgar is the only character who truly undergoes a change in his character. When asked *"What is your study?"* Edgar replies *"How to prevent the fiend and to kill vermin."* (3.4.154-155). All in the audience would know that to prevent the fiend one must study virtue: the four cardinal virtues (justice, prudence, temperance, and fortitude) and the three spiritual virtues (faith, hope, and charity). Edgar is then going to put into practice the first of these lessons by applying Justice to those who have perpetrated evil upon the community.

Edgar, as the lowest most dejected thing of fortune, knows he will return to better days (4.1.3). This gives him hope. He has left a place of privilege to now experience what wretches feel. This has been a humbling experience but he understands the need to keep going and to accept fortune's whims (4.6.217-219)

> *A most poor man, made tame to fortune's blows*
> *Who, by the art of known and feeling sorrows*
> *Am pregnant to good pity.*

He has seen his father blinded and Lear driven mad. He knows the enemy he must face. He is no longer naïve about betrayal, forewarned is to be forearmed. He is also well aware of the need for pity in a just world. Edgar now has a philosophy, *"Men must endure"* (5.2.9). Edgar now has a wish, *"Pray that the right may thrive"* (5.2.2).

Edgar's experiences have been similar to Lear's but his journey will end in wisdom. He comes to understand from his father that to live in the sensual world is to feel. That the world becomes a better place through compassion. That wisdom lies in seeing the world *"feelingly"* and not by removing ourselves from its suffering through disengagement. This is why Edgar's last piece of advice is to *"speak what we feel"* (5.3.323) to be honestly engaged with each other and with the world. To speak from experience.

Through the course of the play we have been exposed to three methods of coping in a harsh world. Edmund, Goneril and Regan chose to match violence with violence, they live like the times, they live like the beasts. They cope on the level of survival of the fittest and their actions, like beasts, are often unconsidered.

Lear begins to see the world as it is but chooses to let things be and sit on the sidelines as an observer. He disengages. This is a selfish decision. He chooses no longer to participate in the world but just to watch it go by. A prison (just like his castle) removes him from the world. Unfortunately his attempted intellectual retreat is interrupted as violence breaks into even this isolation. Gloucester's suicide attempt is very similar to Lear's coping strategy in the sense that both are acts of withdrawal. Both are selfish acts. Both remove them from the world. Neither attempts to make the world a better place for their fellow sufferers.

Edgar stakes out the middle ground. He has learned to live life *"feelingly"*, with compassion. He doesn't hide from suffering or pain but he chooses to use his sensual understanding of the world to make life better for his fellow sufferers. He knows the value of compassion. He will not become a selfish beast or retreat into selfish isolation. He is an earthling and can make the world better through understanding and compassion and the exercise of justice.

Idle Weeds

F.G. Butler in his article *Lear's Crown of Weeds* (*English Studies*, 70, vol.5, 1989, p. 395-406) puts forward a very convincing argument that Lear's self constructed crown (4.4.3-6)

> *Crowned with rank fumiter and furrow-weeds,*
> *With burdocks, hemlock, nettles, cuckoo-flowers,*
> *Darnel and all the idle weeds that grow*
> *In our sustaining corn*

is made of invasive weeds that either stop or destroy the growth of food crops necessary for civilization. It becomes another example of Lear's intent to subvert the rules of civilization, abandon all rules, and hasten its descent into barbarity.

Corn was the staff of life and anything that threatened corn threatened civilization. Lear's crown is made of idle, parasitic, and savage weeds that invade and destroy useful crops replacing them with a green desert full of species that are of no use to humans for either food or medicine. Weeds, because of their speed and efficiency of propagation, quickly turn domesticated land back into wilderness.

Lear has been subverting the laws of civilization from the beginning of the play. His selfishness causes him to exile one daughter and further alienate the two others. When he storms off into the wilderness in an adolescent tantrum he appears to go mad but in the process reveals both his true intentions and his destructive nature (4.6.113; 115)

> *Let copulation thrive;*
> *To't, luxury, pell-mell, for I lack soldiers.*

He, like the weeds he sports, has the less than noble goal of selfish conquest. To reinforce this idea he makes a vow of selfishness. He vows he will not love (4.6.134)

No, do thy worst, blind Cupid, I'll not love.

Lear and Edmund possess very similar characters. Both are agents of barbarism. Both use people for their selfish ends. Neither Edmund nor Lear respect the goal or sanctity of marriage. Edmund has promised himself in two marriages and Lear, when reunited with Cordelia, returns to his retentive ways.

The end of the play echoes the beginning with its alternative take on the wedding vows. Where normally a priest concludes a wedding with the phrase *"What God has joined together let no man put asunder"*, Lear rephrases as a curse. Whomever should attempt to violate his reunion with Cordelia will be punished (5.3.22)

He that part us shall bring a brand from heaven.

Lear is reclaiming Cordelia. He always wanted complete possession of his daughter and now has achieved his goal with the help of a small war. Lear has not evolved from his initial position at the beginning of the play. Lear remains Lear.

Lear has been a bane on society since the beginning of the play violating its traditions but Edmund comes to the idea fresh. Edmund is intent to do harm to society and like Lear and Goneril he does not feel society's rules apply to him [4]. They all are a law unto themselves (5.3.156)

the laws are mine not thine.

Edmund is just another weed (1.2.20-21)

Edmund the base

Shall top the legitimate. I grow, I prosper.

He and Lear are the tares that Satan has sown in God's garden. Lear is the selfish all-consuming Saturn, Edmund a younger version of him. They fit in with the barbarous society around them. Their ravenous appetites engage them in a race to the bottom, to become the beasts they are (3.4.105-106)

> *Unaccommodated man is no more but such a poor,*
> *bare, forked animal as thou art.*

Reconciliation of Opposites

In the Elizabethan Age humans were seen a creatures that existed between the beasts and the angels. They could be of an ascending or descending nature, but of course held both natures within themselves. The characters in the play are clearly divided into these two groups. Kent, Gloucester, Cordelia, and Edgar are of the ascending type defined through their love of truth and loyalty to others. Goneril, Regan, Edmund and Lear are of a descending nature driven by their various self interests and sensual passions.

Humans were born into ignorance but through education and reflection could gain self-knowledge. By understanding their own natures they could employ their virtues in the service of others and by being aware of their vices could avoid possible temptations. Education for all people was a religious necessity.

In *King Lear* circumstances arise both from the whim of fortune and from the influence of the stars. Regardless of where circumstances arose it was a person's free will that was tested. The person always chose their action.

Edgar, when faced with a descending wheel of fortune as circumstances get increasingly worse for him, copes with his adversity because of his ascending nature.

In a world of changing fortunes, patience and endurance are required for events to play out and for opportunities to arise. The readiness is all; "*Fortune, good night: smile once more; turn thy wheel*" (2.2.171).

So ascending and descending types stand ready to take control of events but there is a warning the Fool gives that applies to them all (2.2.261-263)

Let go thy hold when a great wheel runs down

A hill lest it break thy neck with following it; but the

Great one that goes upward, let him draw thee after.

The play is one great circle. Edgar and Edmund who last saw each other with swords drawn pretending to be in conflict (2.1.31) meet once again with swords drawn but now in real conflict (5.3.172)

The wheel is come full circle, I am here.

Lear, too, comes full circle. The father who imagined that he *"gave his daughters all"* (2.2.438) at the beginning of the play has by the end of the play created the circumstances that extract from his daughters all. He has consumed them. He remains and they are all dead. He circumvented the natural processes, those of regeneration, and can be regarded as a monster because of it.

The play subtly examines the conjoined nature of our world. Everything can be represented in circles. Just as the angel and the beast are polar opposites of one circle so are selfishness and compassion the polar opposites of another. The two exist within the one. They are not different things but part of the same thing like our ascending and descending natures are the poles of our own nature. To possess one is to possess them both.

In the play, Love was shown to be disastrous but still two types were represented. Lear, Goneril, Regan, and Edmund all wished to receive love (not give love). They competed for it. Manipulated others with it. Theirs was a selfish love.

Cordelia, Kent, and Edgar give love. Theirs was a selfless love, a compassionate love. Even though all of them had been exiled, cast out from the selfish world of the play, they all felt duty bound to help even at their peril.

The play demonstrates that selfishness is in the end all consuming and leads to mutual destruction. Its polar opposite, compassion, provides a possible solution to this chaos. Compassion is capable of creating a civil society where *"distribution should undo excess and each man have enough"* (4.1.73-74).

Cordelia is eventually murdered, Kent considers himself too old to contribute to society, so the world is left with Edgar to help reform it. Edgar is an everyman, experiencing life, rising from nothing, (2.2.192) *"Edgar I nothing am"*, to become poor Tom (a beggar), then a messenger, a knight, and finally a Ruler. He has learned to *"feel what wretches feel"* (3.4.34). He can avoid the trap of his father and Lear who both could not see the problems of the poor because they could not feel (4.1.71-72). They ruled without compassion. Edgar has suffered and learned to see properly, he knows love and compassion are a better way (4.3.18-19)

> *Her smiles and tears*
> *Were like a better way.*

Civilization depends as much on these as it does on justice. Love for those with family and friends, compassion for those without, and justice for all.

Selfishness and Compassion are the polar opposites of one circle. *King Lear* is a hopeless story with a hopeful solution within.

Chaos and the birth of love

Marsilio Ficino (1433-1499) wrote about love and chaos in his *Commentary on Plato's Symposium on Love*. In it he writes of love's beginning.

"On the Origin of Love

> *In the "Argonautica", when Orpheus, in the presence of Chiron*

190

and the heroes, sang about the beginnings of things, following the theology of Hermes Trismegistus, he placed Chaos before the World and located Love in the bosom of that Chaos before Saturn, Jove, and the other gods" (as transl. by Sears Jayne, I.3, p. 37).

This idea is reinforced later in the text (I.3, p.39)

"Its (Chaos) first turning toward God we call the birth of Love..."

"...Who, therefore, will doubt that Love immediately follows Chaos"

"...Therefore Orpheus rightly called Love the oldest of the gods."

The world of *King Lear* is one of chaos and violence. It may very well be a metaphor resembling the world before the gods; a world that is just turning towards the good. The story could be one depicting the birth of love.

Lear does not appear to change throughout the whole drama, in spite of a few epiphanies. He does, however, do a selfless act in the last scene of the play. He tries to save Cordelia. He does this not out of vengeance towards others but in order to save his own child and at his own peril. This one act reverses an earlier decision he has made (1.1.114)

Here I disclaim all my parental care.

By this selfless protective act he has behaved like a parent instead of like a child. This is Lear's first turning towards the good. This is the birth of love in Lear. With this selfless action he has reversed his vow that he made to Cupid (4.6.134) that he would not love.

Had Cordelia survived, this act of love by Lear may have vindicated her return. She, like all the characters in the play, seems to hunger for love, a parent's love. You see it when they are first reunited. She requests her father's blessing even though he is clearly 'out of his mind' (4.7.56-57)

look upon me, Sir

And hold your hand in benediction o'er me!

She needs to know that he approves of her actions, she needs his blessing. This is true of Edgar as well who also asked for his father's blessing (5.3.194).

The world of the play evolves from one that operates under the King's oppression to one that could operate under a King's blessing, a parent's blessing. The King as caregiver/parent replacing the King as authoritarian ruler.

A Civil Society

The world Lear inhabits is perched between chaos and order, anarchy and civilization. Fear has eroded most of the trust that exists (1.4.321-322)

> Albany. *Well, you may fear too far.*
> Goneril. *Safer than trust too far.*

Goneril, Edmund and Regan are a law unto themselves (5.3.156) "*the laws are mine not thine*" and trust no one but themselves. They, like Lear, are authoritarian rulers. Under such conditions civilization suffers because civil laws do not apply; only the rule of natural law (survival of the fittest) seems to take effect. Fear runs rampant in this world because might is right.

Lear is the father of this world; he has chosen to subvert both marital/civil law and natural law by refusing to relinquish his daughters and thereby preventing the regeneration and dispersal of his family and fortune. He has used threats of disinheritance to control his daughters and forced from them 'vows of love'. Lear, having relegated himself into the group of the old, weak and powerless, quickly finds he must suffer from the conditions he has created. The trust he placed in his daughters was a false hope as they still fear him and his knights. Lear, Goneril, Regan, and Edmund all oppose civilization through their own self interests. They are even incapable of forming the smallest unit of civilization, the family.

Society and reform of the legal system were major concerns in Elizabethan society. Many of these concerns are reflected in G. Bruno's *The Expulsion of the Triumphant Beast* (1584), a dialogue about the reform of the heavens through the expulsion of vice and its replacement by virtue so that the heavens could only reign down virtuous influences upon the earth. In the dialogue, Bruno praises the Roman society as an example of good government (*The Expulsion of the Triumphant Beast*, Second Dialogue, First part, p.149).

"For this reason they (the gods) exalted the Roman people above others; because with their magnificent deeds they, more than the other nations, knew how to conform with and resemble them, by pardoning the subdued, overthrowing the proud, righting wrongs, not forgetting kindness, helping the needy, defending the afflicted, relieving the oppressed, restraining the violent, promoting the meritorious...and honoring the gods...

Whence, consequently, that people appeared more bridled and restrained from vices and of an uncivilized and barbarous nature, more excellent and ready to perform generous enterprises than any other people that has ever been seen."

Bruno saw Rome as an example of good government that encouraged civilization. The laws of the state and laws of religion merged to encourage the progress of civilization.

Bruno was not alone in his beliefs; John Dee also had similar views and even better, the ear of the Queen. Dee wrote *Brytannicae Reipublicae Synopsis* (1570) to outline the current state of the realm and to suggest ways to cure its ills. The document was created by Dee for an elite group of government officials with the encouragement of the Privy Council.

Dee's first suggestion was that all laws *"Ought to be ordered to gither in a Body Methodicall: and not to be a Confused Chaos (and Worse) as they are." (John Dee, The Politics of Reading and Writing in the English Renaissance, p.136).* We can understand this to be a comment on the current state of English law, as a confused body of laws. To create a civil society one needs the rule of law and laws that are available, just, and understandable by all.

In 1592 in his *Compendious Rehearsall* Dee wrote *"The blinded lady, Fortune, doth not governe in this commonwealth, but justitia and prudentia" (John Dee, p.142)*; prudentia was generally interpreted by Dee to mean wisdom *(John Dee, p.136)*. He felt that random luck (fortune) should not be what people depended on to make their lives better but rather every English citizen should have a right to the rule of law and thereby some control over their own destinies.

In 1577 in his *General and Rare Memorials*, Dee held up King Edgar (959-975 C.E.) to Queen Elizabeth to be regarded as the mirror of prudence. Edgar was considered wise because he set up a royal navy (4800 ships) to protect the country and also to create wealth and employment. He also praised Edgar for travelling the country to hear the complaints of the commons *(John Dee, p.143, 170, 171)*. Edgar played the role of the good parent by creating the conditions of safety and justice necessary for civilization.

Dee felt that Edgar displayed not only *"Fortitude"* and *"Iustice"* but *"wisdom Imperiall"* and *"marveilous Politicall and Princely Prudency"*. Edgar's prudence had rested in wisdom *"in tyme of Peace, to Forsee and prevent...all possible malice, fraude, force and mischief Forreyn"*. Dee wished Elizabeth to follow Edgar's example, advice Elizabeth, in fact, did follow with equally good effects on the economy.

Edgar is, of course, Shakespeare's example of a potentially wise monarch. He reflects the same understanding Dee had reflected in his manuscript. Edgar is in touch with the suffering of the people. Their concerns are his concerns. Edgar is the parent figure that Lear is not.

Dee felt that individuals were members of the cosmopolites *"Cosmoploites: A Citizen, and Member, of the whole and only one Mysticall City Universal"* (*John Dee*, p.144). He believed, like others of his day, in the 'ideal of the commonwealth' (a mid-Tudor equivalent to the Welfare State). He believed in the relief of the poor and the defense of communal interests.

These ideas are certainly reflected in Shakespeare's *King Lear*. The play is a clear warning against self-interest and for the need of compassion. Like *The Iliad*, *King Lear* warns against the destruction of civilization by the barbarism of self-interest. In both tales love is the fulcrum. Self-love leading to barbarism and selfless love leading to civilization and the growth of community.

Civilization frees us from the tyranny of Fortune. We control our fates through our own actions. Both Edmund and Edgar realize this in the play. Edmund chooses the path of selfishness that inevitably leads to his isolation and destruction. Edgar chooses the path of compassion that leads to the caring society. Neither is slave to Fortune but each constructs his own future.

A Moral Society

Thomas Hobbes, a moral philosopher, (*Leviathan, or the matter, forme, and power of a commonwealth, ecclesiastical and civil*, 1651) wrote that the natural state of mankind is *"solitary, poor, nasty, brutish and short"* pertaining to the state before central government is formed. He felt that without government man was in a constant state of *"warre of every man against every man"*. Because of the individual's isolation no culture could be produced; no long term projects initiated. Worst of all it meant people lived in *"continual feare, and danger of violent death"*.

The views expressed by Hobbes in 1651 are very similar to the ideas embodied in *King Lear* (1605-1606). These views are not unique in any way. They were taught as a part of moral philosophy (*The French Academies of the Sixteenth Century*, F. Yates, p.116-121). The teachings of moral philosophy often revolved around the correct use of the passions (desires, emotions). The passions were not seen as evil in and of themselves, but rather constituted the raw material, the energy, which it was the task of moral philosophy to direct to the correct ends. Moral philosophy was concerned with the establishment of harmony in the individual soul by self-knowledge (One of Lear's weaknesses is that "*he hath but slenderly known himself*" (1.1.294)). By being aware of one's passions one could through prudent training turn these passions into virtues. Virtues being the mean between two extreme emotions, e.g., fortitude being the mean between fear and recklessness. We see this reflected in Albany's advice to Goneril (1.4.321-322)

> Albany. *Well, you may fear too far.*
>
> Goneril. *Safer than trust too far.*

This idea of virtue comes from Aristotle and can be found in his *Nichomachean Ethics*. Stated more generally, his view is that a moral virtue lies between too little and too much. Shakespeare's Gloucester is aware of this philosophy when he states "*so distribution should undo excess / And each man have enough*" (4.1.73-74).

Moral philosophy was not just interested in the individual but also in the State, through the maintenance of justice and order by Magistrates. A close connection was made between private and public morals because one could easily upset the other. Several speeches of Henri III's Palace Academy were recorded, published, and preserved as manuscripts (Yates, p.107, note 3). The speakers of the Palace Academy (circa 1575) discussed moral philosophy and pointed out dangers associated with such private vices as anger (Yates, p.119).

> "*When anger…is not controlled by reason and turns to rage, it is*

the most mischievous and dangerous pest in the world. Tigers are not more cruel. It has for its end blood and murder; it banishes citizens and makes towns and provinces into deserts. "

To read this quotation is to be reminded of how much Shakespeare is exploiting the works of moral philosophy when writing *King Lear*, a King disposed to anger whose daughters are tigers and who banishes both Kent and Cordelia from his country and who himself is thrown into a windswept desert.

'Just anger' if moderated and directed at the perpetrators of public harm was considered a virtue (Yates, p. 119).

"One ought to be angry with those who trouble the public repose. One ought to be angry with an avaricious magistrate, a thieving captain, with a soldier who ravishes women, robs poor houses, kidnaps labourers, denies God. "

Again to read this is to be reminded of Lear's tirade against injustice and corruption (4.6.146-166) and Edgar's justifiable execution of his brother Edmund who had conspired against a Prince, betrayed a father and a brother and who was false to his gods (5.3.132-133).

Also destructive to civilization is the passion of ambition (Yates, p.120).

"The histories of the Greeks are full of the miseries brought to them by the ambition of conflicting parties; for all ambitious men, whatever they may have said, thought not of making their country happy, but rather of moving heaven and earth to incite barbarians to destroy their opulent cities, just as though one would lead a wild boar into a garden gleaming with beautiful flowers or allow it to wallow in the clear fountains and soil the abode of the pastoral nymphs. "

Ambition destroys the state because the state is made up of many people's interests, all of which must be respected and balanced. Ambition ignores others. 'Just Anger' preserves the state from those that threaten it or unduly threaten the interests of others. Avarice, ambition, and intemperance were all threats to the state and required control. It was the Prince's job to maintain order with just severity.

How much of this work on Moral philosophy was available to Shakespeare is not known but one work he easily could have been exposed to was a work based on the lectures given at Henri III's Palace Academy. This was a work which was greatly in vogue in England and several other countries (Yates, p.123-127). It was dedicated to Henri III, published in 1577, and written by Pierre de La Primaudaye entitled *L'Academie Françoise*. It is a work about four men of Anjou who founded a small private academy. The book was responsible for spreading news outside of France about Henri III's academic movement. The debates in the book followed very closely the debates that took place in the Palace Academy. Certainly Shakespeare's *Love's Labour's Lost* (where a French King and his three friends form an academy) and *King Lear* (with its content of Moral Philosophy) bear some debt to this work either directly or indirectly.

Relations between England and France at the time were friendly. Henri III's younger brother Duc d'Anjou was one of Queen Elizabeth's suitors. The Duc d'Anjou had reformed leanings and was known to many in the Queen's entourage. He led an expedition against Catholic Spain in the Low Countries (Flanders) and fought in the same battle in which Philip Sidney died.

The proceedings of Henri III's Palace Academy would certainly have been of interest to Elizabeth, John Dee (her tutor), as well as several of Elizabeth's staff. There is little doubt that the contents of the debates were known to her and within her circle. Shakespeare's work also reveals that the content was available to him in either a direct or indirect manner.

Conclusion

The world we are presented with in *King Lear* is a hostile world. Nature is hostile; the stars are hostile; most of the characters are hostile; and even love is hostile. It is a world on the verge of destroying itself.

To tame this world, to reclaim this world requires virtue (justice, prudence, fortitude, and temperance). Virtue is a trait that is in short supply but it offers the only real way out of the destructive path set by the leaders in the play.

Despite the tragic nature of *King Lear* it provides an object lesson about the danger of putting one's own self-interests above those of the community. It shows how civilization is perilously close to barbarism and that they are separated by as little as our own self-interest. Hopefully, it also shows that if we can demonstrate a little foresight, patience, and self-control we can create a just world free of fear and capable of caring.

Philip Sidney (*An Apology for Poetry*, p. 75) warned that people may not be moved or even remember a treatise delivered by a philosopher on the nature of virtues or the running of government but that they could be stirred imaginatively by a story.

"*So, no doubt, the philosopher, with his learned definitions, be it of virtues or vices, matters of public policy or private government, replenisheth the memory with many infallible grounds of wisdom, which notwithstanding lie dark before the imaginative and judging power if they be not illuminated or figured forth by the speaking picture of poesy*".

King Lear is such a speaking picture written by Shakespeare to stir the hearts of his audience about virtues, vices, and the running of government. His technique was to deliver the content feelingly. Dee's philosophies on good government are given a pictorial form in Shakespeare's *Lear* where the intellectual becomes sensible.

Footnotes

[1]   Alfred Lord Tennyson, *In Memoriam A.H.H.*, cantos LVI, 1850.

[2]   In the writings of the Palace Academy is an interesting speech delivered by Jamyn (*The French Academies of the Sixteenth Century*, Yates, p.144). In it he is speaking about images relating to the theme of honour. He reveals that the temples of Honour and Virtue were built one behind the other so as to symbolize that the way to Honour was through Virtue. In addition he speaks about Roman iconography:

"In Roman pictures there was always a little Cupid leading Honour towards Virtue, to show that Love likes, follows, and honours virtuous persons."

What makes this text interesting with respect to *King Lear* is that blinded Gloucester (who Lear mistakes for Cupid) follows and honours one of the few virtuous people in the play, Edgar. This may just be coincidental or it may suggest common knowledge. The 'hidden' meanings of Poetry and Painting were, by the 1580s, to some extent an open secret in that they were systematized into large compendiums and available to anyone interested. Pierio Valeriano's *Hieroglyphica* published in 1567 was one such reference.

[3]   The connection between *King Lear* and *The Iliad* is not a difficult one to justify. Genealogically Lear was descended from the great Trojan kings. Geoffrey of Monmouth, Bishop of St. Asaph, wrote *Historia regium Britanniae* near the end of the 12th century (c.1135). He associated Lear (Leir, Llyr, Ler) with the line of kings descended from the Trojan Brute, grandson of Aeneas, and supposed founder of Britain. This was common knowledge in the 17th century.

[4]   Edmund, a bastard, is conceived outside God's natural order, outside of marriage. Because he is an outsider he sees himself operating outside the normal laws of the community, a community he is not part of. He behaves like Goneril, as his own being; as a law unto itself. Neither Edmund nor Goneril can recognize any externally imposed system of morality (5.3.156)

the laws are mine, not thine.

To confirm this Edmund sets himself up as judge, jury, and executioner when he orders the deaths of both Lear and Cordelia.

Bibliography

1) *Holinshed's Chronicle, As used in Shakespeare's Plays*, edited by Allardyce and Josephine Nicoll, Everyman's Library, Dutton N.Y.,1969.

2) *The New Larousse Encyclopedia of Mythology*, translated by Richard Aldington and Delano Ames, edited by Felix Guirand, The Hamlyn Publishing Group Ltd., 1982.

3) *The Iliad*, Homer, translated by Robert Fagels, Penguin Books, 1998.

4) *Shakespeare's Imagery and What it Tells Us*, Caroline Spurgeon, Cambridge University Press, 2005.

5) *The Father and the Bride in Shakespeare,* Lynda E. Boose, Publications of the Modern Language Association of America (PMLA), 97, 1982, p.325-347.

6) *Lear's Crown of Weeds*, F.G. Butler, English Studies, 70, vol.5, 1989, p.395-406.

7) *King Lear*, W. Shakespeare, edited by R.A. Foakes, The Arden Shakespeare, Third Series, Thomson, 2002.

8) *King Lear*, W. Shakespeare, edited by G.L. Kittredge, The Kittredge Shakespeare, Xerox Corp., 1967.

9) *Commentary on Plato's Symposium on Love*, Marsilio Ficino, translated by Sears Jayne, Spring Publications, 1985.

10) *Tetrabiblos,* Claudius Ptolemy, Edited and translated by F.E. Robbins, Harvard University Press, 1980.

11) *Christian Astrology*, William Lilly, London, 1647, Reprinted by Astrology Classics, 2004.

12) *The New Astrology: The Art and Science of the Stars*, N. Campion and S. Eddy, Trafalgar Square Publishing, 1999.

13) *The Elizabethan World Picture*, E.M.W. Tillyard, Vintage, London, 1959.

14) *Three Books of Occult Philosophy*, Agrippa, translated by James Freake, edited by Donald Tyson, Llewellyn Publications, 2004.

15) *Shakespearean Tragedy,* A.C. Bradley, MacMillan and Co. Ltd., 1964.

16) *John Dee, The Politics of Reading and Writing in the English Renaissance*, William H. Sherman, University of Massachusetts Press, 1995.

17) *The Expulsion of the Triumphant Beast*, Giordano Bruno, translated by Arthur D. Imerti, University of Nebraska Press, 2004.

18) *The French Academies of the Sixteenth Century*, Frances A. Yates, Routledge, 1988.

19) *Sir Philip Sidney's 'An Apology for Poetry' and 'Astrophil and Stella': Texts and Contents*, edited by Peter C. Herman, College Publishing, 2001.

Abstract for *Love's Labour's Lost*
Bruno's Labour's Not Lost

Giordano Bruno believed in the Copernican Heliocentric solar system but more importantly he believed in an infinite universe with infinite solar systems. Because of these attitudes he viewed Matter, the building block of the universe, as something much different from the Matter that Aristotle described as making up the Ptolemaic enclosed universe.

Aristotle believed that Matter was corrupt and that it corrupted everything it touched. His was a world born to original sin. Bruno felt that the Creator could not be separated from the creation and that the two were made of the same Matter. Bruno proposed a new theology to match his new physics; a theology that could heal the separation between the Divine and Physical Worlds.

I argue that Shakespeare applied the philosophy as outlined in Bruno's *De la causa, principio e uno* (*Cause, Principle and Unity*) and personified its principles in his own play *Love's Labour's Lost*.

Bruno's Labour's Not Lost

Introduction

Frances Yates, in her book *A Study of Love's Labour's Lost*, points out many works contemporaneous with Shakespeare's play that were or could have been influential to the writing of *Love's Labour's Lost*. She, however, did not fully consider the impact of one particular dialogue that provides an outline to and justification for much of what occurs in the play. It is Giordano Bruno's dialogue *De la causa, principio, e uno (Cause, Principle and Unity)*, 1584.

Giordano Bruno's essay was written during his Oxford sojourn (1583-1585) and was intended as an introduction to his larger work *De l'infinito universo e mondi* but he instead chose to publish it separately (1584) in London. Bruno's first London work *La Cena de le Ceneri (The Ash Wednesday Supper)* presents a clear affirmation of Copernicanism as well as a belief in an infinite universe with infinite solar systems like our own. Bruno felt that this new vision of the cosmos would change our relationship with the Divinity. In his *Cause, Principle, and Unity* Bruno set about presenting a metaphysics to match his newly adopted physics.

The existing Ptolemaic model of a finite universe based on Aristotelian ideas was widely accepted and considered dogma by the Church. Ptolemy's cosmos contained ideas that were inherent to its structure and led to ways in which we viewed our world and each other. In Ptolemy's cosmos the sublunar world (everything below the moon) was seen as *'inferior'* to the Planetary and Celestial spheres above. Our Earth was considered to be made of *'corrupt materials'* (the four elements) whereas the rest of the cosmos was believed to be made of the Fifth element (Quintessence) which was incorruptible.

Bruno, because of his belief in an infinite universe, felt that the sublunar world was made of the same material as the rest of the cosmos and that the Earth was in no way inferior to or corrupt relative to any other Planet or Star. In his infinite cosmos there was no center, and no one place more important than anywhere else. Everything, everywhere equally close to God. Bruno's new understanding of the cosmos necessitated a new theology, a new view of matter, hence a new creation story, a new Genesis.

I intend to demonstrate in this essay that *Love's Labour's Lost* is an allegorical tale exploring this new theology put forward by Bruno in his *Cause, Principle and Unity*. By showing philosophical points of contact between Shakespeare's play and Bruno's dialogue it is possible to demonstrate that the two works are related. I will start by explaining Bruno's alternative understanding of Matter.

What's the Matter in Shakespeare

Rather than presenting Aristotle's view of Matter I feel it is more revealing to present how Bruno viewed Aristotle's ideas as these appear to be the source of Shakespeare's dialectic on the subject.

Bruno saw Aristotle as the *"Prince of the Peripatetics"* and was opposed to his ideas as well as the views espoused by his followers, the peripatetics (*Cause, Principle and Unity*, p. 70, 74). To them he assigned the role of 'woman-haters' because he saw them as promoters of the idea that Matter and women were both corrupt. Aristotle equated women with physical Matter and with sin (ibid., p. 70-71); but men he equated with Form which was considered sinless; for no Ideal Form could be a source of error until it was joined to corrupt Matter. For Aristotle physical matter corrupted the ideal form when it translated it into the physical, sensual, material world. Bruno translated this woman-hating Aristotelian philosophy into the Poliinnio character of his dialogue (ibid., p. 72). It is also this Aristotelian philosophy Bruno sees in Genesis where Adam speaks to God about Eve(Genesis 3.12-13 as remembered by Bruno, ibid., p.71).

"The woman that you gave me, it is she, she who deceived me".

When Bruno broke with the Ptolemaic cosmos he also broke with its underlying Aristotelian ideas. Bruno was to propose a new understanding of Matter, one that was not corrupt or in any way associated with sin. We sense his opposition to Aristotle's views in his First Dialogue (ibid., p. 32) where Bruno discusses how language is used, revealing it to be instinctively opposed to Aristotelian dogma.

"all the vices, imperfections and crimes are masculine and all the virtues, merits, and goodness are feminine. Hence, prudence, justice, strength, temperance, beauty, majesty, and dignity, both in grammatical gender and in our imagination, as well as in our descriptions and paintings, are all feminine."

Shakespeare echoes this use of language in *Love's Labour's Lost* where he constructs a world where the women are morally superior to the men. In Shakespeare's Eden they do not tempt the men and in fact encourage them to keep their vows, for when the women are invited into the King's court they refuse, stating (5.2.345-346)

This field shall hold me, and so hold your vow
Nor God nor I delights in perjured men.

Language is the point of intersection between Bruno and Shakespeare. Bruno in his dialogue re-defines Matter, the substance that makes up the universe, and Shakespeare echoes Bruno's process using words as the building block or matter, of his created universe, the play.

Two excellent articles have been written showing how the women and the men in *Love's Labour's Lost* use words differently (the first by Ralph Berry, *The Words of Mercury*, Shakespeare Survey, Vol. 22, 1969; the second by Malcolm Evans, *Mercury versus Apollo: A Reading of Love's Labor's Lost*, Shakespeare Quarterly, Vol.26, No.2,

1975). What this essay will explain is <u>why</u> they use language differently. Words, the building blocks of the play, will be used to represent either Aristotle's views of Matter or to reflect Bruno's. Shakespeare's use of words will be shown to mimic the sexual differences seen in Aristotle's distinction between male "*Form*" and female "*Matter*" but will also respond to Bruno's re-definition of Matter as both innocent and universal.

Bruno's new view of Matter was as revolutionary as Copernicus's Heliocentric Solar System and its consequences would ripple down through the centuries. Bruno drew from a long tradition when he redefined Matter. He had taken ideas from the Epicureans, from Heraclitus, Anaxagoras, Democritus, Pythagoras, David of Dinant, and Nicolas of Causa. He was taking the ideas and making them his own while at the same time keeping their philosophical currency. For Bruno (ibid., p. 56-57)

"This natural matter is not perceptible...nature's matter has absolutely no form (it is) a single, formless thing".

Modern readers would have no problem understanding what Bruno means in his dialogue. This unseen matter can easily be understood as Energy. The translation between energy and physical matter being described by the mathematical expression $e=mc^2$. The modern reader understands that the '*Big Bang*' turned energy into physical matter and that processes like radioactive decay or nuclear explosions can turn physical matter back into energy. Bruno does not have the physics to back up his arguments but he certainly has the philosophical understanding. His Matter is not perceptible, has no dimensions, is undifferentiated throughout and is capable of constituting both an "*Unseen God*" and a "*Sensual World*". Bruno's Matter made up the corporeal and non-corporeal worlds. "*To be*" or "*not to be*" was just a verbal distinction as the same Matter made up both.

Bruno's imperceptible Matter without dimension was God and when it "*contracted*" it created the physical world (ibid., p. 78-79). God is everywhere because God is everything. The smallest energy packet (photon) contains God just as the largest Star. To exist is to be a part of God; nothing is outside God. Energy in all its forms, as physical material or as heat and light, are all contained in God. Regarding this Bruno quotes Plotinus (*Ennead*, II, 4, 4) (ibid., p.76):

"That thing which is common to both the intelligible and sensible worlds can be termed Matter and that which individualizes or differentiates them can be termed Form."

Bruno saw Time as the midwife to form. The eternal gave rise to transient forms that came and went, changing constantly, but the substrate out of which they were made was always the eternal Matter, God.

Bruno felt Matter produced forms from itself and that it did not receive them from the outside (ibid., p. 81). Matter was both potency and act. The potential to create everything and the programme. It was everything. It was the permanent unchanging principle (ibid., p. 84). Cause, Principle and Unity.

This is a very different understanding of Matter than that held by Aristotle or the Church. This is why Bruno felt his physics needed a new metaphysics. This is why Bruno wished to re-write Genesis. His Matter carried much different consequences for the world.

Genesis is where we will pick up once more with Shakespeare.

Love's Labour's Lost as an "Arsy-Versy" Genesis

Patricia Parker, in her article *Preposterous Reversals: Love's Labor's Lost* (Modern Language Quarterly, Dec. 1993), demonstrates how the play turned traditional relationships on their heads. She demonstrates the *"arsy-versy"* or inverted character of the play by exposing its many reversals. She argues that the play reverses the priority and proper ordering of the genders as recorded in Genesis. For her, Jaquenetta represents Eve in this newly created Edenic enclosure and Costard, whose name means both *"apple"* and *"head"*, represents Adam and becomes the first of the men to fall into sin.

It is not difficult to see Genesis in *Love's Labour's Lost*. The men have created a paradise for themselves. They have formed an ascetic community mimicking the perfection of Eden before Eve came along. At its core is a sexist philosophy. At its core are laws that are set up in denial of human nature. Berowne points this out to the King and his men (1.1.147)

Necessity will make us all forsworn

but in the end they all vow to obey the laws the King has set up.

Costard is the first to disobey. His actions confirm Berowne's prophesy. Costard protests by saying (1.1.295)

I suffer for the truth

thus mimicking Christ's comment but inverting its sense. Costard suffers because of the human truth, the sensual truth of our animal natures while Christ suffered for the divine truth.

Costard ties us to Bruno early in the play. Yates (*A Study of Love's Labour's Lost*, p.105-106) describes and quotes from the dedication to Philip Sidney in Bruno's book *De gli eroici furori* (1585) (*The Heroic Enthusiasts*). Bruno opens with a caution against wasting one's creativity on worshipping women and seeking sensual pleasure and he ends his dedication apologetically by pointing out that he meant no offense to the women of England who are not women but rather nymphs, goddesses and stars. He refers to Queen Elizabeth as *"unique Diana"* who reigns over them.

This dedication touches on *Love's Labour's Lost* on several points. First when Costard is accused of being seen with a woman

(1.1.248-291) he evades the issue by calling her a wench, then a damsel, then a virgin, then a maid all in an attempt to avoid the letter of the law. His verbal gymnastics are to no avail but are reminiscent of Bruno's evasion at the end of his dedication. Closer to the source, however, is Longaville's equivocation (4.3.61-62)

> *A woman I forswore, but I will prove,*
>
> *Thou being a goddess, I forswore thee not thee.*

Second, Bruno refers to Queen Elizabeth as Diana (the Moon). In Shakespeare's play the Princess is referred to by the King as the Moon or described using Moon imagery (4.3.23-40) and (5.2.204-206). Finally, the caution against wasting one's wit in praise of women is reiterated by the Princess herself (2.1.17-19)

> *I am less proud to hear you tell my worth*
>
> *Than you much willing to be counted wise*
>
> *In spending your wit in the praise of mine.*

Bruno's ideas did not just influence the surface text of Shakespeare but they reached into its very structure. Bruno's influence carried many consequences. His reversal of the Ptolemaic cosmos by exchanging the location of the Sun and the Earth (switching from a geocentric to a heliocentric system) is mimicked by Shakespeare in his creation of an arsy-versy Genesis for *Love's Labour's Lost*. Bruno's ideas on both Matter and an infinite universe are also similarly reflected in the play.

Ptolemy's enclosed, stratified, hierarchical world was philosophically replaced by Bruno's infinite universe where everywhere is as important as anywhere else. The idea of an infinite universe cannot lend support to a hierarchy of being; there no longer is a stratified macrocosm to be reflected in the microcosm. In *Love's Labour's Lost* we find women are not the "*weaker vessel*" compared to the men. They in fact are the men's moral superiors manifesting many superior qualities such as honesty, straight-forwardness, and dignity. The clowns in the play do what clowns do in all plays, make fools of their superiors. Parker refers to these role reversals as *"arsy-versy"* when comparing them to the status quo but I believe there is something else going on and I think it has to do with the re-definition of what hierarchy means in an infinite universe. When Armado (high-born) marries Jaquenetta (low-born) there is a sense of inversion but there is also literally a marriage, a joining together of the classes; it can be argued that this last scene (5.2.870-876) reflects that hierarchies are breaking down.

Bruno never suggests that the world does not have qualitative differences; people have different jobs, different educations, and different skills but the rigid hierarchy, the moral hierarchy cannot be justified by Bruno. Shakespeare seems to reflect these values in his play as when Holofernes scolds the Lords (5.2.623)

This is not generous, not gentle, not humble

or when the Princess corrects the King (2.1.108)

To teach a teacher ill beseemeth me.

Those higher up the ladder, as it were, are not closer to God.

A Matter of Ideas

Ralph Berry, in his article *The Words of Mercury,* describes *Love's Labor's Lost "as a delicate and controlled movement towards an acceptance of reality."* Berry sees the different character groups of the play as having different attitudes toward words.

The men he sees as equivocators. They undermine words. The King wants words to match his wishes. Berowne uses jests to devalue words (2.1.214-215)

Not a word with him but a jest
And every jest but a word.

For both the King and Berowne there is a quality of whimsy to their words. The King wants words to match his whims and Berowne uses words in a whimsical way. This equivocal spirit renders their words almost meaningless, except to them. Their oaths aren't worth the air they're imprinted on, for their words are not tied to any reality (4.3.65)

Vows are but breath, and breath a vapour is.

If Words truly are Shakespeare's version of Matter then much can be learned from his created world. The men have created an enclosed world for themselves like Ptolemy's enclosed universe and it smacks of Aristotelian sexism. They have excluded women. They have created an ascetic community. They have created a set of laws that are in violation to their own human natures. They appear to be trying to create a purely rational society based on learning and philosophy.

The King, by removing himself and his men from the rest of the world and from sensual pleasures is actually going beyond Eden; he is trying to create a home for Aristotle's ideal forms; he appears to be trying to re-create Ptolemy's Intelligible Sphere. This is the enclosed, sexist world Bruno describes in his Fourth Dialogue, the world he associates with Aristotle (ibid., p. 71).

"It is not without good reason that the senators of Pallas' realm have judged it well to set matter and woman side by side…

Women are a chaos of irrationality…

[Without doubt], form does not sin, and no form is a source of error unless it is joined to matter. That is why form, symbolized by the man, entering into intimate contact with matter…coupling with it, responds to these words…she is the cause of all my sins."

In the men's world of *Love's Labour's Lost* 'Words serve Ideas' as 'Matter serves Form'. These are Aristotelian concepts; for Bruno they are 'Old School'. Because words serve ideas they have little connection to the real world. They are a plaything, an intellectual toy. Words in the

Intelligible Sphere mean what the men want them to mean. Words are their own amusement devoid of consequence (1.1.173)

I love to hear him lie.

Words are generated to match any situation (1.1.176)

A man of fire-new words.

Words serve the jest, the desire, the idea. This was Shakespeare's interpretation of Aristotle's idea; that Matter served Form. This was the idea Bruno's new philosophy was going to kill. Death would come to Aristotle's view of Matter as surely as Death would visit Shakespeare's play.

A Matter of Fact

Berry points out that the women have the utmost respect for words as symbols of reality. A reality determined by the careful evaluation of the senses (2.1.15)

Beauty is bought by judgment of the eye

and (5.2.849-850)

A jest's prosperity lies in the ear

Of him that hears it.

The women choose to unmask the meaning of words so as to determine the motives and purposes of their originators. They are the detectives of meaning and employ a deconstructionist attitude to everything the men say. The women reason like philosophers to get down to the meat of the matter.

For the women Words serve Reality. They are connected like two sides of a coin. Words limit, carve, and hone reality. Out of all possible meanings words are selected to find the one that is the closest match to reality. A groping process with a purpose, much as science probes into the secrets of nature.

The strategy the women use on the men's superfluous orations is described by Bruno (ibid., p.95):

"when the intellect wishes to grasp the essence of something, it proceeds by simplifying as much as possible"

"Just as a lengthy, long-winded oration cannot be understood but by reducing it to a single conceit."

In the play we can see the women apply this principle when discussing with the men how many miles they measured (5.2.184-200). This is a distance the men should be well acquainted with since early in the play they passed a law involving it (1.1.119-120)

> *Item, That no woman shall come within*
> *a mile of my court.*

When we look at the scene the women in the dialogue keep pushing the men to associate number with measure but the men evade the question by changing the meaning of the word 'measure' from first meaning to travel, then to meaning a dance, then to mean a length of poetry, and finally to mean an increased amount of something.

Berry ascribes this evasion by the men as a way of avoiding reality in that number was used as a symbol of reality in the play (Berry, p.74). In this Bruno would agree, for he also felt that number was inextricably linked to both measure and Matter

"measure is not independent from number, because the understanding of measure cannot be found without an understanding of numbers" (ibid., p.94-95)

and

"all number, diversity, order, beauty and ornament are related to matter" (ibid., p.9).

For Bruno everything was Matter. Matter contained all Forms just as wood contains a bed, a bench, a beam, a carving or anything else made of wood. Matter had infinite potential (potency) to be anything

215

(ibid., p.82-83). Forms floated on the surface of Matter. Matter was the permanent constituent of the cosmos. For Bruno Matter is best understood as a potency that contains all forms, that thing that underlies everything. Bruno's Matter was like our understanding of energy (it possessed no dimension or shape) but when condensed it could give rise to the created sensual, physical world; hence any form.

Forms came and went as things/people were made/born and destroyed/died but underneath it all was the Matter (energy) that went on indefinitely. Forms were produced by the contraction of Matter (energy) and they existed for only a finite time (ibid., p. 78-79) but the Matter underneath the form went on forever. Bruno's Matter was God. Nothing existed outside it and God was everywhere in it. God was Everything, Everywhere, Forever. The Unity. Bruno's Matter was the Ultimate Reality encompassing everything. It was the potency and the act; Form did not exist outside Matter (as Aristotle would have had it) but was inside it, everything was inside Matter as everything was inside God. Bruno said "*Matter is Act, absolute potency and absolute act.*"

Just as Aristotle's Forms cannot exist outside Bruno's Matter neither can the men (symbols of Aristotle's male form) exist outside the real world that is made manifest by the women. This is why Berry perceived the plot of *Love's Labour's Lost* as a movement towards reality. The Forms are being absorbed into Matter. This is why the men must give up their vows, vows that are forcing them to live in the Intelligible world of Forms (4.3.335-336)

> *Let us once lose our oaths to find ourselves,*
> *Or else we lose ourselves to keep our oaths.*

Bruno was making a huge philosophical point when he disagreed with Aristotle. He was saying that Everything was God, but more specifically that the corporeal and incorporeal worlds were made of the same thing. He was saying God, the angels, humans, trees, rocks, even

216

ideas, Everything, was made of the same material. He was saying the Earth was not corrupt but was part of God, that the physical, sensual world was not corrupt. He was denying original sin (ibid., p.78-81).

Shakespeare's play animates these ideas in the Muscovite scene (5.2.79-307). This is a scene of masks and switched identities. It shows how the men are stuck on Form; that thing that lies on the surface of Matter. Their inability to see beneath to the truth is what makes them fools. Bruno describes forms as a type of multiplicity (ibid., p. 93).

"And what creates multiplicity in things is not being, is not the thing, but what appears, what is offered to the senses and lies on the surface of things."

The men come disguised as Muscovites to court the women. The women are not deceived by the masks but perceive the individuals beneath. The men see only the external signs, the surface, the tokens they sent to their chosen one. Since the women too are masked and have exchanged the tokens among themselves, the men court the wrong woman making promises they will again have to break. Berowne comes late to this realization (5.2.468-469)

The ladies did change favours and then we,
Following the signs, wooed but the sign of she.

For the women words are tied to reality, this gives them confidence, their words become acts (just as Bruno's Matter is Act); they came to resolve a suit with the King and have at this point resolved it (5.2.732-733)

Excuse me so, coming too short of thanks
For my great suit so easily obtained.

With the men, words are jests, a way of avoiding reality and hence any meaningful action. They are trapped in their enclosed world having no impact and incapable of making the world a better place.

There is a futility to their lives and an emptiness that can be felt, this is why they attract our sympathy.

Hunting for Fame

Prior to the Muscovite scene is the Hunting scene [4.1]. It is a scene of great significance to Bruno and central to his poem *Gli eroici furori* (*The Heroic Enthusiasts*) (1585). In his book Bruno explains the allegory behind the story of Actaeon, the hunter, who when out hunting stag came across the goddess, Diana, bathing. She turned Actaeon into a stag who was then pursued and attacked by his own dogs. *Love's Labour's Lost* certainly alludes to Actaeon's story but whether it's a general classical allusion or an allusion to Bruno's specific interpretation of Actaeon is the question we need to answer.

The scene begins with a question about the King. The Princess wonders if he was the person who spurred his horse up a steep hill. She states that (4.1.4)

Whoe'er'a was, 'a showed a mounting mind.

The word "*mounting*" could be taken as a sexual innuendo or as an intellectual term meaning aspiring. Her question is answered later in the play by Berowne who identifies the King as having been out hunting (4.3.1)

The King, he is hunting the deer.

Again "*deer*" could be a pun on "*dear*" meaning the Princess. Meanwhile, the Princess has assigned herself the role of "*murderer*" (4.1.8). We know the King has already assigned her the role of the Moon, Diana, from the poems he has written her and conversations he has had about her. So all the pieces are in place. We have the stag hunt, the hunter, and Diana. The classical tale can be seen as a tragedy, a punishment by the Goddess doled out on a mortal but Bruno's interpretation is more in keeping with Shakespeare's story. *Love's*

Labour's Lost is not a tragedy but rather ends in a challenge; the women ask the men to change, to become '*more than they are*'. This matches Bruno's interpretation of the Actaeon legend (*Gli eroici furori*, fourth dialogue or for the English translation see L. Williams and G. Bruno; *The Heroic Enthusiasts*, p. 91-94, my underlining).

"Actaeon signifies the intellect, intent on the pursuit of divine wisdom"

... *"and love it is that moves and urges the intellect, and precedes it as a lantern."*

... *"The great hunter saw, he understood as much as was possible, and became the hunted. He went out for prey, and this hunter became himself the prey, by the operation of the intellect converting the things learned into itself"*

... *"As I understand: because love transforms and converts into the thing loved"*

... *"So Actaeon with those thoughts – those dogs – which hunted outside themselves for goodness, wisdom, and beauty, thus came into the presence of the same...saw himself converted into that for which he was seeking, and perceived, that of his dogs or thoughts, he himself came to be the longed for prey; for having absorbed the divinity into himself <u>it was not necessary to search outside himself for it</u>.*

For this reason it is said "the kingdom of Heaven is in us""

... *"See then, Actaeon hunted by his own dogs – pursued by his own thoughts – runs and directs these novel paces, invigorated so as to proceed divinely and "more easily...towards the denser places", to the <u>deserts</u> and the regions of things incomprehensible. From being such as he first was, a common ordinary man, he becomes rare and heroic".*

The King guided by love for the Princess is asked to become a better man at the end of the play. The Princess requests that he look within himself, that he lead an "*austere insociable life*" (5.2.793) to find the hero within, the person she could love, then to come and challenge

219

her by *"these deserts"* (5.2.799) to be his wife. The play ends on a note of *'becoming'*. It is Bruno's Actaeon we see reflected in *Love's Labour's Lost*.

Nothing Desires What it Already Possesses

Bruno states that Matter (*Cause, Principle and Unity*, p. 86):

"does not desire those forms which daily change on its back" for what can form offer to the *"divine being in things."*

"Matter does not desire form...because a corruptible thing does not preserve an eternal one. Moreover, since matter clearly preserves form, form must desire matter in order to perpetuate itself, and not the other way around. For when form is separated from matter it ceases to exist".

Shakespeare echoes this sentiment. The men (form) clearly are smitten with the ladies (matter); but the ladies point out to the men that their offers of love were not taken seriously (5.2.771-778)

We have received your letters full of love...

And in our maiden counsel rated them...

As bombast.

After this rejection the men are asked to prove themselves 'Worthy of Love'. They are asked to change their natures.

Bruno's dialogue introduces one more idea into this exchange. He has stated *"form must desire matter in order to perpetuate itself"*. This one idea supports two concepts in the play. First it goes a long way towards explaining or justifying the sexual banter in the play and the endless double entendres. Second it introduces a central concept in the play: death. Death as the end of existence, death as the end of perpetuation, death as the end of form. So there we have it; all the central themes are connected; Matter and Form; Female and Male; Life and Death.

Fame and Death

In the first few lines of the play death is introduced. The King also introduces the concept of fame as if it were a remedy for death. His speech is an idealistic and not realistic evaluation (1.1.1-8) (my underlining)

> Let *fame*, that all *hunt* after in their lives,
>
> Live registered upon our brazen tombs,
>
> And then grace us in the disgrace of death;
>
> When, spite of cormorant devouring time,
>
> Th'endeavour of this present breath may buy
>
> That honour which shall bate his scythe's keen edge,
>
> And make us heirs of all eternity.

The Princess in the other <u>hunt</u> scene of the play also talks of fame in the context of death but she sees it as an illusion or a manipulation (4.1.31-35) (my underlining)

> Glory grows guilty of detested crimes,
>
> When for *fame's* sake, for praise, an outward part,
>
> We bend to that the working of the heart;
>
> As I for praise alone now seek to spill
>
> The poor deer's blood, that my heart means no ill.

Bruno's dialogue also deals with ideas of fame and death. He has harsh words for Aristotle and also for Plato, both of whom he felt compromised the truth for personal gain.

"Aristotle...he perceived truth badly. With his harmful explanation and his irresponsible arguments, this arid sophist perverted the sense of the ancients and hampered the truth...out of jealousy and ambition" (ibid., p. 91)

and

"Plato...I mean that the goal of his philosophy was more his personal glory than the truth" (ibid., p. 94).

He does not think this to be true for Pythagoras who he feels followed his ideas to their logical conclusions. So in Pythagoras lies the truth and the truth about death.

"Every production, of whatever kind, is an alteration, while the substance always remains the same, since there is only one substance, as there is but one divine, immortal being. Pythagoras, who did not fear death but saw it as a transformation, reached this conclusion" (ibid., p. 90).

... *"You see, then, how the universe is in all things and all things are in the universe, we in it and it in us"* (ibid., p. 90).

..."*from the Knowledge of true form derives the true comprehension of what life is and what death is ...our philosophy...withdraws the somber veil of the insane belief in Orcus and in grasping Charon, a belief which poisons and detracts from all that is sweetest about our life"* (ibid., p. 6).

The secret of life/death, its transformative quality, seems to me to be the basis of Rosalind's request of Berowne (5.2.829-857). She asks him to use his wit for good (5.2.840-842)

...your task shall be

With all the fierce endeavour of your wit

To enforce the pained impotent to smile.

Berowne misinterprets, he thinks she is asking him to use jests to make the sick laugh (5.2.844-845)

It cannot be, it is impossible.

Mirth cannot move a soul in agony.

She clarifies, she wants him to throw away that jesting spirit (5.2.855) but to still use his wit to comfort them. Just as the Queen asked the King to look inward, Rosalind is asking Berowne to use his intelligence to find the secret of Pythagoras, the secret of life and death, and to share it with the suffering, to give them the comfort of a transformation instead of the somber belief in death and possible punishment.

"Those philosophers who have discovered this unity have found their beloved Wisdom" (ibid., p. 90).

The women represent Bruno's vision of Matter, reformed from Aristotle's corrupt ideas. If the men love the women they will seek the perfection they see in them. They will come to be like the women; they will learn the secret of Pythagoras, they will find wisdom, and come to understand both life and death. The play ends on a note of becoming.

Universal Becoming

"Who does not see that corruption and generation derive from the same principle? Is not the end of the corrupt thing the beginning of the thing generated?...transmutations are circular" (ibid., p. 99).

Love and Death, birth and decay these are the themes in *Love's Labour's Lost*. Love and sex give rise to generation and the bawdy humour of the play. Death is brought up in the context of fame. The Princess shows fame to be an illusion and Bruno and Pythagoras show Death to be one as well. Death, it should be noted, does not end the play rather two songs do; one about Spring, the other Winter. It is a cycle. The play is neither a tragedy nor a comedy but a cycle of becoming. The men are corrupt but now have a chance to reform themselves. In another year they will have one more chance at love.

Intelligible and Sensible Worlds

In Frances Yates' book, *A Study of Love's Labour's Lost* (Chpt. 7, p. 137), she points out a fundamental debate that was going on in the literature of the time and particularly among those of Shakespeare's acquaintance. The Earl of Northumberland and Thomas Hariot both wrote on the topic of finding the balance between love and learning.

How time spent in the pursuit of one deprived them of time for the other. How one seemed to be the product of idleness while the other from hard work.

Philip Sidney's poem *Astrophel and Stella* personified this struggle by showing Astrophel the poet being bullied by Astrophel the philosopher and being sternly told that it was a waste of time to observe the fascinating blackness of Stella's eyes when knowledge was the only goal worth striving for (Yates, ibid., p. 113; *Astrophel and Stella*, sonnet 10).

What was a debate about love and learning carried baggage from Aristotle's and Ptolemy's version of the cosmos. The corrupt Earth was home for the sensual pleasures and God was at home in the Intelligible Sphere beyond the fixed stars.

Returning once again to Frances Yates but this time to a later work, *The Occult Philosophy in the Elizabethan Age* (Chpt. 13,14). Here she re-visits a poem she referred to in her earlier book, a poem written by George Chapman called *Shadow of the Night* (1594). It is alluded to in *Love's Labour's Lost* (4.3.251). She sees it as an example of Agrippa's philosophy of inspired melancholy that he describes in his book *De occulta philosophia* (*Three Books of Occult Philosophy*, Book 1, Chpt. LX)(1533). What is of significance is that Chapman wrote a second poem, *The Banquet of Sense* (1595), a year after his poem on melancholy. Just as melancholy is associated with Saturn (black bile) so is sensuality with Venus. The two poems were meant to work together, to temper one another; one a poetic picture of Saturn the other of Venus (Yates, ibid., p. 168). One mitigating the influence of the other in order to achieve balance (*Three Books of Occult Philosophy*, p. 318, 730). The one poem speaking about a night of meditation with the senses asleep, the other poem speaking about day and the sensuousness of our perceptions as lived out through our five senses.

Both poems should have been known to Shakespeare and both poems superficially influenced *Love's Labour's Lost* with respect to the Intelligible and Sensual spheres. Meditation, thought, and study were associated with Saturn (Yates, ibid., p. 158) and sensual pleasures with Venus. *Love's Labour's Lost* takes place over two days. It begins on Friday (Vendredi – Venus day) and ends on Saturday (Saturn – day) (4.1.6) (see note in Arden; the first two acts occur on Friday and the last three acts on Saturday). Venus and Saturn set the timetable for the play. At the end of the play the songs of Spring and Winter reprise the roles of Venus and Saturn.

The play is set up to evoke the two spheres; the Intelligible and the Sensual. The Intelligible sphere includes the men (examples of Aristotle's ideal forms), ideas, ascetic pursuits, and study. It provides the example of the rational world. It includes Mercury and the intellectual pursuits associated with Mercury like book-learning, memory work, and writing but also includes Saturn and things associated with Saturn such as contemplation, melancholic meditation, reflection, things dark and heavy and, of course, Death (Saturn being Father Time, Cronos, who consumes all his children).

The Sensual sphere includes the women (examples of Aristotle's corrupt matter), reality, the physical world enjoyed and perceived through the five senses. It includes Venus and all things associated with her like Love, dance and theatre but also includes nature's Apollo and the sensual things he is associated with like poetry, song, seasons, light and Life.

Malcolm Evans in his article *Mercury versus Apollo: A Reading of Love's Labor's Lost* (Shakespeare Quarterly, Vol.26, No.2, Spring, 1975, p.113-127) does an excellent job in elaborating on the offices of Mercury and Apollo and in relating them to Berry's observation of how language was used differently by the men and women in the play. Evans contributes to the discussion by showing that the men not only equivocate like salesmen but that they employ intellectual techniques that distance themselves from others. They communicate through '*written*' or '*memorized rhetoric*' that they have composed in isolation and that they have often employed others to deliver. Their work, though personal in nature and addressed to another, does not take into account the response of that other person. Their '*message in a bottle*' approach inevitably leads to addressing the wrong person or to misunderstandings.

Evans sees the women as part of the sensual world and directly engaged in dialogue. They participate in an active game of call and response. They improvise with another breathing, thinking individual to produce the jazz of communication. They are part of a social world, a world requiring the engagement of all their senses.

But even Evan's bigger picture perspective can be subsumed under the rubric of the Intelligible and Sensible worlds.

Acknowledging this overriding theme allows me to return to Bruno, his theology, and what he was hoping to accomplish. Bruno felt his new philosophy of Matter, namely, that the same Matter made up both the Intelligible and Sensible worlds, had consequences; that it could heal the division between Nature and Divinity. Traditionally these two worlds were separated with one being regarded as corrupt. Bruno felt his new philosophy would redeem the physical realm. That physical '*Human Needs*' need not be in violation of '*Divine Will*' because both physical reality and intellectual reality were composed of the same Matter, God (the Unity, the One).

This is what Shakespeare saw in Bruno. A philosophy of healing. Just as Venus could complement Saturn to create balance so could Bruno's philosophy bridge the gap between learning and loving. His play is not about the conflict between the two but their resolution.

Bruno found in Pythagoras the meeting place between the Sensual and Intellectual worlds (*Cause, Principle and Unity*, p.94). *"Pythagoras (his philosophy) was no less suitable and adequate for corporeal things than it was for those things which reason, imagination, intellect and both intelligible and sensible nature can forge."*

Armado becomes the proof of this. He is our glimpse at a happy ending. He has seen the error of his ways (5.2.717-719)

> *For mine own part, I breathe free breath. I have*
> *Seen the day of wrong through the little hole of*
> *Discretion and I will right myself like a soldier.*

rather than ascending to an intellectual heaven he has fallen to the sensual Earth. He will become a man of the soil. The first Adam in this new paradise. He is to be absorbed into Jaquenetta's world as a man of *"russet yeas and honest kersey noes"* (5.2.413)

> *I have vowed to Jaquenetta to hold the plough*
> *For her sweet love three year* (5.2.871-872).

His union offers hope to the others.

Conclusion

Words are Shakespeare's Matter. They are not the corrupt Matter of Aristotle but rather the Matter of Bruno's new philosophy. The Matter that would turn Genesis on its head, free of original sin. Shakespeare is telling a tale of becoming; that is why it has no end. His corrupt men (Aristotle's Forms) are going to be absorbed into the real world (the Matter) that the women bring to the play. It is a Matter free of sin that can give rise to both physical and intellectual reality. The men are going to be challenged to find the God within themselves and to use their wit to discover the secret of wisdom, the secret of life and death, the secret of Matter. The men instead of separating themselves from the world are going to find the Unity of it all.

Bruno is not only in Shakespeare's play he is the source of the philosophy that infuses it. Bruno's *Cause, Principle and Unity* comes alive in Shakespeare's *Love's Labour's Lost*. It provides the solution to the question of the age. The Intellectual and Sensual worlds are not divided/not separated but are made of the same matter and are parts of the same unity. They provide balance to the cycle of life.

Bibliography

1) *Love's Labour's Lost*, William Shakespeare, The Arden Shakespeare, ed.: H.R. Woudhuysen, Thomson Learning, 2001.

2) *Cause, Principle and Unity and Essays on Magic*, Giordano Bruno, edited by Richard J. Blackwell and Robert de Lucca with Intro. by Alfonso Ingegno, Cambridge University Press, 2003.

3) *The Heroic Enthusiasts an Ethical Poem*, Giordano Bruno, trans. L. Williams, Kessinger Publications, 2005.

4) *A Study of Love's Labour's Lost*, Frances A. Yates, Cambridge University Press, 1936.

5) *The Occult Philosophy in the Elizabethan Age*, Frances A. Yates, Routledge Classics, 2001.

6) *Sir Philip Sidney's An Apology for Poetry and Astrophil and Stella: Texts and Contexts*, Philip Sidney, edited by Peter C. Herman, College Publishing, 2001.

7) *Three Books of Occult Philosophy*, Henry Cornelius Agrippa, edited and annotated by Donald Tyson, Llewellyn Publications, 2001.

8) *Preposterous Reversals: Love's Labor's Lost*, Patricia Parker, Modern Language Quarterly, Vol.54, Dec. 1993, p. 435-482.

9) *Mercury versus Apollo: a reading of Love's Labor's Lost*, Malcolm Evans, Shakespeare Quarterly, Vol.26, 1975, p.113-127.

10) *The Words of Mercury*, Ralph Berry, Shakespeare Survey, Vol. 22, 1969, p. 69-77.

11) *The God Particle. At the Heart of All Matter; The hunt for the God particle*, Joel Achenbach, National Geographic, March 2008.

Abstract for *Othello*
Bridling Othello

De magia (*On Magic*) and *De vinculis in genere* (*A General Account of Bonding*) both by Giordano Bruno outline the processes involved in psychological manipulation. These little known works published in 1588 most likely provided Shakespeare with the knowledge his character, Iago, would require in order to bind Othello to his will.

Bridling Othello

Introduction

De magia (*On Magic*) and *De vinculis in genere* (*A General Account of Bonding*) both by Giordano Bruno outline the processes involved in psychological manipulation. These little known works published in 1588 most likely provided Shakespeare with the knowledge his character, Iago, would require in order to bind Othello to his will. By outlining Bruno's methods of manipulation this essay will demonstrate that these works were a source of immense value in Shakespeare's writing of *Othello*.

Bruno's work addresses the subject of manipulation from the point of view of the manipulator. Shakespeare's *Othello* does us the same favour by presenting us with Iago's point of view. Bruno approaches the subject objectively without any ethical or social concerns. *A General Account of Bonding* and *On Magic* are precursors to the science of Applied Psychology and Sociology or more precisely to a subgenre of these fields, that of social control as exercised through the use of mass media, a science that is generally practiced today by advertisers and media consultants.

Bruno's work examines the manipulation of individuals as well as groups (the mass audience). He considers individual manipulation to be much more difficult than mass manipulation. Since Shakespeare's work features the manipulation of one individual by another this essay will focus its discussion on the topic of individual manipulation.

Bruno believed you could control other people by "*binding*" them or forming "*bonds*" with them. By binding their will to yours you could guide their decision-making processes. Bruno felt every bond was fashioned from Eros; those things that we love. He felt this was the "*bond of bonds*" out of which came all others. Love was the source of

231

Desire and desire could be generalized into any number of things; a desire for wealth, power, fame, control, pleasure, or revenge. It was infinitely guidable and easily tuned. Desire allowed one to tap into all the emotions both positive and negative.

"The most important of all bonds is the bond of Venus and of love in general, and that which is primarily and most powerfully the opposite of love's unity and evenness is the bond of hate...

These two feelings, or rather, in the last analysis, this one feeling of love (whose substance includes hate) dominates all things, is lord over all things...love is the bond of bonds."

(*Cause, Principle and Unity and Essays on Magic*, Giordano Bruno, edited and translated by Richard J. Blackwell and Robert de Lucca, Cambridge University Press, 1998, p. 173-174).

In this edition of *Cause, Principle and Unity and Essays on Magic* the essays on magic include translations of *De magia* (*On Magic*) and *De vinculis in genere* (*A General Account of Bonding*). All future quotations will be taken from these sections of Blackwell's translation.

"We have claimed in our treatise De naturali magia (On Magic) that all bonds are either reduced to the bond of love, depend on the bond of love or are based on the bond of love...love is the foundation of all feelings" (ibid., p. 165)

also

"There are two causes of the act of bonding...namely, knowledge of some kind and desire of some kind. If something has no desire at all, then it cannot be bound" (ibid., p. 164).

In Shakespeare's play Iago binds Othello to his will. He manipulates Othello to do things that are against his own best interests. Yet why should we think that Shakespeare would draw from Bruno's essays on magic for information regarding this type of manipulation. The answer is in Act 1. Shakespeare repeatedly draws our attention to the idea that magic can be used to manipulate another's behaviour. The concern expressed, however, is not for Othello but over the fear that Othello has used magic to control Desdemona

> *Is there not charms*
> *By which the property of youth and maidhood*
> *May be abused*
> (1.1.169)

again

> *thou hast enchanted her*
> (1.2.63)

again

> *If she in chains of magic were not bound*
> (1.2.65)

again

> *That thou hast practiced on her with foul charms*
> *Abused her delicate youth with drugs or minerals*
> *That weaken motion*
> (1.2.72-75)

and again

> *She is abused, stolen from me and corrupted*
> *By spells and medicines bought of mountebanks,*
> *For nature so preposterously to err*
> *Being not deficient, blind, or lame of sense,*
> *Sans witchcraft could not*
> (1.3.61-65).

These are but a few of the references pertaining to the use of magic to control another's behaviour but they set a precedence, they prepare the audience. This is Act 1. Shakespeare is introducing the concepts he will be working with. He is looking at bonds. Bonds of friendship (1.3.337-339); bonds of service (1.1.41-42); bonds of loyalty

(1.2.12); bonds of love (1.2.25); bonds between a father and his daughter and between a wife and her husband (1.3.180-189); bonds of hate (1.1.5-6); how bonds are formed (1.3.251-252) and how bonds are broken (1.1.131-132).

The Objects to be Bound

Shakespeare uses Act 1 to look at the three main characters. He quickly sets up Iago as the manipulator, the one we should be watching for, the one who uses others for his own purposes and who shows one face publicly and another privately, *"I am not what I am"* (1.1.64).

He introduces Desdemona, a character that will be repeatedly referred to in the most glowing of terms. A veritable Madonna of innocence and love; *"The divine Desdemona"* (2.1.73).

He also introduces a powerplay that is going to occur for the control of Othello; Iago to destroy him through hate (1.3.385-403) and Desdemona to save him through love (1.3.254-255).

Honigmann in his introduction to the Arden Edition of *Othello* (p. 108) points out that Iago and Desdemona can be regarded as metaphysical characters who compete for Othello's soul. I believe there is some truth to this claim but for me the proof comes in the form of the imagery that is associated with Othello.

Twice in Act 1 the Sagittary is mentioned (1.1.156) and (1.3.116); it is an inn operating under the sign of Sagittarius (the Centaur). Sagittarius is the symbol of the half-man/half-horse, it is the place Othello is to be found. Sagittarius was regarded as representing humanity's dual nature; rooted half in the animal world – subject to fate and uncontrollable passions and half in the spiritual world – with access to reason, moral choice, and enlightenment. These are the characteristics that define Othello; they are also the different qualities Iago and Desdemona appeal to.

The centaur allusion is an important one and purposefully made. The centaurs were the descendants of Ixion (son of the War God Mars). Othello too is the son of war, having been raised in it all his life (1.3.130-134). Iago focuses on the "horse" aspect of Othello just as Desdemona appeals to his humanity. Iago hopes to bridal Othello while Desdemona hopes to influence Othello as his bride.

It is Iago that refers to Othello as a Barbary horse (1.1.109-111)

you'll have your daughter covered with a Barbary horse;

you'll have your nephews neigh to you.

It is Iago that plans to guide him as you would a horse with a bridle (1.3.398-401)

The Moor is of a free and open nature

That thinks men honest that but seem to be so,

And will as tenderly be led by th'nose

As asses are.

The Honest Broker

The play offers a perfect glimpse into the world of Renaissance Magic and theories of how to bind others to one's will. In this play Iago must control or guide the behaviours of three individuals; Roderigo, Cassio, and Othello. To understand how Iago is to accomplish this it is important to first understand Bruno's theory and see how it relates to Iago's problems.

As mentioned earlier Bruno felt love/desire was the "bond of bonds" the source for all the bonds that could be formed between individuals. He also felt that no magic was possible without faith or belief.

"The second bond is also a triple and is needed in the agent, in the action and in the thing on which the agent acts. It consists of faith or

credibility of invocation, of love and of strong emotions in the
application of the active to the passive.

...for a magician is most fortunate if many believe in him and if he
commands great persuasion" (ibid., p.130).

As the quotation states this belief had to be held by both parties.
The magician had to both believe in himself and his cause and the client
had to believe in him. This is why Iago is referred to as "honest" over 15
times in the play by others and he uses the term 6 times when referring to
himself (*Shakespearean Tragedy*, Bradley, p.214). Others believe him to
be honest and he convinces himself he is honest.

Iago can be seen rehearsing deception or justifying his actions
several times in the play. For instance in his soliloquy of (2.1.284-310)
he maintains Cassio loves Desdemona; this may in fact be true. He then
goes on to state that Cassio may have cuckolded him, a fear he but
suspects. It is no great leap of logic to believe Cassio could cuckold
Othello at some later date. For Iago this sequence of potential events is
enough. He believes Cassio to be capable of cuckolding Othello so he
can honestly present the possibility to Othello. Iago along with Othello
can both believe the accusation. The agent, the action (the action must
be believable), and the thing on which the agent acts (Othello) all believe
Cassio is capable of infidelity with Desdemona.

"Given a good general impression and a disposition to be
believed, he can somehow use the power of his soul to arrange, disclose
and explain things for them...

This opens the door to those other impressions which the art of
binding seeks in order to establish further bonds, namely hope,
compassion, fear, love, hate, indignation, anger, joy, patience, disdain
for life, for death, for fate, and all of the powers which cross over from
the soul to change the body" (ibid., p. 142).

So the honest man can guide the believer into believing whatever the honest man tells him and he can guide him using any of a number of emotional states available to him. This is why Bruno felt that:

"...all practitioners of magic...produce no results without a pre-given faith" (ibid., p. 141).

This is why Iago has cultivated his reputation as the honest man, the man you can trust. It is a reputation he needs to do his work. When reading the play it becomes apparent that Iago, for the most part, does give good advice and seldom lies. He gives the impression of the honest broker.

The Power that Binds

Bruno felt that all people could be bound, *Plotinus has asserted, "both the wise man and the fool can be bound"* (ibid., p. 142), but that bonding could be difficult to maintain because of people's changing natures.

"...different people have different functions, habits, purposes, inclinations, understandings and eras. And so ...the same material object can be changed into different forms and figures, such that to bind them continuously one should always use differing kinds of knots.

In addition to this, let us notice the conditions of human life: being young and then old; being of a moderate station, or noble, or rich, or powerful, or happy, or, indeed even envious and ambitious; or being a soldier or a merchant, or one of many other officials who play a role in different ways in the administration of a state, and thus who must be bonded to each other because they function as agents and instruments of the state" (ibid., p. 145).

This meant that one had to use as many bonds (knots) as possible on a subject and that one had to act as quickly as possible; for even the best bonds are only temporary.

This paragraph also speaks of the bonds that pre-exist among people, especially soldiers who have formed strong bonds with each other in order to function as a unit. This is true of Iago and Othello who have served together for many years and have fought side by side (1.1.27-28). Long years of service together have created bonds of trust but time also allows bonds of resentment to grow and for slights to accumulate and for talents to be taken for granted.

Bonding individuals is a difficult business and requires extensive knowledge of the person to be bound. Iago possesses such knowledge. "*...he who knows how to bind needs to have an understanding of all things, or at least of the nature, inclination, habits, uses and purposes of the particular things that he is to bind*" (ibid., p. 148).

"*Bonds are brought to completion by knowledge in general, and they are woven together by feelings in general. I say 'knowledge in general' because it is sometimes not known which sense has captured the object, and I say 'feelings in general' because sometimes that is not easy to define*" (ibid., p. 155).

This discussion informs us that it is easier to bond a close trusted friend than a stranger because we need extensive knowledge of the subject in order to predict their behaviour and understand which 'bait' might attract them. In many ways the art of manipulation plays on people's need to be understood. Understanding, trust and emotional bonding all go together and are the normal parts of a good friendship. Unfortunately they can also be used to exploit the unsuspecting and betray normal human relations. This is why Iago's crime can be seen as so reprehensible; he exploits the people that trust him, he betrays friendship and even the meaning of friendship.

The play opens with Iago manipulating Roderigo to rouse Desdemona's father and make him aware that she may have eloped with Othello. At this point Iago may simply be wanting to deprive Othello of his prize (Desdemona) by stopping the wedding. Since he personally has no way to do this without offending Othello he recruits Roderigo, a friend and former suitor of Desdemona to accomplish his goal. He functions as a background character, never letting Brabantio know his name and leaving before he comes down to talk with Roderigo. Operating in the background Iago has a better chance at manipulating and orchestrating the action.

"At the social level, orators, court officials and those who know how to get things done bond more effectively if they secretly conceal their skills when they act...for to conceal an art while using it is no small part of the art" (ibid., p. 169).

Early in Shakespeare's play we already have a sense of how Iago operates; he befriends, he shares confidences, jokes and then withdraws into the background letting the bound victim engage in any action to be taken.

"...orators create good will with their art when their listeners and judges find something of themselves in it" (ibid., p. 157).
"Mutual agreeableness gives rise to mutual bonds. Thus there are bonds in jokes, in wit... " (ibid., p. 161).

Roderigo is merely a pawn for Iago, he keeps him as his purse; *"Thus do I ever make my fool my purse"* (1.3.382). As of Act 1 he has no other clear plans for Roderigo but Iago knows Roderigo is obsessive in his infatuation over Desdemona, a match Brabantio disapproved of, *"My daughter is not for thee"* (1.1.97), and that this obsession has driven Roderigo to despair. Iago files this information in his mind for future use, after all a suicidal man who does not fear death can be a very useful tool.

Iago has three characters that are of direct concern to him and that he hopes to manipulate for his benefit. His first inkling of a plan is voiced in his soliloquy (1.3.381-403). To bind three personalities is difficult and requires much planning and preparation as well as anticipation of their changing needs.

"Whoever wishes to bind must take note of the fact that some of the things that can be bound are affected more by nature, others more by judgment or prudence, and still others more by practice and habit. As a result, the skilful person obliges and binds the first type of things with bonds provided by natural things, the second type by reasons and proofs, by symbols and arguments, and the third type by what is at hand and is compelling" (ibid., p. 158).

Through the play we will see how Iago takes advantage of these differences. With Cassio, Iago takes advantage of his habits, with Roderigo he uses his natural infatuation for Desdemona to control him and with Othello he attacks his judgment.

Iago knows that Cassio is a 'mean drunk'. Iago's knowledge of Cassio's past habitual behaviour has informed him of this. He uses Roderigo to provoke Cassio once he gets a little more drink into him. Iago outlines his plan in another soliloquy (2.3.45-58). He's not sure of the outcome but figures something offensive to the islanders will result.

This awareness of people's natures is what makes Othello vulnerable to Iago.

"Because of their temperament those who are melancholy are more bound to indignation, sadness, pleasure and love, for since they are more impressionable, they also have a stronger sense of pleasure. They are also more prone to contemplation and to speculation, and in general are moved and agitated more often and more strongly by their emotions" (ibid., p. 161).

Bruno felt those with excess black bile (melancholics) were more easily bound than other temperaments; although the choleric, the sanguine and the phlegmatic all possessed certain weaknesses that could be exploited (see also ibid., p. 161).

240

It is here I must address the colour of Othello. The fact that he is a Moor is important to the storyline, it makes him an outsider but I believe he must be a black Moor for symbolic reasons. Black is the colour associated with melancholy and with Saturn (*The Three Books of Occult Philosophy*, Book 1, Chapter LX and Appendix IV). Othello, like Saturn, represents death and he embodies Bruno's definition of a melancholic personality. From a writer's point of view, having Othello exhibit both a passionate, sensual nature along with strong contemplative powers gave Shakespeare a broad canvas to work with.

The Hunter of Souls

Iago is a much different character. On the outside he is an extravert, apparently everybody's friend; inside he is a cold calculating lizard. Bradley believes there is no mystery in the psychology of Iago; he believes Iago is longing to satisfy a sense of power, a sense of superiority (*Shakespearean Tragedy*, p.229). By being overlooked for promotion his ego has suffered a shock. Although not an ambitious man this assault on his sense of worth, brought on by the judgment of others, has denied him of a reward he felt he deserved. Because of this it has awakened his vengeful side; he is full of righteous indignation. He is now motivated to show them all just how clever he is. Nothing could be more satisfying to Iago now than being master of his General, and controller of Cassio's fate, the man who was preferred to him.

The sense of power and elation felt by bonding others is discussed by Bruno and it certainly aligns with Shakespeare's understanding of Iago.

"He who binds experiences joy and a certain sense of glory, and this is greater and stronger in so far as the one who is bound is more noble, more worthy and more excellent...In praising the vanquished, the victors extol their own victory" (ibid., p. 152).

Bruno also discusses the tools Iago might require in order to bind others.

"The bonding agent has three types of tools. The first type is located within him...i.e., those which belong to the nature of his species; and those which are accidental and acquired...for example, sagacity, wisdom, and art. The second type is located in his environment, for example, chance, good fortune, opportunity, encounters, and arranged meetings. The third type is located above him, for example, fate, nature and the favor of the gods" (ibid., p. 153).

In the list is not only his own cleverness but also opportunity, chance, good luck, and fate. Bradley (*Shakespearean Tragedy*, p. 182) comments that in *Othello* one could get the impression *"that fate has taken sides with villainy"*. One could instead make the more truthful observation that it is only the villain who is attentively waiting on fate in order to take advantage of any opportunity or chance that comes his way. This means that the odds are in Iago's favour since all others are oblivious to the passing of events or to the fact that these events could in any way have been manipulated. The bonding agent (Iago) has made chance and opportunity his servants.

We Cannot All Be Masters

Iago and Desdemona are in many ways very similar characters. Both are bound to Othello and both are held in his affection. Bruno's work informs us of another important point about bonding; that it is a two-way street.

"It is not possible for a bonding agent to bind something to himself unless the former is also bound to the latter, for bonds adhere to, and are inserted into, that which is bound;...However, the bonding agent has an advantage over that which is bound, for he is master over the

bonds, and because he is not affected and influenced in the same way" (ibid., p. 164).

We know all bonds stem from Eros (Love/Desire) and that both Iago and Desdemona are bound to Othello. This subtext in Shakespeare's work has led to interpretations of *Othello* where Iago has been represented as a latent homosexual (Introduction to The Arden Shakespeare version of *Othello,* p.50-51). This reading is possible because of the reciprocal nature of bonds. But bonds stemming from Love should not be misunderstood as Love. The magical bonds of Eros are really bonds of Desire not necessarily physical desire which may only define Desdemona's and Othello's relationship. Iago's desires are more for power and control and they feed on and encourage Othello's similar desires.

Realizing bonds are reciprocal introduces complications to the magician creating bonds. Being aware of the bonds offers some protection because it allows for some objectivity on the part of the magician. But the magician must be more; he must be of almost two minds. With one he must empathize with his victim, imagine their feelings and anticipate their reactions and with his inner mind he must turn off this empathy to coldly carry on his task. The feelings he needs to understand others will interfere with his ability to control them.

I believe this explains Iago's dual nature and his uniqueness as a villain in Shakespeare's oeuvre; *"I am not what I am"* (1.1.64).

Iago and Desdemona both wish to control Othello. Both are using bonds to exercise this control. Desdemona is shown exercising control over Othello early in their courtship (1.3.164-167)

> *She thanked me*
> *And bade me, if I had a friend that loved her,*
> *I should but teach him how to tell my story*
> *And that would woo her. Upon this hint I spake.*

She is the aggressor in the courtship, but she is offering something Othello desires. Othello desires Desdemona so he is an easy catch.

"...bonds and bonding powers are established and maintained in skillful ways...Things move more easily towards that to which they are inclined" (ibid., p. 153)

also

"Nothing is bound unless it is very suitably predisposed" (ibid., p. 157).

Iago and Desdemona offer Othello much different things and so employ different binding techniques. Desdemona is virtually unconscious of what she does to bind Othello. It comes naturally to her. Iago is a manipulator, he uses his own skills, he takes advantage of natural events and fabricates what he must.

Bruno describes how one person can be drawn or bound to two different things.

"There is one type of bonding in which we wish to become worthy, beautiful and good; there is another type in which we desire to take command of what is good, beautiful and worthy. The first type of bonding derives from an object which we lack, the second, from an object we already have" (ibid., p.152).

Othello is subject to control from these two seemingly opposite forces because in the first instance he wishes to be like Desdemona (worthy and good); this is why he is attracted (bonded) to her. She possesses aspects of character that he admires, that he wishes to learn from. But he also wants to secretly control her (command her) perhaps because of fears of losing her. She has brought order and gentleness into his life, but he fears the chaos that would come if she left, if she abandoned him. These fears make him subject to the other type of control, the kind that Iago can exploit.

"That the same thing bonds contraries in the same way"

"Consider, for example, the bonds of physical love, which seem to be both a fire and snare at the same time, which drive one to shout and to be silent, to joy and to sorrow, to hope and to desperation, to fear and to boldness, to anger and to gentleness, to weeping and to laughter...all things contain contraries" (ibid., p. 148).

So Desdemona and Iago can be seen pulling on these contraries from opposite sides, like the proverbial angel and devil. Both are exploiting Othello's desires. Unfortunately for Othello Iago is conscious of what he is doing while Desdemona is not. She relies on human nature and Othello's own natural defenses to prevent another from taking control over his will. These defenses seem to lie in obsessiveness and singleness of focus.

"Resistance to being bound."

"The more that a soul is bound to one object, the more it turns away from and rejects others...For, indeed, a more pleasant action excludes a less pleasant one; the soul that is intent on hearing neglects vision; he who observes more attentively becomes deaf; when we are either very happy or sad for some reason, we are little concerned with the other...

As a result, when the orator breaks the bond of love by laughter or envy or other feelings, he binds by hate or contempt or indignation" (ibid., p. 158).

This ability to focus on just one aspect of a situation, tunnel vision, allows Othello to realize how much he loves Desdemona when he is with her (4.1.202-203)

I'll not expostulate with her, lest her body and beauty
Unprovide my mind again.

Her beauty lessens his resolve so he resolves not to see her. His awareness of her ability to beguile him means that he will avoid seeing her and also means she is not afforded a chance to defend herself against Iago's allegations.

This tunnel vision also gives rise to another type of situation such as that which occurs in (3.4.50-99) where Desdemona and Othello talk at cross-purposes. Desdemona is focused on getting Othello to meet with Cassio while Othello is obsessing over the handkerchief. They are not talking with each other but over each other. They are so focused on their own goal that they cannot hear the other. This lack of communication will result in tragedy since Desdemona has not picked up on Othello's mental state; a mental state that is obvious to any outside observer such as Emilia (3.4.100)

Is not this man jealous?

Emilia understands love has a dark side. So does Bruno as he discusses how easily one emotion can become its contrary.

"It is not difficult to change that which can be bound from one type of bond to its contrary...Even though I was once bound in thought by a teaching, the bonds of contempt and indignation may come later when that opinion has been studied in a better light" (ibid., p. 162).

If someone you trust betrays you, the journey from love to hate becomes exceedingly short. This is something Iago knows, something he has lived.

Desdemona and Iago mirror one another in another significant way. The play begins with Desdemona's wedding/elopement and the iteration of her obligations as wife and daughter (1.3.180-189). The play ends with Iago's and Othello's commitment ceremony (a mock wedding). Here Othello renounces his love (3.3.451-452)

Yield up, O love, thy crown and hearted throne
To tyrannous hate!

He then kneels, declares his hate to be permanent, Iago kneels, declares he will aid Othello in his bloody business and then pledges (3.3.482)

I am your own forever.

Iago wants what Desdemona has; to be master of his master (2.1.74)

She that I spake of, our great captain's captain

or

Our general's wife is now the general (2.3.310).

He pines for it the moment he makes the statement to Roderigo that

We cannot all be masters (1.1.42).

This ceremony has granted his wish. The bonds shared between Othello and Iago now draw the two closer together increasing their trust and dependence on one another. As Bruno points out (ibid., p. 176) *"Bonds create a desire for some sort of gratitude"* and Othello is grateful to the man who enslaved him

Now art thou my lieutenant (3.3.481).

Potions and Charms

Act 1 makes frequent references to magic potions and charms but it is not Othello that uses them, rather it is Iago. He employs both potions and charms in manipulating and binding the different personalities.

Cassio is the first person Iago manipulates using a potion and his potion of choice is alcohol (2.3.45-48)

If I can fasten but one cup upon him,
With that which he hath drunk tonight already
He'll be as full of quarrel and offence
As my young mistress' dog.

Later references to potions are not so literal but refer to a 'doubt' infected upon Othello's imagination. This 'doubt' alters Othello's perception of events and slowly robs him of his reason (just like a potion would). Iago makes several references to Othello's increasingly obsessed imagination (3.3.328),

The Moor already changes with my poison

and later (4.1.44-45)

Work on,

My medicine, work!

Iago is practicing natural magic, a form of magic that uses natural products and natural processes to achieve its goal. It was very close to medicine, and science grew from its principles. Natural magic was considered acceptable magic and even the Church did not outright ban it.

When Iago binds Othello he binds using both charms (the handkerchief) and by infecting doubt and images on Othello's imagination. Both are powerful tools employed in binding and both have been discussed by Bruno.

The Handkerchief's Poisonous Magic

"*...sometimes incantations are associated with a person's physical parts in any sense; garments, excrement, remnants, footprints and anything which is believed to have made some contact with the person. In that case, and if they are used to untie, fasten, or weaken, then this constitutes the type of magic called 'wicked', if it leads to evil...If it leads to final destruction and death, then it is called "poisonous magic"*" (ibid., p. 106).

The handkerchief carried great emotional significance for Othello. It was his mother's and even more than that it was a touchstone to a story, one of fidelity (3.4.57-62)

That handkerchief
Did an Egyptian to my mother give,
She was a charmer and could read
The thoughts of people. She told her, while she kept it
'Twould make her amiable and subdue my father
Entirely to her love.

Othello believed in its magic and so it was indeed magical (3.4.71)

'Tis true, there's magic in the web of it.

When Iago takes advantage of it he uses it as a symbol proving the intimate contact between Cassio and Desdemona. Bruno's understanding of tokens combines these two ideas; intimate contact and magic.

"The different type of bonding agents."

"Some things bond by their own power. Other things bond because…they are aided by something else to which they are attached" (ibid., p. 150).

In this case the handkerchief is aided by Othello's attachment to it and it being a symbol of his devotion. It has magical properties because Othello has associated magic with it.

"…he who wishes to bind ought to focus in some way on the awareness in that which can be bound. For, indeed, a bond accompanies the awareness of a thing just like a shadow follows a body" (ibid., p. 157).

Iago focuses Othello's awareness on the handkerchief. Its location becomes of primary importance to him. By keeping Othello focused on the handkerchief Iago can guide Othello's interpretation of events. The handkerchief's absence means something and who has it means something because Iago tells Othello it does. The closer Othello focuses on the handkerchief the less he pays attention to the events around it.

"A thing is bound in the strongest way when part of it is in the bonding agent, or when the bonding agent controls it by one of its parts. To show this with just one example, necromancers are confident that they exercise control over entire bodies by means of the fingernails or the hair of the living, and especially by means of footprints or parts of clothing" (ibid., p. 157).

In our case Iago (the bonding agent) has control over the handkerchief. It is a part of Othello that represents his devoted love. It is a part that Othello has attached great significance to, he believes in it. Because of this the handkerchief already has a bond with him.

"...he who wishes to bond should be careful to use means which effectively bind the object, that is, he should employ the bonds which already hold it" (ibid., p. 163).

Iago, wisely, has chosen an object that holds Othello's attention and he uses it to focus his thoughts. Othello will not be able to weigh his options because Iago is going to limit how Othello thinks.

Phantasy and the Power of the Imagination

"Fourthly, the bonding arising from imagination."

"The role of the imagination is to receive images derived from the senses and to preserve, combine and divide them. This happens in two ways. First, it occurs by the free creative choice of the person who imagines, for example, poets, painters, story writers and all who combine images in some organized way. Second, it occurs without such deliberate choice. The latter also happens in two ways: either through some other cause which chooses and selects, or through an external agent" (ibid., p. 138).

In our case the "external agent" has a name, Iago. He guides Othello's imagination. He fills it with unwanted and unforgettable images of his wife's infidelity (3.3.397-399) *how satisfied, my lord?*

Would you, the supervisor, grossly gape on?

Behold her topped?

also (3.3.404-406)

What shall I say? Where's satisfaction?

It is impossible you should see this

Were they as prime as goats, as hot as monkeys.

These images of Desdemona's wantonness and of Othello's worst fears are designed to stick in his mind. Even though these events never occurred, they occupy and preoccupy his thoughts. This is shown by Othello's response later in the play where he recalls this image as a non sequiter... *"You are welcome, sir, to Cyprus. Goats and monkeys!"* (4.1.263).

Bruno assures us that controlling someone's imagination or guiding its imagery is of primary importance

"...in the act of binding, the imagination must be stimulated or else one can hardly motivate anyone by other means." (ibid., p. 141).

"Are not humans bonded to higher and immaterial things, as well as to imaginary things, and especially to things beyond experience?" (ibid., p. 153).

"For that which can be bound to be truly bound, a real bond is not required, that is ...An apparent bond is enough, for the imagination of what is not true can truly bind, and by means of such an imagination, that which can be bound can be truly bound" (ibid., p. 164).

In understanding the imagination it is important to remember that the Senses fed their information into the Common Sense and that it was from the Common Sense that the Imagination would draw its information. Reason and the higher mental functions would then speculate on synthesized information provided by the Imagination. This is why Bruno claims:

"Since the sense happen to be bound and obligated in all these ways, magic and medicine must pay very special attention to the workings of the imagination. For this is the doorway and entrance for all the actions and passions and feelings of animals. And to that linkage is tied the more profound power of thought" (ibid., p. 141).

So in the practice of bonding it was more important to control the imagination than someone's thoughts or actions for if you controlled their imagination the subject themselves would form the desired thoughts and perform the appropriate actions; in short they would become a slave to your will with the bonus that they would do it all of their own volition. This left the magician at arm's length from any action taken allowing him to slip into the background.

"...fantasy and opinion bind more things than does reason, for the former are indeed stronger than the latter. To be sure, there are many who love without reason, although there is some cause which motivates their love, and, as a result, they are bound but do not know what binds them" (ibid., p. 152).

"...all physical changes originate from the powers which are prior to thought and which are its principal and efficient causes" (ibid., p. 142).

So the best control over a subject is exercised by influencing their imagination. The actions that follow are of their own choosing but of the magician's design. This is how Iago operates. He stokes the furnace of Othello's imagination. We see this when Iago tells Othello that Cassio has *"lied with"* Desdemona (Iago plays on the ambiguity of the phrase "to lie" as meaning either "to tell a fib" or "to have sex with") (4.1.32-34).

Iago. *He did –*
Othello. *What? What?*
Iago. *Lie.*
Othello. *With her?*

Iago. *With her, on her, what you will.*

Iago allows Othello's imagination to fill in the blanks (*what you will*) knowing his imagination will create the worst scenerio. He has done this before when he initially set up Othello (3.3.94-210). By slowly releasing information Iago gives that information the taint of sin, the sense that it is secret information.

The imagination is the best agency to bond with but not the only one.

"The gates through which the bonding agent attacks."

"There are three gates through which the hunter of souls ventures to bind: vision, hearing, and mind or imagination. If it happens that someone passes through all three of these gates, he binds most powerfully...The one who is bound encounters the bonding agent through all the senses up to the point that a perfect bond has been made" (ibid., p. 155).

Gates of the Senses

"The gates of bonds. The senses are the entrances through which bonds are cast. And vision is the most important of them all...Different bonds enter through different windows" (ibid., p. 168).

When Iago is binding Othello he tries to bond in as many ways as possible. He tries to control Othello's imagination. He tries to control what he sees. He tries to control who visits him and when. By controlling as many of the circumstances as possible that surround Othello, Iago hopes to limit Othello's view and guide his actions.

"Something is perfectly bound if it is bound in all its powers and components. Hence, he who binds should count these items carefully so that, in wishing to bind as completely as possible, he can tie up many or all of them" (ibid., p. 164).

Othello gives credibility to Iago's gossip by demanding more and more proof rather than just dismissing the ideas. Iago has hooked Othello and when Othello demands *"ocular proof"* (3.3.363) it affords Iago the opportunity to create a visual bond.

The visual bond comes in the form of the handkerchief which is also an emotional bond. The handkerchief is innocent on its own but Iago has woven it into an imaginative narrative suggesting it to have been given as a gift/token from Desdemona to her new lover. Iago guides Othello's senses (4.1.93-188); he hears what Iago wants him to hear (another bond set), he sees what Iago directs his eyes to (another bond set). He directs Othello's response to the information. Othello sees the narrative and not the evidence.

Iago knows he must act swiftly because bonds are not stable and they change with time.

Opportunity Knocks

"The kind of proportionality which we regularly experience in eating and in sexual intercourse is found in every act of bonding. For we are not attracted and bonded by these desires and loves at all times, or in the same way, or in the same degree, or with the same variations of time. The reason is that our physical constitution...fluctuate and change with time. Therefore, the moment for bonding must be predicted ahead of time...and the opportunity must be quickly seized when it presents itself." (ibid., p. 153)

Iago watches his victims and nurses them along but when a chance comes in his favour he leaps on it (2.3.383).

Dull not device by coldness and delay!

Iago knows the clock is ticking the moment a bond is set because bonds are not stable.

"...*bonding powers are continually changed and altered as forms, circumstances and natures are altered*" (ibid., p.147).

"...*things alternate between bondage and freedom, between being bonded and escaping from a bond, or they transfer from one type of bond to another...But complete stability is opposed to the nature of things...for it is quite natural to desire to break from bonds, while just a little while ago we were open to being tied to them by our own voluntary and spontaneous inclinations*" (ibid., p. 159).

This temporary nature of bonds accounts for the speed at which the plot moves after Othello is infected with doubt. Iago delivers emotional blow upon blow on Othello, never giving him a chance to reflect nor does Othello seek respite with Desdemona for she is tainted in his imagination. Alone with only Iago to guide his senses he is rendered senseless.

Why he hath thus ensnared my soul and body?

There is little doubt that Iago has sufficient motive to want to see Othello destroyed and as Bradley has pointed out there is no mystery in the psychology behind Iago's indignation. However, justifying an action and explaining your reasons for hating someone still does not dismiss the mystery of hate itself. Unfortunately Iago's deceptive nature and failure to give clear answers at the end of the play only deepens this mystery (5.2.300-301)

> *Demand me nothing. What you know, you know.*
> *From this time forth I never will speak word.*

The truth is that Iago's hate is as inexplicable as is Desdemona's love. Iago's desire for control is explicable, his motive is understandable but his hate is a mystery.

"The blindness of the bonding agent."

"The explanation of bonds is, for the most part, hidden, even to the wise, for what use is it to appeal to...meaningless words when we see a person who hates nothing more than another person who is his genial companion, while at the same time and without reason, he also loves that person more than anything else?" (ibid., p. 152).

Bruno believes that Love and Hate are a form of knowledge, something that can be balanced with Reason, but not fully understood.

"...love, like all emotions, is a very practical form of knowledge...Therefore, he who wishes to bind believes that Reason has neither a greater role nor a more important role than love in binding" (ibid., p. 163).

Because of love's indefinable nature it becomes a wild card in binding leading to variable results.

"What it is that bonds to love and hate or contempt is hidden to the functions of reason...Thus the condition of things that can be bound is unfathomable to casual and routine examination" (ibid., p. 162).

Iago's inexplicable hate should not be overemphasized any more than Desdemona's mysterious love for Othello. Love/Hate cannot be explained but they can be understood and in the context of the play both are understandable.

Obedient to the End

When one thinks of obedience in the context of the play *Othello* one thinks of Desdemona. She is young, innocent, compliant, and even offers excuses for her husband's bad behaviour. She is, *"Truly, an obedient lady"* (4.1.248). Yet it is Othello that is the one who is obedient to both the Senate and Iago's aims. Othello has the sense of a soldier about him; he takes orders. It is possible he sees this quality of obedience in himself and in Desdemona and that he comes to despise it.

It is possible that the anger he shows towards Desdemona is really directed at himself.

The reason I suggest this is that when the order comes from the Senate relieving Othello from command and replacing him with Cassio (4.1.234-236) he flies into a fury and the subject of his anger is obedience (4.1.253-261)

> *Ay, you did wish that I would make her turn.*
> *Sir, she can turn, and turn, and yet go on*
> *And turn again. And she can weep, sir, weep.*
> *And she's obedient: as you say, obedient,*
> *Very obedient. – Proceed you in your tears. –*
> *Concerning this, sir – O well – painted passion! –*
> *I am commanded home. – Get you away.*
> *I'll send for you anon. – Sir, I obey the mandate*
> *And will return to Venice. – Hence, avaunt! –*
> *Cassio shall have my place.*

Othello is showing Lodovico how obedient Desdemona is and how obedient he is (*"I obey the mandate"*), he is furious with her but even more so with himself for being the Senate's lap dog, a realization he has just made. He sees the futility of his life; when war was possible he was the acceptable/disposable choice to govern Cyprus, but now that the danger has been averted he is to be replaced by Cassio, a man he had to discipline for attacking Montano, the previous governor. The fact that Montano doesn't bring up Cassio's misbehaviour (2.3.193-199) and dismissal (2.3.245) implies that Cassio must be favoured by the Senate. This goes to undermine Othello's authority even more. It makes a mockery of his appointment and dismisses any actions he took while governor. He sees himself for what he is, powerless and obedient. He does what the Senate wants; Othello go to war, Othello be governor, Othello step down. The Senate is humiliating Othello just like Othello is humiliating Desdemona in this scene. Both he and Desdemona become pathetic in his eyes. The disrespect he shows her is really directed at himself (self-loathing). His self-esteem has reached a low point. Unfortunately, this event works against Desdemona for Othello sees himself as powerless to control any situation, even his own marriage and sadly he perceives Cassio as the beneficiary of both his losses.

Othello is a man of war, a man of action, but it seems he cannot even control his own household. Because of his impotence and frustration he seems unable to clearly evaluate the situation.

"However, they think that these impressions of the internal sense are the real things. Thus, it happens that they refuse to be recalled to a healthier point of view by actual witnesses, whom they prefer to reject in favor of their own imagination" (ibid., p. 139).

Neither Emilia (4.2.1-19) nor Desdemona (5.2.58-61) can break Othello of his delusion of Desdemona's infidelity.

"But it does sometimes happen that a person is so tied to one object that his awareness of other things is weakened" (ibid., p. 147).

His loathing of Desdemona is matched by his own self-loathing. He kills Desdemona for being unfaithful but he kills himself for being everybody's puppet. By so doing he has released himself from all the bonds that held him.

"Bonds are so subtle...They change from moment to moment...It is necessary to study the sequence of the changes...do bonds of anger follow the bonds of indignation, and the bonds of sadness follow the bonds of anger" (ibid., p. 154).

Seeds of Bonds

Othello states of himself that he is not a jealous man (3.3.186-192)

'Tis not to make me jealous

258

To say my wife is fair, feeds well, loves company,

Is free of speech, sings, plays and dances well:

Where virtue is, these are more virtuous

Nor from mine own weak merits will I draw

The smallest fear or doubt of her revolt,

For she had eyes and chose me.

Yet such a jealous beast grows in him so quickly. One gets the sense that he "*protests too much*". For as Bruno observed:

"...it was said above that part of what is in that which is to be bound must be present in the bonding agent. A completely chaste girl...is not bound to sensory pleasure...for in all actions there must be some seed, but not all seeds are fruitful everywhere" (ibid., p. 178).

For the seed of jealousy to grow in Othello's imagination there had to be a fear, a sense of inadequacy, a sense that he did not fit in with this culture, a sense that he could not be truly loved.

This hint of self-doubt is present in everyone. It is why we all can be bound. Even more frightening than Iago's exploitation of Othello's weakness is Bruno's advice on how to bind all humans. To read his ultimate secret stated so clearly sends a shiver up your spine. It is a philosophy many advertising agencies operating today have embraced as a way to achieve their ends. It makes you fear for your children's self-esteem.

"The foundation of the capacity to be bound."

"...if one could extinguish self-love in an object, it would be subject to any and every type of bonding" (ibid., p. 159).

Conclusion

Bruno's essays *On Magic* and *A General Account of Bonding* were intended as instruction manuals for teaching the art of manipulation to those interested. Shakespeare has dramatized much of the content of those works in his play *Othello*.

Shakespeare's use of arcane knowledge to give structure and depth to his plays is a pattern he has repeated in many of his works. In *Othello* Shakespeare has used the plot provided by Cinthio's *Hecatommithi* (The third decade, story 7) (see Appendix 3, *Othello*, The Arden Shakespeare) to give him both characters and a storyline to improvise upon; but it is Bruno's works that give Shakespeare the knowledge required to make the plot believable. Bruno tells Shakespeare how one character can manipulate another. Shakespeare's Iago embodies Bruno's philosophies.

When looking at Bruno's influence on Shakespeare you are looking at how a philosophy is incorporated or merged into a text; you are not looking at how a descriptive passage, for example, is altered and inserted onto a text. Bruno's influence is not observable floating on the surface of the text as, say, Biblical references are but rather they provide Shakespeare with the philosophical depth to draw his poetry from. It is the source to a body of ideas that adds weight to his poetry.

Bruno's influence does not necessarily affect Shakespeare's imagery so much as it affects what Shakespeare's plays may mean. Bruno's contribution is a contribution of content not poetic description or imagery. This is why influence is difficult to show; Bruno's ideas live in the heart of the work; they are bred into its bones.

To see how Bruno's ideas influenced Shakespeare requires an examination of the ideas embodied in Shakespeare's work. With *Othello* Iago gives us the window we need to see Bruno. The principles Iago follows in binding Othello are the principles Bruno has outlined in his works. The number and the quality of the ideas drawn from Bruno's two short works (71 pages in translation) easily makes the argument of influence; one that is difficult to deny. Bruno provided a well of ideas that could be tapped into enriching Shakespeare's poetry. The content allowed the poetry to address issues of substance and freed him from superficial description; it made art possible.

For Shakespeare, Othello is a fatally flawed man (5.2.342)

one that loved not wisely, but too well.

For Bruno, Othello is a man who violates moderation (ibid., p. 174)

"...the laws of prudence do not prohibit love, but love beyond reason".

The comparison shows the two authors share content but not superficial similarity. Shakespeare versifies Bruno. The two are joined by their ideas.

Bibliography

1) *Othello*, W. Shakespeare, Edited by E.A.J. Honigmann, The Arden Shakespeare, 3rd edition, Thomson Learning, 2002.

2) *Cause, Principle and Unity and Essays on Magic*, Giordano Bruno, Edited and translated by Richard J. Blackwell and Robert de Lucca, Cambridge University Press, 2003.

3) *Eros and Magic in the Renaissance*, Ioan P. Couliano, translated by Margaret Cook, The University of Chicago Press, 1987.

4) *Shakespearean Tragedy; Lectures on Hamlet, Othello, King Lear, Macbeth*, A.C. Bradley, MacMillan and Co. Ltd.,1964.

5) *Three Books of Occult Philosophy*, Henry Cornelius Agrippa, edited and annotated by Donald Tyson, translated by James Freake, Llewellyn Publications, 2004.

Conclusion to *In Sheep's Clothing*

Having read through a collection of essays such as these one cannot help but wonder what Shakespeare was up to. For he was certainly up to something.

The pattern revealed through the essays shows an author who is incorporating not just ideas and attitudes of his time but specific attitudes and specific ideas from specific sources and he is incorporating them rigorously into his own works.

These essays have revealed extensive knowledge of what can only be described as the subversive literature of his time. The common factor that keeps reappearing in this literature is Giordano Bruno. He is the nexus out of which all this literature can be traced.

Shakespeare may have met Bruno while Bruno was in England (1583–1585). Bruno can certainly be directly linked to people of Shakespeare's acquaintance (Fulke Greville and Philip Sidney). Bruno's works were published by people known directly by Shakespeare (Richard Field and Thomas Vautollier) and these essays demonstrate that there is really no doubt that Shakespeare was at least well acquainted with the published Bruno.

Bruno was in England when Shakespeare was between nineteen and twenty-two years old. Bruno and his ideas would have been very attractive to anyone interested in counterculture. Bruno was counterculture. He turned the Aristotelian world on its head. He smashed the Ptolemaic model of the Cosmos. He popularized Copernican ideas and he understood the consequences of these ideas. They led to an infinite universe of infinite worlds. They redefined the Matter that made up the universe. Bruno was the tipping point between the Medieval and the Modern world. He represented change on almost every front. By smashing the Ptolemaic world he also smashed the existing model of the Macrocosm. Bruno was smart enough to realize that this would in turn change all our attitudes about the microcosm and about us. His philosophies changed religion, science, and society. He was a very dangerous man. He was executed as a heretic the year Shakespeare wrote *Hamlet*, his Copernican eulogy to an ascending soul based on the *Hermetica*.

What makes Bruno interesting to us as well as to Shakespeare is that Bruno sat on the edge between two worlds. All the philosophers he read belonged to another age; all his points of reference were in the past and he was trying to imagine a future using their terminology. When you read Bruno's work he is ratcheting between old ideas and modern concepts without the vocabulary he needs. He embraces Copernicanism and yet he speaks of the soul ascending through the planetary spheres which were based on Ptolemy. He knows the rules have changed, he knows the symbolic language of the past is no longer appropriate but without it he has no metaphors to explain what he means. Without these metaphors he cannot dialogue with the past. Bruno is at the cusp, some of the old ideas will still work with his new conception of the universe and some won't but he doesn't yet know which are which. Only time will tell.

For a young author being exposed to a new world, new concepts, the potential to develop a new vocabulary would have been enormously seductive. A chance to tell stories not yet heard. A chance to become the new voice to describe this new world.

Shakespeare's early play *Love's Labour's Lost* lives up to this ambition. Its structure comes from Bruno's *Cause Principle and Unity*. Bruno has redefined matter. He doesn't know what it is but he knows it's not Aristotle's four elements and he knows it makes up this world and the planets and God. He knows the world is not corrupt. He knows it is free of Original Sin; and so does Shakespeare.

Shakespeare uses his words as Bruno's matter to create his play and Bruno's world. Both free of Original Sin. Both places where Eve carries no taint of sin. Shakespeare turns Genesis on its head just as Bruno did when he realized that the world was made of the same matter as God. Shakespeare, like Bruno, is trying to create a metaphysical story that will match the new physics. The end of the Ptolemaic cosmos; the beginning of the infinite Copernican universe must redefine the stories we tell of our world and our relationship with God. The old model no longer works. Shakespeare is going to help tell these new stories. He's going to create a new metaphysics, write the new bible for this new world.

What is surprising with *Love's Labour's Lost* is that it is not a tentative exploration of a few new ideas but a full embrace of Bruno's ideas. *Love's Labour's Lost* is Shakespeare's Genesis, an early example, a template, for his many plays; each following its pattern. They fully embrace a philosophical idea and subsume it into their structure. All very complex ideas, like Cabala which is swallowed into *The Merchant of Venice*.

Not all ideas are Bruno's but he was a keystone figure for the Hermetic Movement. Bruno was a great source to tap for he carried with him influences of many leading philosophers of the past. He respected their ideas and referenced them as sources. Bruno adapted and modified the Mnemonics theories of Simonides that Shakespeare exploits in *Macbeth*. Bruno embraced the magical ideas of Ficino and Pico della Mirandola. Shakespeare was obviously drawn to this source material for we can see Ficino's understanding of both Love and Magic reflected in *A Midsummer Night's Dream*, we can find Pico's 'Christian Cabala' in *The Merchant of Venice* and his *Oration on the Dignity of Man* in *The Winter's Tale*.

Conclusion

What I hope I've shown in this collection of essays is that Shakespeare was using a 'Hermetic programme' to construct his plays. A programme was the mythological or metaphorical framework for a piece. Its purpose was to give a unity to the structure of a work. By following the overall metaphor or myth chosen it was possible to select characters and an appropriate plot to carry this symbolic content. It made sure that the characters were cut from the same cloth as the plot and that both could serve the overarching myth.

Shakespeare was burying the best of what Hermetism had to offer in his plays. Perhaps he feared a return to more repressive times when such thoughts would not be tolerated. He was burying treasure in his works. Each play a new philosophy; each play a new idea for a new world.

www.ingramcontent.com/pod-product-compliance
Lightning Source LLC
Chambersburg PA
CBHW061942070426
42450CB00007BA/937